Estranging the Novel

Estranging the Novel

Poland, Ireland, and Theories of World Literature

KATARZYNA BARTOSZYŃSKA

Johns Hopkins University Press
Baltimore

© 2021 Johns Hopkins University Press
All rights reserved. Published 2021
Printed in the United States of America on acid-free paper
2 4 6 8 9 7 5 3 1

Johns Hopkins University Press
2715 North Charles Street
Baltimore, Maryland 21218-4363
www.press.jhu.edu

Library of Congress Cataloging-in-Publication Data

Names: Bartoszyńska, Katarzyna, author.
Title: Estranging the novel : Poland, Ireland, and theories of world literature / Katarzyna Bartoszyńska.
Description: Baltimore : Johns Hopkins University Press, 2021. | Includes bibliographical references and index.
Identifiers: LCCN 2020040859 | ISBN 9781421440644 (hardcover ; acid-free paper) | ISBN 9781421440651 (paperback ; acid-free paper) | ISBN 9781421440668 (ebook)
Subjects: LCSH: Polish fiction—History and criticism. | English fiction—Irish authors—History and criticism. | Comparative literature—Polish and Irish (English) | Comparative literature—Irish (English) and Polish. | Poland—Civilization. | Ireland—Civilization.
Classification: LCC PG7099 .B37 2021 | DDC 808.3—dc23
LC record available at https://lccn.loc.gov/2020040859

A catalog record for this book is available from the British Library.

Special discounts are available for bulk purchases of this book. For more information, please contact Special Sales at specialsales@jh.edu.

Johns Hopkins University Press uses environmentally friendly book materials, including recycled text paper that is composed of at least 30 percent post-consumer waste, whenever possible.

All I wish is, that it may be a lesson to the world,
to let people tell their own stories their own way.
 -Laurence Sterne, Tristram Shandy

CONTENTS

Acknowledgments   ix

Introduction: *Unreal Histories*   1

1 The Problem with Happily Ever After: *Swift and Krasicki*   16

2 The Terror of Worlds Unfolding: *Potocki and Maturin*   39

3 Queer Tales and Seductive Paintings: *Żmichowska and Wilde*   75

4 Impossibly Free: *Gombrowicz and Beckett*   102

Conclusion: *Toward a "Weak" Theory of the Novel*   125

Notes   135
Bibliography   161
Index   179

ACKNOWLEDGMENTS

This book began, more years ago than I can really wrap my head around, as a dissertation at the University of Chicago. Jim Chandler believed in the idea even before I did, and he has patiently shepherded it along its path, giving my ideas wing through his insightful and generous feedback, even long after I'd left the nest. Françoise Meltzer was a rock star, truly, and always treated me more like a colleague than a student. Bożena Shallcross and Lina Steiner were supportive and smart readers who ensured that my connection to Polish literature was not only personal but scholarly. I was also incredibly lucky to study alongside so many truly brilliant and wonderful people, who are still some of my best friends today. Dustin Simpson, Gerard Cohen-Vrignaud, Jonathan Ullyot, Joshua Adams, and Maggie Fritz-Morkin taught me many things, and certainly made me a much better poker player.

I spent many happy summers at Notre Dame's Irish Seminar, and was honored to be invited to present a very early version of the first chapter of this project there. And a Keough-Naughton Fellowship provided significant support during a later stage. Generous invitations to give lectures at the Centre for Fictionality Studies in Denmark and the Institute of Literary Research at the Polish Academy of Sciences gave me the opportunity to test some of the arguments in front of international audiences. I have received generous and helpful feedback from listeners at numerous conferences, especially at meetings of ASECS, ACLA, and SNS. A special shout-out to Sandra Macpherson, who included me in an "Against History" panel at ASECS in 2015, which turned out to be a major milestone in the very, very slow process of figuring out how to frame the argument.

At my first job at Bilkent Üniversitesi, Mustafa Nakeeb was a supportive and jovial chair, and I benefited from lengthy conversations over lunch and late into the evenings with Daniel Leonard, Daniel DeWispelare, Colleen Kennedy-Karpat, Ipek Çelik, Alexis Rappas, Margaret France, Chris Love, Denis Ferhatović, Michael Meeuwis, Mihaela Harper, Andy Ploeg, Michael Subialka, William Coker, Ayşe Çelikkol, Cory Stockwell, Costa Constantino, and Louise Barry.

At Monmouth College, Mark Willhardt was both a great chair and a great friend, and, crucially, he fought hard to get me proper parental leave, and a more manageable schedule after my return. I am grateful to have worked alongside smart, interesting, and kind colleagues, and to have found excellent writing buddies in David Wright, Carina Olaru, Michelle Damian, Mike Nelson, and Zach Erwin. Special thanks to the English Department assistant in 2017, Bree Perschall, who cheerfully waded through hours of tedious work on my bibliography, and even pretended to enjoy it.

My new colleagues at Ithaca College came into my life just as I was completing this book, but they managed to squeeze in disproportionate amounts of encouragement in the final stages. Thanks especially to Jen Spitzer, Chris Holmes, Dyani Johns Taff, Derek Adams, Alexis Becker, Dan Breen, and to Claire Gleitman, who provided me with the perfect epigraph for the introduction.

Some of the material in this book has been published in different forms, in various articles, and I am grateful for permission to use that material. An early version of the first chapter appeared in *Comparative Literature Studies* (Pennsylvania State University Press) as "Persuasive Ironies: Utopian Readings of Swift and Krasicki." Parts of the introduction and chapter two appeared in *Comparative Literature* (Duke University Press) as "Constructing a Case: Reflections on Comparative Studies, World Literature, and Theories of the Novel's Emergence." Some early thoughts on Jan Potocki appeared in *Nineteenth-Century Contexts* (Taylor and Francis) in an article entitled "From Fantastic to Familiar: Jan Potocki's *Manuscript Found in Saragossa*."

My anonymous readers at Johns Hopkins University Press have given me helpful suggestions for sharpening the argument, and I am lucky to have worked with an excellent editor, Catherine Goldstead, and a marvelously thorough and understanding copyeditor, David Goehring. I might not have been able to work at all, if it were not for Susan Lipson, Maureen Fayen, Venus Evans-Winters, and the loving staff of the Wonder Playschool and Wonder Academy. And then, so many delightful people have offered feedback or encouragement in response to various pieces of this project at different steps along the way, and it meant the world to me: Laura Martin, Josh Landy, Caroline Levine, Nathan Hensley, Nigel Hatton, Catherine Flynn, Barry McCrea, Grace Lavery, Tobias Boes, Jan Mieszkowski, Abigail Zitin, Andrea Haslanger, Heather Keenleyside, Sarah Tindal Kareem, Joanna Niżyńska, Tim Bewes, Luke Gibbons, Jed Esty, Julie Orlemanski, Jonathan Kramnick, Jeff Deutsch, Ula Klein, Emily Kugler, Amanda Johnson, Nicole Garrett, Rebecca Colesworthy. And Srinivas Aravamudan, who is dearly missed.

My friends are my heroes. Jennifer Carroll has taught me so much, even while insisting that the debt runs in the other direction. Ligaya Beebe's place in my life has always been beyond what words can describe. Ruchama Johnston-Bloom is quite possibly the most interesting person I know, and the best movie date. For long hours at the kitchen table together, or absurdly long conversations via text, there is no one quite like Kelly Kaihara. The inimitable Harold Gabel methodically puzzled through many dilemmas with me, often over the delicious meals he cooked. Derek Stephenson regularly reminds me what really matters. The good people of hpk-mayhem grew up with me and schooled me in the art of making effective arguments. Krzyś Pijarski and Kasia Bojarska (truly the Greater Kasia) are the hippest couple I know, and a seemingly endless source of creativity and enthusiasm. Anna Kornbluh, consummate hostess and tireless architect of better collectives, has encouraged me to actually say things. And I truly don't know if I would, or could, have finished this book without my fabulous Sweater Squad, Stephanie Insley Hershinow, Kathy Lubey, and Gena Zuroski, who inspire me, support me, and text me every damn day, thank god.

My family is a powerful source of love and strength. My incredible aunties—Audrey, Anna, and Edith Siler, Simone Wright, Margaret Ford, Filomena Stroup, and Ida Watanabe—make every Thanksgiving a holy day (along with Don and Scott Watanabe), and it's always a joy to see Sandie Liebman and Stan Hoffman. Lena Maminajszwili seemed like the most sophisticated woman alive to me when I was a child, and still does. Ania Maminajszwili brightened every room with a quietly resolute goodness, and I am grateful that the icon she painted keeps watch over my desk. Gosia Wołyńska trekked to various Warsaw libraries to scan texts for me, and her tireless struggle to make the world a better place gives me faith that eventually it will be. Kazik Kunicki unfailingly reminds me of all the humor in Polish literature. Doris Perry gave me a room of my own in her house, and her fierce protectiveness, among many other gifts. My grandmother, Aleksandra Jasińska-Kania, was the first to have the insight of the Polish-Irish resemblance and has always been a model of what it means to be a committed intellectual. Zygmunt Bauman was an enthusiastic supporter of this project, and I wish he could have seen its publication. Albin Kania and Anna Bartoszyńska, I know, would be proud, and I miss them all the time.

My parents, Joanna Kania-Bartoszyńska and Tomek Bartoszyński, have given me absolutely everything, and they continue to do so. In so many ways, this book could not have been written without them. Antonio Perry feeds me, finds everything I lose, and makes me laugh. He has given up more for this book than anyone else, while regularly reminding me that there was a worthwhile life outside of it. And finally, Julian Bartoszyński Perry ended up being my first major (coauthored) work after all, and he will almost certainly be my best.

Estranging the Novel

Introduction
Unreal Histories

>STELLA: Stanley is Polish, you know.
>BLANCHE: Oh yes. They're something like the Irish, aren't they?
>STELLA: Well—
>BLANCHE: Only not so—highbrow?
>
>—Tennessee Williams, *A Streetcar Named Desire*

On an anecdotal level, there are some obvious similarities between Poland and Ireland: both are countries on the peripheries of Europe, largely Catholic, with lengthy histories of political oppression and traditions of exile and immigration. Even the stereotypes about them are similar, as the above quote from Tennessee Williams illustrates: their proclivity for potatoes and strong liquor, an alleged stupidity that has made them the butt of jokes and ethnic slurs, a storied and martyrological obsession with the past, and a darkly comic sense of humor.

Their literary traditions are markedly similar as well: each has a proud poetic heritage, from early folk ballads to the lyrical bards of the Romantic period and the Nobel laureates of the twentieth century who draw on, resist, and reinvent that legacy. A robust national theater, one that was often a stage for political action. A notable link to the Gothic, one that is often seen as emerging from the violence of their histories. A penchant for satire and double-edged irony. A quirky delight in mind-bending philosophical games. A seemingly underdeveloped nineteenth-century novelistic tradition, arguably lacking any true masterpieces of realism, but an exuberant and well-regarded explosion of activity in the twentieth century, resulting in an impressive array of experimental, post/modernist creations.

Even more intriguingly, we find a series of apparently anomalous pairs, works in both literatures that seem to emerge out of nowhere, offering strange twists or innovations on forms typical of the time, such as the travel narrative or the Gothic novel. These texts, ostensibly freakish within their own contexts, as well as within the broader map of the novel's evolution, are, however, strikingly similar to each other, suggesting that their oddness is not a strange one-off or random occurrence, and that the similarities between the Polish and Irish traditions are more meaningful than they might initially appear.

In this book, I argue that the resemblance is indeed quite meaningful—but not in the way one might think. Rather than suggesting that these traditions offer models of uneven development, or evidence of historical trauma fracturing literary form, the shared features of Polish and Irish prose serve to illuminate blind spots in theories of the novel's development. A study of the resemblances between the literary trajectories of Poland and Ireland, and the rise of the novel there, turns out to tell us a lot about how we talk about the development of the novel in general, and especially how we talk about it in "peripheral" parts of the world—indeed, how we construct those peripheries in the process of doing so. To read these two literatures alongside each other is to realize that the problem of world literature is born of a neglect of literary form. An examination of their resemblances becomes an opportunity, not only to learn about the evolution of the novel in Poland and Ireland, or even the development of the novel as such, but also to reflect on the ways we construct literary histories, imagine the project of "world" literature, and develop our sense of the novel as a genre. Rather than being detours on the path to realism, the apparently odd pairs that dot these literary histories should be seen as notable explorations of literary form—roads not taken, perhaps, but whose contours give us a better understanding of the novel and its potential.

❧

For a long time, the standard account of the development of the novel was a story about the rise of realism in English literature. A story of increasingly realistic fictions supplanting wondrous tales of princesses and dragons. A story of a burgeoning middle class, the growth of individualism, and the emergence of the nation-state, and of democracy. . . . Various historical accounts have focused on different features, but there is a consistent link between fiction and sociohistorical developments, one that frequently relies on an implicit notion that the central feature of the modern novel is its interest in representing reality.[1] It is a story that emerges together with the English novel itself: alongside the works by Defoe, Fielding, and Richardson that are often considered to be the earliest English novels, we see the steady presence of a critical tradition that valorized realism (or the "novelistic," as opposed to the "romantic"), and insistently linked it to modernity, connecting tales of quotidian reality to advanced, developed societies.[2]

This narrative has not been wholly uncontested,[3] and indeed, in recent years it is arguably on the wane. On the one hand, there is a greater awareness of the central position that English literature occupies in research on the novel, and a sense of resistance to the universalizing way in which it is treated (the fact that the history of the novel tends to be the history of the English novel, with only occasional nods to French, Spanish, or Russian writing[4]). This has led to more active and effective advocacy for reading literature from all over the world, and the emergence of a subfield of "world" or "global" literature that strives to clarify and define theoretical frames for it.[5]

On the other hand, the strong focus on realism has also increasingly been called into question. Not only have the contributions of other modes of writing (such as the romance, the oriental tale, or the Gothic) received increased attention, but the operative distinction between so-called romantic and realistic (or novelistic) writing that has so long structured the field of eighteenth-century studies has increasingly come to seem untenable and illusory.[6] This shift is manifested in new approaches to the novel: instead of tracking the emergence of features deemed "realistic," scholars are focusing instead on aspects such as the idea of worlding, exploring how fictions build worlds of their own, at various levels of remove from the worlds that produce them, or on the examination of fictionality, considering how novels conceive of themselves and their relationship to reality.[7]

This book will demonstrate that these two critiques, which have proceeded largely in isolation from each other, need to be connected: a broader geographic perspective requires a more capacious understanding of the novel and its various forms. And a more expansive approach to the novel demands a greater awareness of different ways it has been approached in different places around the world.[8]

Indeed, as I argue, research on the novel in countries other than England and France has been stymied by laboring under a normative model of the genre's development. As names such as "minor," "peripheral," or "postcolonial" make clear, the category of these traditions is generally defined relationally, and often in terms of their geopolitical or historical circumstances.[9] And the research on them follows suit, particularly in work on the novel: there is frequently a sense that the critic is tasked with explaining why these traditions do not follow what is seen as the typical trajectory of the novel's development. Because the dominant story of the novel's rise is a historicized account, the explanation for the particular course of its development in a given "minor" literature is likewise sought in history.

It seems obvious that a more global approach to literary studies must be attuned to shifting sociopolitical relationships and the power dynamics underlying cultural production and reception. At the same time, however, efforts to analyze the effects of these power structures can implicitly reproduce them, describing a world republic of letters characterized by relationships of center and periphery, and subtly assessing the (quality of the) literature from those places accordingly—casting writing from the Global South or periphery as "underdeveloped" or flawed, particularly when it fails to conform to models set by the "center."[10] This leads to a model like the one Franco Moretti offers in his "Conjectures on World Literature," which seemingly reverses the terms by saying that it is in fact the "center" that is anomalous—in the sense of uncommon—but nonetheless seeing it as setting the standard, meaning that the novel's diffusion in the world is "a compromise between foreign form and local materials," the foreign form being, of course, the novel itself, which is being exported to other places. This compromise, moreover, is often portrayed as a chaotic or schizophrenic effort, where "the historical conditions reappear as a sort of 'crack' in the form; as a fault line running between story and discourse, world and worldview: the world goes in the strange direction dictated by an outside power; the worldview tries to make sense of it, and is thrown off balance all the time."[11]

The problem with such a view is that it hardly does justice to the dynamics of literary development in the so-called center, not to mention that it delegitimizes the literature of the periphery as being a series of flawed imitations, and implicitly makes the influence unidirectional. Moretti himself acknowledges this in *Distant Reading*, which reprints the original "Conjectures" but retreats from it, acceding that world economic systems do not map neatly onto systems of world literature.[12] But the real problem is that this kind of reasoning produces a subtly circular account: a given kind of novel (realist) is linked to a specific sociohistorical context (British). When a different historical context is examined, it is found to produce a different kind of novel . . . because of differences in the historical context. The possibility that the apparent strangeness of some of these novels is not a schizophrenic struggle to adapt an imported model, but a conscious experiment with literary form that is itself worthy of interest and attention is rarely considered.

Notably, the difference between the works in minor traditions and the alleged standard of novelistic form is registered primarily as difference—the "local materials" are not literary techniques, but history itself, or some aspect of the social context—rather than as an experiment with form that is worthy of attention and exploration. The fictions are considered from a normative perspective that gauges them in relation to an expected model of novelistic development, thereby occluding a more careful and nuanced understanding of their alleged divergence—that is, an attentive reading of the formal features of these works.

A redemptive reading mines texts from the Global South for content that would render them of anthropological interest as "representative," offering a glimpse of "the African experience," village life, the position of women, and so on. If form is considered, it is usually examined with an eye to how it encodes or represents sociohistorical conditions.[13] Surprisingly, this is even more noticeable when those forms are not mimetic: breaks with realism are usually discussed first and foremost as symptoms of historical trauma. Thus, for instance, the Warwick Research Collective's account of combined and uneven development, which includes discussions of "irrealist" features such as anti-linear plot lines, unreliable narrators, and contradictory points of view, sees all of them as techniques for registering the lived experience of capitalism and uneven development within the world system.[14] Although there may well be strong correlations between irrealist features and the imposition of various forms of capitalist production, the central emphasis, and interest, of such arguments seems to be the capitalist world system, rather than the literature it (allegedly) produces. The problem with such a view is that it subtly suggests that novels from "other" parts of the world become worthy of attention primarily when they help us see or understand something about economic or political realities, or offer ways of conceptualizing socioeconomic development—rather than because they are powerful or interesting works of literature.[15] Although historicism offers many valuable tools for reading literature from the periphery, it needs to be balanced with a more robust formalism, not only to better understand the texts themselves but also to avoid reinforcing the frameworks that make these traditions seem peripheral in the first place.

The case of the resemblances between Poland and Ireland allows us to see how this reasoning plays out—and provides an opportunity to reconsider it. Examining Poland and Ireland in relationship to each other, rather than to a perceived mainstream, opens up the possibility of defining the terms of such a comparison in fresh ways, seeing what new features are suggested by a different frame, and revealing how an understanding of the literature in both places has been conditioned by a consideration of their sociopolitical histories.[16] Aspects of each that had appeared unique prove not to be, and assumptions as to causes are called into question, even as seemingly anomalous or strange facets are normalized by being placed among new company.

Of the various commonalities that Poland and Ireland share, the one that is simultaneously the most obvious, yet the most controversial, is the particular nature of their peripheral status. As dominated regions within Europe—that attained nationhood in the early twentieth century—they do not fit neatly into categories defined by postcolonial theory. But the resemblance between them has been repeatedly invoked throughout their history. In the eighteenth century, for example, Wolf Tone, cofounder of the Society of United Irishmen, wrote that "the two most miserable and oppressed countries of Europe always looked to Napoleon for liberation. He never gratified their hopes; yet, by raising Ireland, he might have crushed forever the power of England, and by assisting Poland, placed a curb on Russia."[17] And as John Merchant has documented, in the late nineteenth and early twentieth centuries, members of the Młoda Polska movement actively drew on the work of Irish nationalists.[18] Despite these repeated comparisons, both sides also often see themselves as unique, particularly in the specific forms of subjugation they have endured, and scholars regularly speak of each as singular. In his work on representations of Eastern Europe during the Enlightenment period, for instance, Larry Wolff repeatedly describes the idea of a gradation from civilization to barbarity as being on a west-to-east axis, apparently overlooking the fact that the Irish were frequently portrayed as savage or uncivilized during this time.[19] Similarly, David Lloyd writes that "if it remains true that Ireland's history offers peculiarly significant paradigms for developments in Europe and elsewhere, this is no doubt due to its anomalous position as at once a European nation and a colony,"[20] ignoring Poland's claims to a similarly anomalous paradigm.

It must be noted, of course, that Lloyd is correct, insofar as Poland was never a colony: during the Partitions, it was occupied territory, erased from the map of Europe (aside from the short-lived Duchy of Warsaw), and under Communism it was a satellite state. So in this sense, Ireland is indeed unique. This is why, in the Polish case, critics use the term *post-zależność*, post-dependence, rather than postcolonial.[21] Nonetheless, the resemblances between Poland and Ireland are strong enough to make a comparison reasonable. Indeed, they demonstrate that such comparisons are necessary, because some of the features the two places share are the very ones that make them exceptional in relation to postcolonial studies.

Most obviously, there is the fact of sheer proximity: although they may have had inferior status, both were nonetheless always intrinsic parts of Europe.[22] Historians are careful to emphasize this: R. F. Foster, for instance, writes that "a glance at social conditions in Ireland in the onset of the eighteenth century reveals that Ireland was a truly European society—both by virtue of its structure and because its development was constricted by factors that were general in Western Europe," though he clarifies this later by saying that "Ireland in 1700 bore all the marks of a highly centralized European kingdom, albeit a kingdom that was subsidiary to the kingdom of England."[23] Similarly, Piotr Wandycz argues that East Central Europe should not be seen as wholly external to Europe, and having "imported" the Enlightenment:

> Even if East Central Europe had undergone a certain orientalization and turned its back on the West in the course of the seventeenth century, even if Sarmatism and the "extra Hungarian non est vita" (there is no life outside Hungary) attitude prevailed, the region was an integral part of Europe. The stimuli it had received in the past, whether Christianity, Renaissance, Reformation, or Counter-Reformation had been fully absorbed. . . . The issue was not that of transplanting foreign and incompatible ideas, but rather of receiving and digesting them without risking loss of identity.[24]

There is also the question of race, which is a complex one: although both are now seen as largely "white" today, they have also, at various moments, been constructed as racially Other.[25] Also, as Joe Cleary notes in his discussion of Ireland's position in postcolonial theory, the Irish were both victims of and participants in the British imperial project, emigrating to other colonies and serving as part of the administration.[26] While the Poles never had an active overseas colonial project, they did have fraught relations with ethnic and religious minorities within their own territories.[27] Cleary argues, further, that Irish nationalists did not conceive of themselves as colonial subjects, and did not identify with non-European colonials, which is (largely) true in the Polish case as well.[28]

However, it is also important to note the historical differences between them. The massive size, and ethnic and cultural diversity, of the Polish-Lithuanian Commonwealth presents a contrast to the Kingdom of Ireland, as does its position between several powerful neighbors as opposed to one. There is also the difference in the fate of their respective languages: colonialism had an absolutely devastating effect on the Irish language, whereas Polish emerged from the Partitions relatively unscathed. The language politics are therefore extremely different. Notably, most of the Irish authors I discuss write in English, whereas all but one of the Polish authors wrote in Polish.[29] Several scholars have read the work of Irish authors writing in English as examples of "minor" writing in Deleuze and Guattari's sense of the term, or as texts "haunted" by English.[30]

However, many of the formal features that are seen as stemming from this fact are also visible in Polish fiction, despite the difference in language politics. Rather than serving as a counterargument to such theories, this curious situation is an instructive reminder, both that there are meaningful differences between the two places, and that causality is a complex matter, especially as regards the relationship between culture and history.

Regarding their literary trajectories, it is widely agreed that neither tradition follows the typical path of the novel's development. Most notably, neither develops a strong realist tradition in the nineteenth century.[31] In scholarship on the development of Irish literature, we find a sense of embarrassment or shame about nineteenth-century fiction: as Joe Cleary has pointed out, "Studies of the nineteenth-century Irish novel have long been conditioned by the search for an Irish *Middlemarch*, and by the attempt to explain why there is not one."[32] Polish critics similarly observe, albeit without any noticeable sense of embarrassment, that the novel does not become a major genre in Polish writing until later in the nineteenth century.

The explanation for this "failure" or anomalous trajectory is frequently sought in history. For instance, Zdzisław Najder, writing about the emergence of the Polish novel, points out that Poland had a different kind of reading public from the strong middle classes that are usually seen as "producing" the mainstream European novel, and notes that the novel emerged in Poland "at a time of unprecedented political and ideological turmoil."[33] In his *History of Polish Literature*, Czesław Miłosz explains that historical conditions "prevented [writers] from analyzing contemporary life in a sufficiently detached way."[34] Similarly, Terry Eagleton, explaining the lack of a realist tradition in Irish writing, argues that "the realist novel is the form *par excellence* of settlement and stability, gathering individual lives into an integrated whole, and social conditions in Ireland hardly lent themselves to any such sanguine reconciliation."[35] David Lloyd gives a more pointed account, arguing that colonial force imposed certain structures of both organization and, more generally, thought, which refused alternate possibilities, rendering other models not just unlikely, but "unrepresentable."[36] The notion that both places have literary histories that are somehow anomalous, and that the best explanation for that difference is sociohistorical, is considered uncontroversial—it is so widespread as to be a truism.

It should be noted that these kinds of accounts, which seek to explain specificities of form by reference to political conditions, are not simply born of critics, but are clearly espoused by authors of the time as well: writing in 1824, for instance, Maria Edgeworth famously proclaimed that "it is impossible to draw Ireland as she is now in a book of fiction—realities are too strong, party passions too violent, to bear to see, or care to look at their faces in a looking glass. The people would only break the glass and curse the fool who held the mirror up to nature—distorted nature in a fever."³⁷ In fact, when Polish author Maria Wirtemberska presents what appears to be the opposite argument, writing in the preface to her 1816 novel *Malwina* that the book "przypomni, że nie ma tego rodzaju pisma, do którego język polski nie byłby zdolnym" ("may serve to remind readers . . . that there is no genre of writing of which the Polish language might not be capable"), she illustrates a similar point.³⁸ There is a sense among many authors that the novel is not obviously a native form, but one that may require a kind of translation, proof that it can be applied to this context. There is indeed evidence, in other words, that writers of the time experienced their sociohistorical conditions as a constraint on their aesthetic choices. This is not, however, a sign that these traditions were "backward" or "undeveloped." Indeed, the sense of self-consciousness rather suggests authors very much engaged with questions of representation and form, thoughtfully reflecting on different approaches to storytelling.

But if (literary) history has decreed that Polish and Irish literature were lagging behind in the nineteenth century, burdened by historical violence and incomplete processes of modernization, it finds itself with a strange problem in the early twentieth century, when both traditions suddenly appear to be at the forefront of literary innovation, leaping ahead to modernism and the avant-garde techniques that will become au courant all over Europe. This surprising burst of development can be seen in one of two ways: either it serves to contest the apparent backwardness of nineteenth-century writing from both places, or it offers a vivid example of uneven development in literary traditions.

We find an example of the former view represented by a certain strain of Irish literary criticism that attempts to recuperate nineteenth-century Irish novels by suggesting that their apparent flaws reveal them to be forerunners of the fragmented forms of modernism.³⁹ Such arguments usefully demonstrate that metrics of literary development are in the eye of the beholder: the fractured narratives that look like failure in the context of emerging realism can seem quite successful as early modernist experiments. The teleological bent of such arguments is deeply problematic, however, and essentially replaces one set of privileged criteria with another: there is still a fixed endpoint in the path of literary development (now invoking modernism instead of realism), and the works that count are the ones that provide clear signposts en route.

To see these two traditions as models of uneven development, on the other hand, is to leave untouched the premise that nineteenth-century Polish and Irish writing is largely uninteresting, as well as the broader assumptions about the emergence of the novel that are increasingly seen as questionable: that the development of nineteenth-century fiction was first and foremost the rise of realism, and that it took place primarily in European centers of power. It is not coincidental that theorists promoting such models are typically studying twentieth-century writing: it is a view that is generally uninterested in the "pre-development" period, willingly consigning it to the dustbin of history. Such a perspective does not challenge the standard paradigm of the novel's rise so much as supplement it: rather than contesting the general theory of how the novel came to be, it explains why it did not do so in the same way in Poland and Ireland. It thus reinforces a sense of center and periphery, conceding a normative teleology of the novel and acknowledging the Polish or Irish case as anomalous.

But what if we were to decenter that model altogether? What the case of Poland and Ireland offers us is, instead, a path to thinking outside the framework of that case, toward a more transnational, or global, vision of the novel form. Rather than accepting what have been perceived as the relevant data points to understanding the rise of a specific genre, we can allow the particularities of these two places to guide us toward a new way of conceptualizing the novel and its many faces: not in teleological terms, but in hermeneutic ones. That is the project of this book: to use a comparative examination of the Polish and Irish literary traditions as a tool to pry open and reconsider the history of the novel's rise. As we observe the various formal innovations of works from these traditions that go unnoticed (and therefore unappreciated) in our dominant theoretical paradigms, we begin to perceive the structural inadequacy of rise-of-the-novel narratives: their necessarily selective and limited view.

To take seriously the two lines of critique aimed at the current paradigm for thinking about the novel's rise is to risk finding ourselves adrift in a sea of texts. If both the geopolitical and formal parameters by which we formerly charted development are called into question, what is left? Perhaps the question is not simply: How can we integrate texts from other parts of the world into an account of the novel's development? Or: How can a history of the novel include a richer sense of its generic features? Or even: How can models of literary change integrate, or make allowance for, social or political circumstances? But, more broadly: What do we want from our accounts of literary development? Indeed, we may go so far as to ask whether literary change should be described in terms of development at all, given the unavoidable sense of progression and teleology inherent in such a perspective. As Eric Hayot has pointed out, if our notion of the novel's development is one based on histories of influence and innovation, "we are essentially doomed by the fact that Haroldo de Campos read James Joyce, and not the other way around, to tell a progressive story of aesthetic innovation in which the contributions of the non-West remain supplemental, or constitute thematic appendixes to form."[40] Recent critiques by Nicholas Paige, Eric Hayot, and Julie Orlemanski highlight the inherent flaws of theoretical accounts of "rising" fiction, pointing out both their historical inaccuracies and their problematic underlying assumptions. All three critics urge us to resist the impulse to craft sweeping narratives of progression based on a few specific variables, calling instead for a more hermeneutic approach, one that would be both more restricted in its claims, and more capacious in its sense of the literary field. I return to the broader question of the history of the novel in the conclusion, where I take up both Orlemanski's and Hayot's interventions, but I want to linger with Paige for a moment longer here, to flag some of the insights from his research that have served as the foundations for my own project.

Nicholas Paige's work on the French novel challenges the ostensible interest in innovation in accounts of literary history, demonstrating that the texts generally seen as important or groundbreaking often failed to have any influence on their literary milieu, sometimes even for hundreds of years. He thereby reveals the sleight of hand underlying many accounts of the novel's rise: the illusion of direct ancestry or causality that emerges from critical accounts that carefully select the works they deem meaningful or important, singling them out from among their contemporaries.

Paige advocates for an approach to fiction that would see it as a collection of writing practices first and foremost—"techniques invented and modified, sometimes quickly and sometimes not, through a difficult-to-specify dialectical relationship with what people think literature can and should do"[41]—rather than in relation to other ideas or movements of the time.[42] This perspective is historical without being historicist, and occasionally seems almost to preclude consideration of how sociocultural conditions play a role in formal change. Although Paige takes pains to make clear that literature is not an autonomous realm divorced from history, economy, and science, he interrogates the kinds of evidence that historicist arguments build their case with, arguing that "tracing the rise of identifiable practice makes a kind of sense that the divination of rising ways of thinking does not."[43] His work thus serves as a useful corrective to the temptation of drawing overly simplistic links between novelistic form and sociohistorical context, inviting us to reconsider how such arguments are constructed.

Pointing out how undertheorized the process of change or development in literature really is, Paige notes that our current practice of literary history tends to select for features the critic identifies as important: "We see our canonical novels of the past as an archipelago connected to the mainland of now, whereas they may be only a series of data points acting as hosts for our perception of patterns—patterns we perceive based on our knowledge of what is to come."[44] Literary history, in other words, is rarely a true history of communal practice. More frequently, it charts a course between works that the critic sees as offering interesting contributions or innovations to a particular progression that she or he finds noteworthy or relevant.[45]

It is on such grounds that I build my argument for the importance of works from "minor" traditions to the history of the novel, and perceive a theory of the novel inscribed in this archipelago of twin anomalies in Polish and Irish fiction spanning the eighteenth, nineteenth, and twentieth centuries. Observing that the theory of the novel is often less historical than it purports to be and is more typically an engagement with a specific theoretical problem or question that a given critic traces across a given chronological span,[46] I argue for a more inclusive vision of the novel on both geographical and formal terms. Rather than tracking one particular progression, I offer a series of snapshots across a long historical arc, reading texts against the grain of the theoretical paradigms of their specific periods, as a way of illuminating the limitations of those conceptual frameworks. Insofar as I trace a development, it is in the accumulation of various approaches that I observe embodied in practice over time, without positing a necessary relationship between them. The project I have undertaken in this book is to respond to the provocation offered by these mysterious pairs in Polish and Irish fiction, examining the account of the novel that emerges when they are strung together like beads on a necklace. What if they are seen not as anomalies, but as natural outgrowths, works in dialogue with their own traditions and a broader republic of letters? Such a perspective validates their formal innovations as significant to our understanding of the novel form and its capabilities.

In distinction to the standard history of the novel as the rise of realism, this book charts a path among works that are resolutely "irrealist," a term Michael Löwy uses to describe "the absence of realism rather than an opposition to it,"[47] novels that are more interested in the texture and contours of fictionality than in straightforward mimesis or fidelity to the "real" world.[48] In their self-conscious interest in the mechanics of fiction, simultaneously drawing on and reworking the techniques or themes prevalent in the "mainstream" works of their time, they show us new aspects of those ostensibly "normal" novels, revealing them, perhaps, to be much stranger than they had originally seemed. These novels also demonstrate that the political power of literature is not limited to realist interventions or commentaries on the world, but it can emerge from alternative ways of producing meaning.

Each chapter considers a different pair of texts, demonstrating how the standard narrative of the novel's rise produces readings of them that fail to engage with or recognize some of their most interesting aspects. Reading the pairs together decenters such accounts, shedding the normative expectations that have burdened prior interpretations, rendering their oddity approachable and opening up an account of what it contributes to the text—the work that these apparently bizarre aspects perform. In the features that have been seen as discordant or anomalous, I find a nascent theorization of what a novel can do—an inquiry into various aspects of its capabilities.

The first chapter examines the pioneering novels of the Polish and Irish traditions, Ignacy Krasicki's *Mikołaja Doświadczyńskiego przypadki* (*The Adventures of Mr. Nicholas Wisdom*) (1776), and Jonathan Swift's *Gulliver's Travels* (1726). Swift's satire is typically excluded from discussions of the early novel, but both Swift and Krasicki use irony in a complex way that serves as a meta-inquiry into how novels strive to persuade their readers, examining the oscillation between distance and attachment. Both take the form of satirical travel narratives, with characters that voyage to places that seem perfect, but not quite perfect enough to keep them from leaving and returning home. Not only do these two novels reveal the fundamental tensions at the heart of Enlightenment dreams of universal reason and utopian fantasies; they also brilliantly demonstrate the specific powers of fiction to deliver such a critique, illuminating the novel's peculiar power to straddle contradiction.

The second chapter investigates the orientalized Gothic novels of Jan Potocki and Charles Maturin, *Rękopis znaleziony w Saragossie* (*The Manuscript Found in Saragossa*) (1805–1815) and *Melmoth the Wanderer* (1820). I argue that these two authors provide ample evidence for claims that the Gothic as a genre was central to the development of fictionality by virtue of its self-conscious examination of consensual illusion. Their inquiry into the workings of fiction runs deeper, however, emerging most forcefully in the architecture of interrelated stories that is generally seen as their oddest trait. Using these baroque networks of tales, Maturin and Potocki illuminate the way that stories build worlds—indeed, that an image of the world is one underwritten by fictions, thereby demonstrating the specific contributions of the literary to discussions of worldedness.

The third chapter considers Narcyza Żmichowska's *Poganka* (*The Heathen*) (1846) alongside Oscar Wilde's *The Picture of Dorian Gray* (1890). Both are stylistic hybrids that use the device of a haunted or magical portrait as an entry point into an examination of the relationship between painting and prose, and love, beauty, and goodness. Their peculiar combination of ornate description, supernatural horror, and theatrical set-piece scenes of dialogue produces a skewed sense of time, making the work of plotting visible as a queer formalism. Both texts explore the relationship between fiction and virtue, ultimately negating the notion of idealism as the source of the novel's ethical critique.

The fourth chapter examines Witold Gombrowicz's *Ferdydurke* (1938) alongside Beckett's Trilogy, particularly *Molloy* (1955) and *Unnamable* (1958). These are novels that take the examination of fictionality to the extreme, dizzying evocations of *im*possibility. Unlike the works discussed in the previous chapters, these are stories set in worlds that are openly abstract, foregrounding metafictional investigations while remaining rooted in the consciousness of characters that are warmly, recognizably human. Reworking the notion of *Bildung* and its sociopolitical implications, they examine how fiction, in its radical ability to represent worlds where the law of non-contradiction does not obtain, offers a space of freedom.

The conclusion returns to the broader theoretical questions of the book, synthesizing the close readings of the chapters into an argument about how we construct the history of the novel on a global scale, and its relationship to the way we chart the emergence of modernity. The novel as a genre has long had a privileged relationship to the emergence of the modern, often seen as at the very least reflecting the process, if not actively shaping it. Examining the various approaches to theorizing modernism and modernity of recent years— "singular," "alternative," "uneven," and "global"—by scholars such as Eric Hayot, Susan Stanford Friedman, Ning Ma, and Paul Saint-Amour, I illuminate their underlying assumptions about form and the role of fiction. Joining Julie Orlemanski's call for a hermeneutics of fictionality rather than a history, I argue for a new approach, one that is equally able to accommodate works not written in a realist vein: a "weak theory" of the novel.

To chart a course through the texts I examine is to write a different kind of story of the novel, a study of how authors have tried, in various ways, to test the limits of the form and consider its capabilities. Although the focus is on their formal properties, my claim is not that these works should be seen in an ahistorical light, but rather that the lines connecting sociohistorical context to literary technique may need to be redrawn. If the interest in literature from previously neglected parts of the world has been driven in part by a sense of historical obligation or redress, it may need to temporarily bracket the question of historical conditions in order to focus more closely on the fictions themselves, if only in order to historicize more effectively.

The observant reader will have noticed that I have entirely eschewed the question of influence: it is largely tangential to my project.[49] Although some of the authors I study were familiar with each other's work, most of them probably were not. I examine these pairs together because they are similar, and my interest in that resemblance is less in how it came about than in what we can learn from it. The case I am making for these texts, and their importance to the theory of the novel, is straightforward: that they are interesting books that offer noteworthy contributions to the form. To appreciate the contribution of these novels to a broader history of literature, however, it is necessary to remember that the novel is intended not only to represent our world but also to create new ones, and to remember that fiction's capabilities extend far beyond verisimilitude.

What does the resemblance between Poland and Ireland really mean? Maybe nothing. What it really shows us is the kind of features we select or find notable when we survey the world, or histories of literature—the material we use to build a case. But maybe, too, it can help us see differently—to allow different stories to teach us different ways of reading.

CHAPTER ONE

The Problem with Happily Ever After
Swift and Krasicki

The two works that arguably launch the Irish and Polish novelistic traditions, respectively, are Jonathan Swift's *Gulliver's Travels* (1726), and Ignacy Krasicki's *Mikołaja Doświadczyńskiego przypadki* (1776) (*The Adventures of Mr. Nicholas Wisdom*). Clearly drawing on traditions of travel narrative and utopias, and, of course, appearing in the wake of Daniel Defoe's *Robinson Crusoe* (1719), their satirical nature sets them apart from the "naive" realism seen as definitive of the early novel. But their engagement with Enlightenment ideals and utopian aspirations marks them strongly as products of their time, and commentaries on it.

Indeed, the utopian novel can be seen as the most apropos of all Enlightenment genres: at a time that seemed to enshrine the emancipatory power of reason and its ability to rationally organize human society, what could be more fitting than a fiction whose ostensible goal was to serve as the embodiment of a philosophical ideal, the dream of a perfect society brought to life? The novel seems like an obvious handmaiden to the utopian project, rendering the brave new world tangible and familiar while also acting as its advocate, persuading readers of its virtues. Swift and Krasicki, however, do exactly the opposite: their works not only serve to critique utopian ideals, they also call into question fiction's ability to deliver utopianism's message, or indeed, any kind of lesson at all. Their novels illustrate the ultimate disjunction between the human and the abstract, a problem that is at the heart of political theory itself. This contradiction is echoed on a formal level by the tension between irony and identification, the two dominant modes of fictional pedagogy. The peculiar work of Swift's and Krasicki's novels is the way they collapse the apparent contradiction between these two modes, calling into question the ostensible opposition between them, and thereby opening a reflection on fiction's methodologies of education. Their offering to a history of the novel lies in the way they simultaneously illuminate the limits of fiction's powers of political pedagogy, and its ability to educate by portraying those limits. What these novels show us is that fiction's unique power is its ability to do contradictory things at the same time, a power that allows it to illuminate the ironies of the human condition.

The story of *Gulliver's Travels* is widely known among scholars of the novel. Gulliver, an Englishman, sets off to sea and travels to a series of wondrous places: Lilliput, a world in miniature; Brobdingnag, the land of giants; Laputa, a floating island hovering over a realm called Balnibarbi; and finally, Houyhnhnmland, where the ever-rational Houyhnhnms rule over the brutish Yahoos. Though greatly impressed by the Houyhnhnm system of governance, Gulliver is sent away and returns to England, where he consoles himself by spending time with two horses. *Mikołaja Doświadczyńskiego przypadki* follows the adventures of a young nobleman named Mikołaj, whose dissolute ways lead him to sea, to escape his debts. Shipwrecked on the island of Nipu, he learns about the islanders' way of life from Xaoo, his friendly host, and comes to find it superior to that of Europe . . . until he finds some money and a boat, and makes his escape. Returning to Poland, he tries to enact political reform but fails, so he retires to a quiet life on his estates, cheered by a new marriage.

Gulliver's Travels was published only seven years after *Robinson Crusoe*, yet it is rare to see Jonathan Swift described as an important figure in the rise of realism.[1] There are various explanations for this omission: although the more whimsical elements of *Gulliver's Travels* seem like the obvious reason,[2] juxtapositions between Swift and Defoe tend to underline Swift's satirical qualities, using them to disqualify him from being considered as a key forefather of novelistic fiction. Indeed, irony presents a problematic case for scholars of the early novel. For John Richetti, for instance, irony is antithetical to the work of realism, because it is a distancing technique that disengages the reader from the characters.[3] In a different vein, J. Paul Hunter argues that the parasitical nature of parody renders it derivative, thereby disqualifying such texts from being considered as originary. Thus, Hunter writes that "*Gulliver's Travels* is not a novel in any meaningful sense of that slippery term that I know," though he goes on to acknowledge that "its generic status would be difficult to establish without having the novel in mind. Swift's masterpiece is, in fact, so conceptually dependent upon the novel that it is almost impossible to imagine the existence of the *Travels* outside the context of the developing novelistic tradition."⁴ This dependence, I argue, is not one-sided. It is through their ironic reflections, and their reflections on irony, that these two authors offer signal contributions to the development of the novel form. Although Swift and Krasicki frequently hold their protagonists at arm's length, offering them as objects of ironic scrutiny, they also make a bid for readerly identification and sympathy. Both authors trouble the apparent opposition between absorption and appraisal, inviting reflection on how fiction persuades its readers. The work of their novels depends on an attachment to the characters, though it is a provisional one, frequently interrupted by moments of detached critique.

These vacillations between identification and critique stem, in both texts, from a reckoning with the irony that is at the heart of travel fiction, the disjunct between representation and experience. These dichotomies are structurally identical: a logical contradiction that we can perceive but not escape. Both novelists cannily connect this ironic structure to the broader problem of giving life to the theoretical, and they show us what this difficulty reveals about efforts to imagine utopia. As they demonstrate, the inability of the universal to meaningfully encompass the individual casts doubt on political projects of universal freedom, which must ultimately be a freedom of the individual, and of self-determination.

I will discuss each of these interlinked ironies in turn: first, the problem of travel literature, then, the problem of attachment, satire, and fictional pedagogy, and finally, the impossibility of utopia.

The contribution of travel literature to the early novel is well established. Travel narratives have a vested interest in evocative description and detail that is clearly aligned with the goals of verisimilar fiction. More intriguingly, travel writing was an important site for contemplating the referential status of the emerging category of fiction, as it increasingly blurred the lines between fiction and reality, with stories ranging from the blatantly impossible to the perfectly probable.⁵ Notably, even the most outlandish of journeys was described in terms that mimicked the stylistics of their factual counterparts.⁶ In this way, travel narratives played an important role as a testing ground for the exploration of the referential status of novelistic prose.⁷

As well, travel writing was a realm where the use of fiction was noticeably activated in the service of philosophy or political theory. Describing foreign cultures and political systems provided an opportunity to reflect, implicitly (and often ironically), on one's own home, as texts such as Montesqueiu's *Persian Letters* (1721) or Diderot's *Supplement to the Voyage of Bougainville* (1796) make clear. Stories of travel were unabashedly novels of ideas, where invention and documentation merged to produce a space of reflection.

Postcolonial scholarship has standardized the notion of travel narratives as part of a system of imperial domination. It is in travel literature that foreign countries are first seen, mapped, and known, making them a crucial tool in the "impressive ideological formations that include notions that certain territories and people *require* and beseech domination."[8] Describing the writings of Count de Ségur, an early traveler to Eastern Europe, for example, Larry Wolff says that "the attentiveness of the observer could never be politically innocent. Russia and Poland both offered themselves to the eyes of Ségur, and the armies of Napoleon would take up that offer in the next generation."[9] This is even more explicit in the Irish case: much of the travel writing about Ireland was in the form of surveys commissioned by the British.[10]

Part of this political work is, of course, in the way that places are represented. Both Poland and Ireland figure frequently in travel narratives as barbaric outposts of civilization. Amusingly enough, one sixteenth-century traveler, Fynes Moryson, even compares them along these lines: "In truth, myself having in *Poland* and *Ireland* found a strange cheapnesse of all such necessaries, . . . this observation makes me of an opinion much contrary to the vulgar, that there is no more certaine signe of a flourishing and rich commonwealth, then the deare price of these things (excepting the yeeres of famine), nor any greater argument of a poore and weake State, then the cheap price of them."[11] Swift was well aware of the entrenchment of negative stereotypes about the Irish: "What we call the Irish Brogue is no sooner discovered, than it makes the deliverer, in the last degree, ridiculous and despised; and from such a mouth, an Englishman expects nothing but bulls, blunders and follies,"[12] as well as the perception of the country as a distant, savage sort of place: "As to *Ireland*, they know little more than they do of *Mexico*; further than that it is a country subject to the King of *England*, full of Boggs, inhabited by wild *Irish Papists*. . . . And their general opinion is, that it were better for *England* if the whole island were sunk into the sea."[13] Although accounts of Poland were not uniformly derogatory in nature—Warsaw was a glittering, decadent capital, a destination for adventurers such as Cagliostro or Casanova[14]—there were enough negative accounts to solidify a stereotype of Poland as a wild, uncivilized place. "But when one enters Poland, one believes one has left Europe entirely . . . dirty villages; cottages little different from savage huts; everything makes one think one has been moved back ten centuries," wrote one traveler.[15] A writer from Poland or Ireland, in other words, is likely to be fully cognizant of the imperial undertones of travel writing, and its deleterious effects.[16]

Yet, as Virgil Nemoianu has argued, it is reductive to see travel writing purely in such negative terms.[17] Doing so ignores not only the work of travel writers from the periphery, but also, what is especially crucial, their efforts to use the form for their own utopian explorations. Krasicki and Swift are exemplary in this regard, evincing a clear awareness of travel literature's potential for harm while also appreciating its benefits. Indeed, both authors exploit the potential—and paradoxes—of travel literature as a genre for their critiques of utopia.

Travel writing is an obvious model for utopian literature: the structure of travel narrative offers the perfect justification for devoting so much attention and detail to the inner workings of a fictional society. Indeed, the premise of the utopian novel practically requires an audience conceived of as foreign, for why else would the descriptions be necessary? Utopian fiction is, one could say, travel writing taken to its most philosophical form. The hypothetical space of fiction can serve as a laboratory setting where philosophical and political theories are put to the test, as authors imagine how their abstract principles could be brought to life. What is more, the novel can be instrumental in bringing about this improved form of society: depicting a preferable way of life, it can persuade readers of its merits, giving them a tangible goal to strive for.[18]

Or rather, this is what utopian fiction should do, in theory. In practice, it rarely seems to work out that way. In fact, it is precisely in its efforts to render utopian life vivid and realistic that so many of the novels fall flat. Fredric Jameson complains, for instance, that in utopian literature "the perspective is utterly anonymous. The citizens of utopia are grasped as a statistical population; there are no individuals any longer, let alone any existential 'lived experience.'"[19] The characters become a uniform, undifferentiated mass, no longer recognizable as human. It is a curious conundrum, for this is the very problem that fiction ought to ameliorate, rendering the experience of utopian life tangible. What it reveals is the difficulty inherent in the encounter between the theoretical and the concrete. The universal is necessarily abstract, a purely formal category: if it is to contain everything, it cannot be too particular. Thus, the author is pushed to consider humanity in its most essential form, threatening to strip away any individuality. The problem of utopian writing is how to embody theoretical ideas about the way society functions in a recognizable human form, to bring ideas to life. And travel writing, rather than solving this problem, actually compounds it, for the disjunct between abstraction and lived experience is the paradox at the heart of all travel narratives.

As a genre, travel literature attempts to deliver virtually what it simultaneously insists must be experienced personally: the experience of travel. This contradiction is made particularly explicit when authors complain about the damage wreaked by other travel narratives that have been propagating false information about a given locale, and when they argue vehemently that literature is not to be trusted. These are works that insistently privilege lived reality over abstract, or literary, knowledge, simultaneously attempting to make the experience of reading a novel akin to the act of travel and protesting the impossibility of their task.

Many texts simply ignore this paradox and take it as given that *their* work will not suffer from such flaws. They acknowledge the problem and proceed as if their own accounts are faultless, because at the very least they have shown themselves as conscientious and aware of the potential dangers that lie ahead. The narrator in Krasicki's later novel, *Historia* (1779), is a representative example: he not only makes a point of correcting stereotypes about the places he visits, but also derides written histories and warns readers never to trust official accounts.[20] In other words, he dives into paradox with hardly a backward glance: historical narratives are unreliable and their misleading accounts have dangerous effects, but his own work can be relied upon to provide a faithful account. In *Gulliver's Travels* and *Mikołaja Doświadczyńskiego przypadki*, Swift and Krasicki treat the issue in more complex ways, using travel writing's inherent problematic as an opening onto the broader question of the clash between abstraction and reality and what it means for utopian thought.

Early on in *Gulliver's Travels*, Swift shows Gulliver to be simultaneously aware of the virtues of travel—its ability to educate and enlighten—and immune to its effects. When his description of England to the King of Brobdingnag is met with horror, Gulliver's own faith in his homeland is not shaken. Rather, he says, "But great allowances should be given to a King who lives wholly secluded from the rest of the world, and must therefore be altogether unacquainted with the manners and customs that most prevail in other nations: the want of which knowledge will ever produce many *prejudices* and certain *narrowness of thinking*; from which we and the politer countries of Europe are wholly exempted."[21] The potential wisdom to be gained from a journey lies in its ability to unsettle one's views, leading to the acknowledgment of a different perspective. Gulliver, unable to distance himself mentally from the politics of his home and recognize them as flawed, can readily dismiss the King's view precisely because the King has *not* traveled widely, never mind the fact that Gulliver's own voyages have served only to reinforce previously held beliefs. The irony here is readily discernible and makes it quite clear that simply going to a different place does not automatically confer wisdom on the traveler.

Mikołaja Doświadczyńskiego przypadki takes a different approach, though a similarly problematic one. Mikołaj, in an encounter reminiscent of that between Gulliver and the King of Brobdingnag, takes the criticisms to heart, even if he is not fully persuaded. Rather than attributing the disagreement to his companion's lack of travel, Mikołaj is impressed by his friend's wisdom despite this lack:

> Upokarzał mnie rozum Xaoo: nie mogłem skombinować, jak człowiek, który w Warszawie nigdy nie był, Paryża nie widział, mógł przecię rozsądnie myślić, mówić i konwinkować nawet człowieka, który nierównie więcej od niego i widział, i słyszał. (99)

> Xaoo's reasoning humbled me. I could not fathom how a person who had not been to Warsaw and had not seen Paris was able nonetheless to think and speak sensibly and be convincing, even in comparison with someone who had both seen and heard incomparably more than he. (71)[22]

Here, Mikołaj simultaneously illustrates the merits of travel—allowing one to encounter others whose ideas may be persuasive—and also implies that it is not necessary, for after all, Xaoo has attained this wisdom without ever leaving home. Perhaps it is simply a matter of reading the right books after all?

Thus we are confronted, in these two scenes, with the paradox of travel writing, the impossible contradiction between its insistence on the necessity of lived experience and its simultaneous desire to deliver that experience through narrative. This tension ripples through travel writing's narrative mode—its combination of vivid description and abstract rumination. As I will explain, it is also structurally analogous to the problem of utopian planning and its efforts to bridge the universal and the particular. And, as these two scenes begin to demonstrate, it is echoed in the apparent tension between detachment and identification, or satire and sincerity, the two primary strategies of novelistic pedagogy, to which I now turn.

In the scenes described above, the reader is clearly intended to read Gulliver and Mikołaj ironically, to understand what they fail to grasp, and to note their arrogant assumption of superiority. Mikołaj's case is slightly more complex, because of the distance introduced between character and narrator: proclaiming himself humbled, and clearly stating what he was not capable of understanding at this moment (how a person who had not traveled could nonetheless have wisdom), he suggests that he now *does* understand it, and thus, implicitly, that we should too. We are invited, in other words, to trust him as a narrator, and to identify with him as a character in order to be led through the process of education that he has presumably achieved. But even Mikołaj the narrator does not make the connection to his own situation as a traveler—he fails to grasp the full irony of the scene. The reader who does perceive that irony is thus distanced from Mikołaj the narrator, who thereby also comes to seem not so different from Mikołaj the character after all. Yet the narrator's implicit assertion that he has learned and changed does make a claim on the reader, inviting sympathy and connection. It is the very kind of sincere avowal that irony typically works to deflate. We see here, in other words, a faint tension between detachment and identification, a vacillation in our attitude toward Mikołaj. We are simultaneously expected to trust him, to take his words to heart and learn from them, *and* to learn from his ignorance, to discern the veiled irony of the text and understand what Mikołaj fails to grasp.

These two strategies are seemingly at odds with each other: surely, we should either identify with our protagonist or remain sufficiently detached to be able to see his or her limitations, and learn from them.[23] Ian Watt describes a similar problem in *Gulliver's Travels*, discussing the tension between Gulliver as ironic persona and lifelike character. As Watt explains, the ironic persona can function in one of two ways: either as the target of critique, exemplifying the failing that the text derides, or as a collaborator, voicing the conclusion the reader is intended to draw, albeit in a naive way, "with some apparent inferiority to ourselves as a witness."[24] In both cases, however, the reader remains in a position of cool detachment that is very different from the attitude solicited by an individualized character, to whom the reader becomes attached, as if to a real person.[25] The striking innovation of both Swift and Krasicki is to explore the tension between these two postures, precisely by collapsing it, and to connect this dichotomy to the problem of utopian planning, on the one hand, and fictional pedagogy, on the other.[26]

Mikołaja Doświadczyńskiego przypadki can ostensibly be read as a narrative of conversion, whereby the protagonist moves from naivete to wisdom as he learns about the world, but this process of *Bildung* is continuously threatened by Mikołaj's stubborn stupidity. The novel's repeated efforts to enact change in the young man elegantly highlight the challenge of education in general, but especially through fiction, by inviting the reader to consider how Mikołaj finally learns (or fails to). As we see, intellectual argument, the method seemingly most replicable for the novel, has limited power to change his ways; instead, he must learn through experience. Here again the paradox of travel literature resurfaces, now turned to the problem of education: the novel shows us that we cannot learn by being told what we are to know—we must experience it for ourselves. But the power of fiction to deliver such transformative experience is questionable at best, requiring a powerful identification with the protagonist.

We see a clear example of this dilemma in Mikołaj's changing attitude toward money. In the early portions of the text, most of Mikołaj's problems are of a financial nature, and his desire for money threatens to destroy him. When he arrives at the island of Nipu, he is seemingly educated and reformed of this love for gold until he discovers a shipwreck that contains, among other things, a pile of treasure. It is here that we see the limits of abstract intellectual argument, for despite his better judgment, he simply cannot resist the allure of money, the very thing that nearly ruined him in the first place:

> Złoto, lubo w tej wyspie do niczego niezdatne, ułudziło mnie zupełnie. Stałem się chciwym bez nadziei zysków, trwożnym w zupełnym bezpieczeństwie. . . . Jużem się był przyzwyczaił do sposobu życia Nipuanów; jużem zaczynał doznawać skutków szacownej spokojności. Kruszec złota nie dość że mnie uczynił nieszczęśliwym w Europie, dognał mnie za światem . . . widząc, że się żadnym sposobem przezwyciężyć nie mogę, przedsięwziąłem na owej zachowanej z okrętu łodzi puścić się na zgubę oczewistą prawie, byle z tej wyspy wynieść. (140–141)

> The gold, though utterly valueless on Nipu, had utterly beguiled me. I became greedy without hope of profit, and I felt anxious while enjoying complete security. . . . I had actually grown accustomed to the Nipuan way of life. I had begun to value the sacred tranquility of the place. But that metal known as gold was not content to make me miserable in Europe alone; it now pursued me the world over. . . . Realizing that I could not prevail upon myself, I resolved to leave the island in the boat I had salvaged from the wrecked ship, even though I was almost certain that this would bring about my ruin. (101, translation amended)

Although greed and the desire for luxury are faults explicitly derided by the Nipuans, and Mikołaj seems to agree with their teachings on an abstract level and appears to enjoy a world without money, when confronted with the glint of gold he is overwhelmed by what even he can recognize as an irrational desire. He flees the island without a word of goodbye, as though he were escaping a prison instead of a paradise. Although he will later claim that it was patriotism and a yearning for home that led to his departure, the baser motive is much more credible. Clearly, abstract knowledge can only go so far: human caprice is far more powerful.

Mikołaj is ultimately converted from his earlier greed, but in a very different way: after leaving Nipu he is enslaved and forced to work in the mines, leading to a painful awareness about where wealth comes from and the suffering it causes. If the lovers of gold were made aware of how much suffering people undergo to provide them with this metal, he argues, they would change their ways.[27] Although he quickly converts his suffering into a life lesson via abstract reasoning, it is clear that it is the physical pain that has changed his mind. This incident, again, casts serious doubt on the power of literature to deliver, in writing, lessons that are bought with experience. The techniques that are seemingly being used to persuade the reader are repeatedly shown to be inadequate to the task of educating the main character.

But the novel has another tool at its disposal: satire. Here, instead, the reader is invited to learn by perceiving what the character does not, by drawing their own conclusions from the givens of the situation, rather than by reading an explanation and being persuaded. The mechanisms of such pedagogy, however, assume a detachment that separates the reader from the character, inviting a more critical perspective. And so we see in Krasicki's novel that Mikołaj is just as often the target of critique as he is the vehicle. Indeed, he is practically a paragon of human intractability. Although he does learn some things, he repeatedly reverts to his previous beliefs and must be trained out of them anew. The glaring discrepancy between the ideas apparently espoused by the novel and the behavior of its hero at crucial moments, and the persistent repetition of such scenes, clearly signals to readers that they are meant to view the young man more critically.

The most obvious example is Mikołaj's persistent tendency to stereotype people. It is in Nipu that Mikołaj begins to question his assumptions about the "savagery" of others. His initial encounters with the Nipuans lead him to think they are a rather primitive race, and he decides that he can best express his gratitude for their hospitality by making them aware of their own barbarism. As he is on the verge of doing so, however, they turn the tables, praising his progress in becoming more civilized and adapting to Nipuan culture. He is thunderstruck with astonishment, and so begins the novel's long-running critique of developmental notions of human civilization. But this is a lesson that Mikołaj never seems to learn. Although he does ultimately recognize that the Nipuans are not "savage," this recognition fails to translate into a broader cultural relativism, or even increased self-awareness of his own assumptions about others. When he arrives in the New World and an Indigenous person offers him assistance, Mikołaj declares himself "zdziwiony takowym procederem dzikiego człowieka" (152) ("surprised that a savage would act in such a manner") (111). The irony of the scene is not lost on the reader, particularly because the local man immediately offers a lengthy disquisition on the topic, which is later repeated in the text by the Margrave de Vennes. Not only does Mikołaj need to be reminded of it again by the Margrave; upon hearing it, he remarks that he is surprised to hear such profound ideas from a man who looks, at first glance, like a dandy—launching the Margrave into yet another lecture, and clearly marking Mikołaj as the object of criticism.

The novel thus finds itself in a somewhat paradoxical position, striving to educate its readers and simultaneously illustrating the limitations of abstract argument. While Krasicki shows that reasoned discourse cannot guarantee a lasting transformation in his protagonist, he seems to retain some faith that, if repeated often enough, such speeches may ultimately convert his readers. The novel therefore attempts to form its claims in multiple modalities: not only by abstract argument but also through vicarious experience, and, when that fails, through ironic detachment. While readers cannot be made to work in the gold mines, for instance, they can, perhaps, be moved through fiction to a new understanding. The power of such a plea, however, is ambiguous at best, and is dependent on the extent to which the reader can identify with Mikołaj and his experiences. At the same time, Mikołaj is also clearly a *negative* example in some cases, whom the narrator is gently mocking for his narrow-mindedness and inability to learn.[28] Thus, the novel must likewise contain long passages of didactic screed (delivered by other characters) to set the reader on the correct path, or a glaring gap between the ideas it repeatedly seems to espouse and the protagonist's behavior. In other words, the novel simultaneously asks the reader to identify with the protagonist *and* read him ironically. This is the problem at the heart of literature's pedagogical potential: it has two strategies of persuasion, and they are at odds with each other. What Krasicki's text so fascinatingly demonstrates is that fiction can in fact accommodate both, even at the same time.

The same is true of *Gulliver's Travels*, though less obviously so. For much of the novel, as in the encounter with the King of Brobdingnag recounted above, Gulliver seems to be a straightforwardly ironic figure; a self-important, bumbling Englishman. Many of the text's political critiques are mounted in a satirical vein, allegories of various aspects of Irish colonialism, which Gulliver observes without significant comment. For the most part, it seems that the reader is expected to retain a circumspect distance from Gulliver (whose misanthropic qualities frequently render him rather unappealing). But he is not uniformly distasteful: his functioning as ironic persona is complex,[29] as an examination of the text's layered critiques of colonialism, which grant him varying levels of awareness, makes clear. The ending of the novel, however, and the critical debates as to its meaning, reveal how tenuous the ostensible detachment from Gulliver is, and how closely linked to the way the meaning of the text is perceived.

Some of the novel's more significant critiques of colonialism are to be found in the third section, in the discussion of the flying island of Laputa, which rules over the land of Lagado.[30] Gulliver notes, but does not comment on, the imperial aspects of the island, remarking, for instance, that "I was assured by a great minister that if the island had descended so near the town as not to be able to raise itself, the citizens were determined to fix it forever, to kill the King and all his servants, and entirely change the government" (Swift, *Gulliver*, 164). At such moments, he is a vehicle for the novel's critique, naively gesturing to an issue that he does not seem to fully understand, and that the text leaves unstated, yet visibly present for a discerning reader. Similarly, observing the poor state of agriculture in Lagado, Gulliver learns that it is the product of reforms instituted by people inspired by Laputan theory—a clear reference to politics of

Swift's time, and his writings on the mismanagement of Irish land,[31] but which Gulliver merely reports, without analysis. Though not himself implicated in the critiques contained in these scenes, Gulliver also does not necessarily share the views implied. He simply passes on information, which the reader is invited to interpret within a broader context.

At the end of the novel, however, he does discuss colonialism quite explicitly, as he deliberates whether Britain ought to conquer Houyhnhnmland. Swift cleverly manages to make Gulliver of two minds on the issue: on the one hand, he is wholly devoted to the Houyhnhnms, and would support them should they choose to intervene in the affairs of Europe: "But instead of proposals for conquering that magnanimous nation," he says, "I rather wish they were in a capacity or disposition to send a sufficient number of their inhabitants for civilizing Europe" (288). Secondarily, however, he argues against a British project to occupy the places he has visited in his other voyages, in words that would ring true even in a non-fictional context: "As those countries which I have described do not appear to have any desire of being conquered, and enslaved, or murdered or driven out by colonies; nor abound either in gold, silver, sugar, or tobacco; I did humbly conceive they were by no means proper objects of our zeal, our valour, or our interest" (289). Here Swift lays bare the fundamental drive behind the colonial enterprise—greed—and the violence that accompanies it. He does say that Britain is of course exempt from such a description, in words where Swift's irony surely overwhelms Gulliver's sincerity. But unlike the scenes mentioned in the previous paragraph, Gulliver is allowed some degree of reflection and insight. It is a moment where Gulliver is allowed to (naively) articulate Swift's position, granting him, in other words, a moment of credibility—which is then rapidly undercut, at least for some readers, as he delivers a florid paean to British rule. Thus, as with Mikołaj, we notice that our relationship to the character is on unsteady ground: he is not as straightforwardly ignorant, or noxious, as we may have supposed; he may be closer to us than we had realized.

But there is another layer to the critique of colonialism, one that is far less apparent, and that positions Gulliver somewhat differently. The real irony of the text, and its most stringent indictment of colonialism, is that at the novel's conclusion, Gulliver can be read as the ideal colonial subject, unquestioningly seeing himself and those of his kind as inferior to the more "civilized" race, with a conviction that overturns even his familial bonds,[32] and worshipping his masters to such a degree that he even serves their representatives in their home country, though they are clearly inferior to the real thing.[33] In his complete dismissal of his wife and children—his repulsion toward them, even—Gulliver can be seen as having completely internalized the structures of (colonial) authority. His despondent existence is thus the logical conclusion of the colonial system: banned from the utopian center because of his species, he wastes away miserably at the periphery. And compelling as Gulliver's explicit critique of colonialism in the final pages may be, it is this subtle ironic twist that serves as the more powerful condemnation. Swift does not use Gulliver's own voice to articulate this argument against Houyhnhnm society—quite the opposite. You have to read Gulliver ironically to understand the point. At the same time, however, to read Gulliver in a purely ironic light is also not sufficient: if the reader is completely detached from him, the force of the critique is partly lost. To recognize the tragedy, one must feel sympathy for Gulliver's abject state. In other words, as in Krasicki's text, the reader is required to both identify with the protagonist *and* maintain a certain detachment from him.

This duality is most apparent at the ending of the text, or rather, in the critical disputes as to its meaning. Part of this debate, summarized by James Clifford as the "hard" and "soft" schools of interpretation, is whether Houyhnhnmland is meant to be a truly utopian space: either it is, and there is true pathos in Gulliver's misery at being cast out, or it is not (because the Houyhnhnms are not human, and their standards are unattainable), and Gulliver's hatred of other humans is a humorous absurdity.[34] In other words, either one is to identify with Gulliver, and share his sadness, or one is meant to read him ironically, and appreciate the comedy of the ending.[35] As I discuss in the next section, there are clear signs that Houyhnhnmland is not truly utopian, but certainly, Gulliver does not realize this and is miserable over his exclusion from it. That some readers share his ignorance and see the ending as a testament to the tragic inferiority of humans makes clear that a (too) strong identification with Gulliver is possible. This is not simply a misreading, I maintain: those who recognize that Gulliver is wrong about Houyhnhnmland would themselves be mistaken if they remained utterly detached from Gulliver and indifferent to his woes. Indeed, they would become the overly arrogant protagonist of their own drama, failing to discern the irony of our shared human predicament.

As the following section explains, these novels are showing us the flaws inherent in utopian reasoning as such, in ways that implicate us, the readers, as well, and they are genuinely mourning them. Crucial to this critique is this vacillation between detachment and sympathy in both texts. We are shown the paradox and our own implication in it, but we can only perceive it if we read with both sympathy *and* detachment. Fiction's two primary modes of education, soliciting an identification that attends to the sincere avowals of the text, and a distanced observation that perceives its ironies, are not opposed, but (paradoxically) complementary. Indeed, this is precisely the unique power of fiction's ability to articulate ideas: that it can accommodate both modes at the same time. As we shall see, this duality is mirrored yet again in the fundamental paradox of utopian reasoning: the tension between collective and individual freedom.

One of the issues that troubles utopian writing is whether people are simply too flawed to ever achieve the Good Life. Both Swift and Krasicki consider this problem, illuminating a core irrationality in humankind. While the conclusion of *Mikołaja Doświadczyńskiego przypadki* speaks to the difficulties in persuading people to change their own system of government to a superior one—to enact a utopia—it cannot be ignored that Mikołaj was not banished from Nipu but left of his own volition, and for wholly irrational reasons. The problem in this case is not only to convince people to create a utopian world, but also to persuade them to stay put once they have one. As Krasicki shows, this is a difficult proposition, for human nature is fickle. Swift likewise speaks of such human caprice: describing the island of Laputa in the third voyage, Gulliver notes that travel is strictly regulated, for the female inhabitants would otherwise flee. While this may be read as simple Swiftian misogyny,[36] it nonetheless further speaks to the impossibility of a rationally organized life:

> The wives and daughters lament their confinement to the island, although I think it is the most delicious spot of ground in the world; and although they live here in the greatest plenty and magnificence, and are allowed to do whatever they please, they long to see the world, and take the diversions of the metropolis, which they are not allowed to do without particular license from the King; and this is not easy to be obtained, because the people of quality have found by frequent experience how hard it is to persuade their women to return from below. (154)

Here we see again the irrational desire to leave "the most delicious spot of ground in the world," even for a life of misery. Although Gulliver deduces from this that "the caprices of womankind are not limited by any climate or nation, and that they are more uniform than can be easily imagined" (154), one cannot help but notice that Gulliver himself is cursed with a similar capricious wanderlust: "the thirst I had of seeing the world, notwithstanding my past misfortunes, continuing as violent as ever" (143); "my insatiable desire of seeing foreign countries" (75); "I continued at home with my wife and children about five months in a happy condition, if I could have learned the lesson of knowing when I was well" (205). Man's instinct to roam, it seems, is unconquerable, making him ineligible for a tranquil utopian existence.[37]

A perfect world would seem to require, in turn, perfect inhabitants, and as these texts make clear, humanity falls rather short in this regard. This problem is articulated in *Mikołaja Doświadczyńskiego przypadki* by the Margrave de Vennes, in much simpler terms, namely, as pertains to the difficulty of making friends:

> Nie trzeba wyciągać po ludziach ostatniego stopnia doskonałości, bo takim sposobem nie znajdziemy żadnego, którego byśmy uznali godnym naszego przywiązania; . . . Nie znajdziesz WPan Nipuanów w Europie; musisz jednak żyć z ludźmi . . . Mniej niedoskonały niech tylko będzie celem troskliwości takowej, będziesz szczęśliwym, bo znajdziesz przyjaciół. (163)

> If we require the highest degree of excellence in people, we will not then find anyone deemed worthy of our affections. . . . There are no Nipuans in Europe, but you must live among people. . . . Grant a few imperfections in those you care to know well, and you will be happy, for then you will find friends. (119)

Collective existence demands compromise and a willingness to accept the faults of others. Reading over these words, one also thinks of poor Gulliver returning home from his voyages and settling into a deeply misanthropic life, unable to bear even the scent of his wife and children, spending most of his time attempting to chat with his horses. But this speech by the Margrave is not simply a guide to making friends; it is also an implicit claim about human nature as such and the realities of collective life. A utopian society is one that requires "the highest degree of excellence in people"—conformity to a standard of perfection that humankind is incapable of.

It is noteworthy that, in his speech, the Margrave draws a distinction between Nipuans and people. One could replace Nipuans with Houyhnhnms and arrive at a message equally applicable to *Gulliver's Travels*. The implication is that Nipuans and Houyhnhnms are a different sort of creature from humans, able to achieve a standard that man cannot. Indeed, in the final voyage of Swift's novel, this would seem to be the case. It is not whim that sends Gulliver back to England but inadequacy of a different sort: he is not a Houyhnhnm. This would seem to be a further confirmation of man's inadequacy to utopian life, but in fact it opens onto a somewhat different interpretation.

It is not exactly because Gulliver is not a Houyhnhnm that he cannot remain in their country; rather, it is because he occupies an ambiguous position in the organization of Houyhnhnm society. Somewhat too refined to be a Yahoo, he is nonetheless not a Houyhnhnm and never will be. He therefore does not meet the requirements to be a true citizen of Houyhnhnmland and, as such, becomes a threat. The Houyhnhnm assembly decrees that it is "not agreeable to reason or nature" (256) for him to live in a Houyhnhnm home as a companion, and dangerous for him to be placed among the Yahoos, for his rudimentary powers of reason could lead him to organize the Yahoos in rebellion. Thus, he is exhorted to leave. Rather than being a claim about mankind's qualifications (or lack thereof), this is an example of a flaw in the utopian scheme: its inability to tolerate ambiguity. In a rationally ordered society, matters are black and white: there can be no third term.

We see manifestations of this problem in both Krasicki's and Swift's novels. The rigid organization of the utopian world makes any possibility of difference or change dangerous. What these works illustrate, furthermore, is the way in which anything that does not belong to the utopian scheme becomes wholly negative, an embodiment of evil. In the Laputan society encountered in Gulliver's third voyage, this attitude is evidenced by their paranoid study of astronomy: the people fear that which they can neither control nor fully calculate. In the voyage to Houyhnhnmland, the point is made more explicitly, in the distinction between Houyhnhnms and Yahoos. It is here that utopia's totalitarianism, and violence, emerge.

Krasicki subtly points to the violence in the utopian scheme through the character of Laongo, who serves as a condensed version of all threats posed by Otherness. Laongo, we are told, traveled to distant islands and returned with plans of reform. When discovered, he and his followers were stoned to death. A pile of rocks marks the site, and a ballad keeps its lessons alive for future inhabitants. Just how strongly engraved the memory of this primordial violence is on the minds of Nipuans is made clear when Xaoo, recoiling in horror at Mikołaj's descriptions of a corrupt European legal system, cries "Bądźcie błogosławione, święte ręce, któreście stosami kamieni przywaliły Laonga i towarzyszów jego! Takich by nas zbrodni nauczyli wezwani od niego cudzoziemcy!" (129) ("blessed be those sacred hands that crushed Laongo and his accomplices with stones! The outlanders he summoned would have taught us to commit the crimes you describe") (93). The brutality of the language, and the matter-of-fact way in which it is uttered, is jarring, forcing the reader to confront the violent repression necessary to any utopian scheme, its inability to tolerate dissension in any form.

It is not only explicit rebellion that Nipuans fear, but innovation more generally—and therefore, travel. Laongo's crime is his attempt to foment rebellion, but the cause is clearly located in his voyages to other countries. Here the problematic union of travel writing and utopian literature becomes clear once again, for while it is obvious that Mikołaj can benefit from his voyages, in that they bring him to Nipu and allow him to learn about their way of life, it is also clear that the Nipuans, believing they have found the ideal way of life, can in no way benefit from encounters with others.

Xaoo initially asks Mikołaj a series of questions, striving to find out as much as he can about the European way of life. Having learned about Mikołaj's way of thinking, he then proceeds with his own lessons, the project of "civilizing"

Mikołaj. Gulliver's Houyhnhnm master is similarly eager to learn about Europe, mostly because he is astonished to discover a Yahoo with some grasp of logic. He likewise, however, seems more intent upon explaining the flaws of these systems to Gulliver than entertaining them as genuine alternatives. But this curiosity on the part of certain utopians—surely akin to the caprice and wanderlust of the protagonists, albeit in a more restrained form—is notable, hinting as it does that travel (both to and from utopia) truly *is* a threat to their way of life. Xaoo states this threat explicitly, explaining the problem of travel by saying that foreign places will either be better or worse than one's home; if they are worse, what good does it do to see them, and if better, what does one gain other than a newfound discontent with one's own lot? Though he agrees that one may indeed learn things that will benefit one's home, he claims that this knowledge will inevitably lead to the importation of foreign vices as well, for evil is more appealing to the weak human spirit than is virtue. This is particularly striking, for it is an implicit acknowledgment that humans are not naturally virtuous creatures: they must be disciplined to be good. While travel does hold out some possibility for improvement, this possibility is outweighed by its potential harm.[38] More importantly, Xaoo says, travel feeds man's restlessness rather than satisfying it, making it clear that a successful utopian society depends upon the suppression of human passions in favor of a virtuous existence. It requires discipline and complete submission to its laws and principles. An encounter with different forms of life leads one to question these norms and is therefore a threat to the entire society.

This danger is apparent even in the highly disciplined society of the Houyhnhnms. Commentators on Swift have pointed out that Gulliver's Houyhnhnm master, in his willingness to play the role of host, violates Houyhnhnm customs.[39] Though he explicitly derides Gulliver's beliefs, declaring him a "perfect Yahoo" (219), he nonetheless seems to enjoy his company and conversation. This conflict suggests that he is not wholly impervious to outside influence. What is more, though he ultimately accedes to the Assembly's ruling and bids Gulliver depart, there is a trace of regret in his final words. The leniency he had verged on exhibiting validates the utopian fear of outsiders, showing as it does that even a perfectly reasonable creature can become personally attached to a Yahoo.

The aberrant nature of this fondness is vividly clear when compared to the fate of the other Yahoos. In Houyhnhnmland, anxiety about otherness is taken to a terrifying extreme. Set against the Houyhnhnms, the Yahoos come to represent all that is evil, and indeed, they are portrayed as thoroughly nasty creatures. This can be seen even in Houyhnhnm language: "The Houyhnhnms have no word in their language to express anything that is *evil*, except what they borrow from the deformities or ill qualities of the Yahoos" (252). This moral distinction, however, is cast in very different terms: whereas the Houyhnhnms are creatures of pure reason, the Yahoos are bestial and irrational.[40] The terms of the debate are set as those of reason itself, wholly impersonal. "So compelling is Houyhnhnm reason that it is presented as entirely other than force":[41] passionless, disinterested, and impermeable to argument. With such variables, the validity of exterminating the Yahoos brooks no disagreement. Even Gulliver, biologically kindred to them (to the extent that he develops a strong sense of repulsion toward himself, though self-immolation never seems to cross his mind), thinks nothing of using Yahoo skins and tallow to outfit his boat. The murder of the Yahoos is not a matter of personal distaste but a logical conclusion. Indeed, the Houyhnhnms "have no conception of how a creature can be *compelled*, but only advised, or *exhorted*; because no person can disobey reason without giving up his claims to be a rational creature" (257), and Gulliver's master, though he hates the Yahoos, "no more blamed them for their odious qualities, than he did a *gnnayh* for its cruelty, or a sharp stone for cutting his hoof" (228). In contemplating the massacre of the Yahoos, they are merely acting out the dictates of reason. In this final episode, the utopian argument is raised to its horrifying logical conclusion: genocide.

By defining the ideals of the Houyhnhnms as reason itself, Swift makes their society the essence of utopianism. The horses are faithful devotees of universal reason, a principle seemingly removed from any particular culture or location. In other words, the structure of Houyhnhnm society is theoretically a timeless, universal template. It is not only a rationally ordered world, but also one that is structured around pure logic. By illustrating the flaws in this society, its inhuman face, Swift casts doubt on the utopian dream at large.[42]

Although he clearly illuminates the inhuman quality of pure logic, Swift's purpose in describing the Houyhnhnms is not to completely renounce reason itself. Reconstructing the claims nested in this voyage, however, is not so simple. Certainly, the argument is not for a wholly irrational, anarchic society. The satire is more open-ended: it does not formulate an argument so much as it articulates a problem, one that it cannot provide a solution for, and perhaps one that cannot be solved. Swift simultaneously reveals the tyranny of reason—its tendency to slip into totalitarianism—and its potential benefits. The Houyhnhnm mode of life is not entirely disavowed or held up as a purely negative example. Swift insists upon the specific merits of this alternative vision, even as he exposes its flaws. However, unlike his *Modest Proposal*, which does (ironically) gesture to some legitimate steps for reform,[43] no such affirmative message can be clearly gleaned from *Gulliver's Travels*.

The same is true of *Mikołaja Doświadczyńskiego przypadki*. Krasicki never suggests what could be changed about Nipu that would make Mikołaj stay there, nor does he ever articulate a specific critique of it as a place. In fact, up to the very conclusion of the novel, Mikołaj continues to see it as perfect, without ever expressing any intention of returning. Agnieszka Śniegucka has argued that Mikołaj's departure from Nipu is precipitated by his realization that utopia makes self-realization impossible, and while one could say that the novel opens the possibility of such an epiphany in the reader, there is no evidence of any conscious awareness of it in Mikołaj.[44] Nor are there clear recommendations for how a better society could be achieved.

Both novels, in other words, never explicitly state their critiques, nor do they offer viable alternatives. Rather, they depict utopias as both problematic and untenable (even though the characters are committed to them). They refuse the possibility of a middle way, even as they show that the extremes are unacceptable.[45] Indeed, how can one logically formulate a solution that is capable of accommodating a certain amount of irrationality—precisely that which cannot be understood, or predicted, via reason?

The problem with utopian modes of government is their attempt to map out an all-encompassing logical system that will apply universally. The argument these two novels make is that when theory and experience collide, the results are unforeseeable. The individual cannot be fully encapsulated within the general except by brute conquest: the demand for freedom exceeds the best-laid plans.

This critique is not only to be found in the content of these texts but is also performed by them. The open-ended nature of their form of satirical argument highlights the very blind spot of utopianism that they critique: that it relies on universalizing pronouncements. Satire is not simply a different way of articulating a logical claim. It operates ironically, never stating its arguments openly. A utopian society, however, is predicated on transparency and clearly articulated premises. It is unable to tolerate ambiguity, which is satire's proper residence. Satire is, in this way, utopian—not in the literal sense of proposing a better world, as we have seen, but in the metaphorical one, representing a kind of hope in the face of impossibility.[46] Gesturing ironically to the hidden meanings behind its claims, it suggests that there *is* an ultimate resolution to the problems that it articulates, albeit one that cannot be simply stated. But while this kind of ironic resignation may be possible for an individual (or a novel), it cannot function as the basis for governing society.

In an essay on nationalism and irony, Terry Eagleton argues that it is precisely those who are politically oppressed under the guise of the Enlightenment's notions of abstract universal equality who come to understand what such universalism truly represents. Universalism, he writes, must emerge from the particular and be consented to and internalized. In places that are politically oppressed, universalism will appear visibly alien, external to the individual, as a threat to local particularity. Upon being brutally dispossessed of their local culture, an oppressed group becomes alienated from itself, and therefore poised to assume the transcendent cosmopolitan subjectivity that the Enlightenment allegedly represented—in order to claim their right to self-determination. The oppressed subject begins with the perception of a lack that renders it non-self-identical, which opens onto a broader social dimension that poses the question of what general conditions are necessary for the fulfillment of their particular needs. Mediated through the general in this way, individual demands become relativized, transformed by an awareness of the particular within the general. The paradox of bourgeois Enlightenment, Eagleton argues, is that its universalism is enshrined in a right to particularity: "The only point of enjoying such universal abstract equality is to discover and live one's own particular difference. The *telos* of the entire process is not, as the Enlightenment believes, universal truth, right and identity, but concrete particularity."[47] To become aware of this, however, is to be forced into a recognition of an ironic dialectic that "cannot be *lived* as simple, seamless unity."[48] This ironic awareness is precisely what is achieved in Swift's *Gulliver's Travels* and Krasicki's *Mikołaja Doświadczyńskiego przypadki*, albeit in somewhat different ways.

While this lesson about the impossibility of universal standards condemns poor, hapless Gulliver to a rather unfortunate ending, Mikołaj's prospects seem rather cheerier, albeit also somewhat half-hearted. Mikołaj returns from his travels brimming with wisdom and an ardent desire to apply it to the troubles that have beset Poland. Eager to bring about reform, he travels to Warsaw and attempts a career in politics, but with no success: people are not persuaded by his arguments. He is surprisingly unperturbed by his failure, saying simply, "Nie udało mi się w Warszawie: ale ja się dlatego ani na Warszawę, ani na rodzaj ludzki nie gniewam. Każdy człowiek ma swój właściwy sposób myślenia; mój nie godził się z Warszawą, pojechałem więc myślić do Szumina" (187) ("I did not succeed in Warsaw, but this did not make me angry at Warsaw or the human race. Everyone has his own approach to things. Mine was not in agreement with Warsaw's, so I went to Szumin to think") (136). He returns to his estates and attempts, as much as possible, to live life in accordance with the Nipuan principles he has learned to value.

This is a surprising turn in the text, an extremely anti-climactic moment: the narrative momentum is completely deflated, as all the travels would seem to be for naught. Yet the novel concludes with an insistent note of contentment, albeit on a small scale. Travel *has* conferred benefits on Mikołaj, but they are of an individual, rather than collective, nature. Instead of attempting to force his views on others and enact political change, he returns to his estates to live out his own concrete particularity. Sante Graciotti sees this ending as a moment where utopian ideals are confronted with reality: the result is not the dissolution of utopian principles, but rather a shift whereby they are kept alive in the individual's mind and personal life.⁴⁹ Graciotti acknowledges that this shift weakens the utopian claims that the text makes, but he argues that this loss is offset by the increase in realism. Such a reading, however, fails to account for the flatness of the ending. The sense that *il faut cultiver se jardin*, that there is no possibility of enticing the collective to pursue a better life for all, is not merely a shift, but also, in an important sense, a failure. Though it may appear unsatisfying to many readers (indeed, I share Agnieszka Śniegucka's view that the sudden appearance of the romance plot at the end of the novel seems obviously compensatory⁵⁰), the finale of the text is a necessary conclusion to Krasicki's overarching argument: a vivid illustration of the coercive lining of dreams of universal freedom.

There is an intriguing precedent for the resigned, pessimistic view of utopia in these two novels, Krasicki's in particular, and I want to briefly tarry over it, because it is a text that has increasingly been put forth as an important source text for Enlightenment fiction and philosophy: Ibn Tufayl's twelfth-century Arabic novel, *Hayy ibn Yaqzan*.⁵¹ Tufayl's novel is often discussed in relation to *Robinson Crusoe*, both being stories of a man living alone on an island.⁵² Although definitive proof that Defoe read the text cannot be found, Nawal Muhammad Hassan has collected what amounts to quite plausible evidence that Defoe was familiar with it, and he has detailed some of the similarities between the two novels.⁵³ Fedwa Malti-Douglas argues, however, that such comparisons are exaggerated, noting the significant differences between the two works.⁵⁴ Although *Mikołaja Doświadczyńskiego przypadki* is superficially quite different, lacking the solitary castaway plotline or the religious dimension of *Hayy ibn Yaqzan*, there is a striking similarity in the conclusions of the two stories, and, I argue, a broader agreement in their philosophical position on the possibilities of utopia, which suggests that Krasicki's novel is the more meaningful counterpart to Tufayl's work. Both texts propose that although individual enlightenment is possible, collective improvement is not, offering endings that are resigned, rather than happy.

Hayy ibn Yaqzan chronicles the adventures of its titular protagonist, who grows up alone on an unpeopled island,⁵⁵ and is raised by a deer. After the deer dies, he gradually reasons his way to a higher understanding, and finds happiness through his connection to God. In the final ten pages of the book, however, there is a curious plot twist, as a man named Asal arrives. Asal has come from a neighboring land, where he was the follower of an increasingly popular religious sect. As he progressed in his studies, he came to believe that men ought to live in solitude, and thus, he found himself on this island. The two men become friends: Asal decides that Hayy is a man of God, and Hayy becomes interested in society and other humans (whom he has never met before) and decides that he would like to help them. So they return to Asal's home and meet with a group of particularly devout men, hoping to bring about their salvation.

But the men of the mainland are not converted. In the words of the text, "the more he taught, the more repugnance they felt, despite the fact that these were men who loved the good and sincerely yearned for the Truth. Their inborn infirmity simply would not allow them to seek him as Hayy did, to grasp the true essence of His being and see Him in His own terms. They wanted to know Him in some human way."[56] Hayy and Asal quickly realize that their goals are futile, and, telling these ignorant men that they are on the right track, depart, returning to their desert island, where they live, it seems, blissfully ever after.

This is a happy ending—for Hayy and Asal. Indeed, it is probably the closest we come to a true utopian text; a story of how one man—and his one friend!—achieve the Good Life.[57] But it is also, arguably, a failure of the utopian project. The knowledge gained by the two men is neither universal nor transmissible. In fact, the narrator of the novel repeatedly makes clear that that knowledge cannot even be properly conveyed to readers, for words cannot describe it, despite the fact that "nothing revealed here contradicts what is revealed by reason" (96). As the example of the unconverted makes clear, there is no guarantee that even those who are both devout and willing to learn will be able to grasp this liberatory knowledge. In other words, the novel suggests that knowledge is attainable through reason, but that it is an individual process, one that cannot be straightforwardly transmitted to others. So, it can lead only to individual, rather than collective, benefit.[58] A novel can show us this process, but cannot, despite its best intentions, guarantee a replication of it—as it shows us through the protagonist's failure to win over others.

Both *Hayy ibn Yaqzan* and *Mikołaja Doświadczyńskiego przypadki*, then, are texts that seem, at first, to celebrate Enlightenment reason and human perfectibility. But both are careful about the scope of potential benefits, and surprisingly pessimistic about the possibility of more widespread reforms. In this caution and pessimism, they make explicit what is arguably a lurking unease within Enlightenment thought, a thread running through all of its utopian fictions. For indeed, one is hard-pressed to find *any* truly successful utopian texts, *particularly* in the Enlightenment period, ostensibly a historical moment most suited to them.[59]

Krasicki's story offers a similar conclusion to Ibn Tufayl's regarding the possibility of persuading others, but embedded in his novel is a more extensive critique of the dangers of utopian efforts than is present in ibn Tufayl's work, a critique that shares the concerns articulated in *Gulliver's Travels*. Both Swift and Krasicki set forth some of the tensions between the Enlightenment's interest in cosmopolitanism, the free exchange of ideas, and the dynamic development of society, as compared to the rigid nature of abstract theory and the static bylaws of a society whose minutest details are the results of rational calculation. Both point to the violence of utopian societies and their stark, brutal intolerance of dissension or difference. In showing that people are not suited to utopian life, they illuminate both the flaws of capricious humankind and the rigidity of social planning, bemoaning both.

❧

Utopian literature is meant to be an embodiment of a philosophical argument that also serves as a necessary corollary to it. If the ideas are sound, then one should be able to put them into practice, and fiction is a means of doing so. These two novels by Swift and Krasicki, however, do precisely the opposite: they show that it is in their embodiment that the ideas of utopian society are revealed as untenable. Lived reality, rather than neatly embodying the abstract, has an unfortunate tendency to exceed or contradict it. Irony ultimately deals the death blow to utopianism, for the clearly reasoned tenets of utopian society prove unable to countenance irony, the playground of human caprice, and thus the locus of freedom.

But, as Swift and Krasicki show us, it is through fiction that the true limitations of the utopian project can emerge. Although literature would seem to provide a unique opportunity to make the utopian argument in a different way, through vicarious experience rather than reasoned discourse, the paradox of travel literature reveals the contradictions inherent in this approach, the use of literature to bestow experience that the text insists words cannot convey. In the same way, it shows us the impossibility of persuading someone by simply telling them what you want them to know. Nonetheless, these novels *do* impart certain philosophical lessons to their readers, precisely through their portrayal of protagonists who fail to learn. The argument made by these books depends upon a blend of irony and identification, revealing the limitations of straightforward realism for political critique.

As they demonstrate the problems that beset fiction's efforts to persuade, Swift and Krasicki simultaneously illustrate fiction's unique capabilities to reveal those problems, because of its ability to collapse the seeming opposition between detachment and sympathy. The contradiction between detachment and absorption is one of many straddled by these books, echoing the tension between theory and practice, or between individual and collective. Illuminating the common structures of these nested contradictions, *Gulliver's Travels* and *Mikołaja Doświadczyńskiego przypadki* show us something new about the novel form itself.

CHAPTER TWO

The Terror of Worlds Unfolding
Potocki and Maturin

Perhaps the most striking case of a singular affinity between Polish and Irish literature is that of Jan Potocki's *Rękopis znaleziony w Saragossie* (1804/1810/1847) (*The Manuscript Found in Saragossa*) and Charles Maturin's *Melmoth the Wanderer* (1820). Rarely discussed alongside each other,[1] both books, with their roving geographies, supernatural effects, and tangled webs of stories-within-stories-within-stories, are regularly described as odd—"freakishly irregular,"[2] as one introduction to *Melmoth* puts it—and yet, of all the texts that I discuss in this book, these two are the most central to a better understanding of the novel form, precisely because they are so absorbed in investigating it themselves. Most obviously, both works playfully explore the way fictions solicit belief in the unreal, thereby examining the effects of fictionality and the question of whether it deludes or corrupts readers. As I explain, however, the intricate architecture of both texts, their interlaced and overlapping tales, extends these inquiries by offering a complex reflection on how specific literary techniques can abstractly model worlds.

Neither book fits neatly into any particular tradition, be it national or generic. Maturin was an Anglo-Irish Protestant clergyman, and his novel is sometimes seen as a foundational text of the Irish Gothic,[3] or alternatively, in relation to the English Gothic, particularly that genre's more psychologically oriented works.[4] Potocki's case is even more complicated: though Potocki was a Polish nobleman, he wrote the novel in French (the language used by much of the Polish aristocracy at the time). Published in fragmentary form during the author's life, a complete edition first appeared only in 1847, when it was translated into Polish by Edmund Chojecki. Although it was long believed that Chojecki's translation came from an original text since lost, scholars now agree that he personally undertook the task of uniting two different manuscripts from 1804 and 1810.[5] Regardless of which version Potocki himself would have considered the "correct" one, it was Chojecki's edition that circulated in Polish literature in the nineteenth and twentieth centuries, and that was used by Rene Radrizzani to produce a complete edition in French in 1989 (which in turn served as the basis of the English translation in 1995).[6]

Neither book appears among the texts generally associated with the novel's rise. Rather, scholars tend to identify the turbulence of their historical contexts—for Maturin, the 1798 Rebellion and Act of Union of 1800, and for Potocki, the French Revolution and the disaster of the final Partition of Poland—as central to their Gothic effects, and, in Maturin's case especially, to the embedded story structure of the novel,[7] and to see these qualities as divergent from, if not in opposition to, the current of emerging realist fiction. *Rękopis znaleziony w Saragossie* is frequently read as part of the French fantastic tradition, or among proto-postmodernist works, in the category of "world literature."[8] But Potocki is also always claimed as a native son in histories of Polish literature, where he is typically given a section to himself, as a singular entity.[9] French critics similarly tend to focus heavily on Potocki's biography, regularly referring to both the man and his novel as a "mystery" or an "enigma."[10] Indeed, the author's remarkable life, and mysterious death, certainly set him apart: an explorer and ethnographer, Potocki traveled extensively throughout Europe, North Africa, and East Asia, penning travel narratives and archaeological studies. As evidenced by the cabbalistic themes in the novel, he seems to have had an interest in the occult: he may or may not have been a Freemason,[11] and he allegedly committed suicide with a silver bullet painstakingly carved from his own sugar bowl. Although Maturin's life is somewhat less remarkable, he does cut an odd figure: a clergyman who relished tales of terror and the supernatural, and whose continuous financial struggles and embattled position in Ireland seem to have made him a bitter and irascible man.[12] The personal quirks of both men draw more attention, perhaps, because of the remarkable texts they created: baroque architectures of interwoven tales with more than a hint of Orientalist exoticism, coupled with a wry, quasi-Romantic perspective that seems both melancholic and skeptical of the promises of the Enlightenment.

Although the two novels are indeed outliers in many ways, focusing on their strangeness can serve to ostracize them, and thereby to minimize their engagement in a broader history of the novel's development. Reading them alongside each other serves to highlight, instead, their shared interest in philosophical questions of fiction's form and function that were prevalent at the time. The role played by Gothic fiction in the novel's emergence is increasingly recognized, and both of these texts lend further credence to these claims, although their use of the supernatural is unique, and quite complex. But although such effects seem like the central focus of these novels, their real interest, I argue, lies elsewhere, in more extended reflections on the question of what fictions do and how they affect their audience. Through their peculiarly unique forms of worlding, these two novels illuminate the complex relationships between worldbuilding, storytelling, and the world itself: they show us that our experience of the world is not as a container, or spatial extension, but as a dense network of stories, which are always, at least in part, products of imagination.

To (briefly) recount: *Rękopis znaleziony w Saragossie* describes the adventures of Alfons van Worden, a young member of the Walloon Guards, who is traveling through Spain to meet his regiment. Warned that the region—the Sierra Morena—is haunted, he stops for the night at a desolate inn. At midnight, two attractive women appear and claim to be his Muslim cousins, Emina and Zubeida. They tell him that he must abandon his Christian faith, prove his bravery, and assume his rightful place at the head of the Gomelez clan. Succumbing to their erotic charms, he awakens the next morning under a gallows, beside two corpses whose ghosts, he has been told, haunt the plains. As his travels continue, he meets up with an assortment of travelers—a priest, a possessed man named Paszeko, a gypsy named Pandesowna, a cabbalist and his sister, Rebeka, and a mathematician named Velásquez—and they pass the time by telling stories. Pandesowna is the primary narrator, and his stories become a labyrinthine maze of tales within tales, as the characters in his stories begin telling stories of their own. These stories become a different form of encounter with the exotic world that Alfons has found himself in, serving to shape his impressions of this strange landscape and help him make sense of his experiences, as he struggles to understand whether his cousins are people or demons, and to evaluate what he should do next.

Melmoth the Wanderer follows a similar scheme: a young man, John Melmoth, travels to the West of Ireland, to the home of his dying uncle. On his deathbed, the uncle demands that John destroy a portrait of an ancient ancestor (Melmoth the Wanderer), who he says is still living, despite being over one hundred years old, as well as a mysterious manuscript. John reads the manuscript, which chronicles a set of eerie encounters between the Wanderer and a man named Stanton. The atmosphere grows increasingly ominous, as the mysterious relative seems to lurk in the vicinity. The next night, a shipwreck brings a sailor named Monçada to the house, and it emerges that he, too, has met the terrifying ancestor. Asked to tell his tale, Monçada launches into a narrative that contains many other stories within itself—the tales of other people he meets (and the stories they hear), and the content of a manuscript he is at one point forced to copy, all of which turn out to be about Melmoth the Wanderer,[13] who repeatedly appears at moments of crisis, tempting suffering people with a horrific offer. As in *Rękopis znaleziony w Saragossie*, it is through the accumulation of these seemingly disparate tales that a bigger picture emerges.

Although there is ostensibly a main plot line, a central question, animating both texts (who is the Gomelez clan, and are they supernatural beings, in *Rękopis znaleziony w Saragossie*, and who is Melmoth the Wanderer, in *Melmoth the Wanderer*?), the hurried finale of each, and the sheer volume of seemingly tangential material, serve to minimize that plot, directing attention to the other tales instead. Individually mysterious, when assembled into a larger whole the stories produce a different kind of effect: the image of a vast, interconnected world. Scholars have suggested that processes of globalization have produced new forms of fiction in the late twentieth century, techniques that reflect new notions of worldedness in our current age.[14] I argue that the interlaced stories of Maturin and Potocki are a much earlier example of such forms, offering peculiarly self-conscious reflections on the ways that fictions world, both within the text, and outside of it.

Gothic fiction has long been seen as a kind of detour on the road of the novel's rise—a continuation of the romance mode, albeit with the addition of horror, a genre largely governed by formulaic plots and escapist thrills. Although Horace Walpole's preface to *The Castle of Otranto* framed the novel as an experiment, an effort to reconcile imagination and credibility that served to bridge the gap between what were often seen as the "romantic" and "realistic" strains of the novel, the extravagantly fantastical element of Gothic works has long excluded them from serious consideration as important contributors to the development of fiction. More recently, however, scholars such as Deirdre Lynch, Nicholas Paige, Katherine Ding, Sarah Tindal Kareem, and Peter Otto have suggested that Gothic novels played a key role in the genre's emergence by virtue of their careful investigation of techniques of illusion.

Such arguments generally focus primarily on the way Gothic novels represent the supernatural or other explicitly unreal phenomena. Thus, for instance, Nicholas Paige argues that the Gothic played a crucial function in literary history by pioneering techniques of what came to be modern fictionality, using supernatural and otherwise impossible events to explore how literature could be "*realistic* without being *real*."[15] These narratives, he argues, served as laboratories to explore referentiality in fiction, the relationship between reality and the imagination. Deirdre Lynch makes a similar argument about the Gothic's contribution to the novel's development: "As *modern* romances, whose stories of superstition and delusion illuminate how fiction is grounded in consensual illusion, they also help complete the rise of the novel."[16] By representing things that were obviously unreal, it is argued, these novels provided a space to examine what fiction did, and how.

Melmoth the Wanderer and *Rękopis znaleziony w Saragossie* serve as good examples for such arguments, for both narratives are so highly self-conscious about their representation of the supernatural that they often seem more interested in examining literary mechanics than in actually producing illusion. In both novels, the supernatural is repeatedly questioned and undercut: the central characters struggle to understand exactly what is happening to them, whether it can be rationally explained, and how they ought to respond. Curiously, however, although many of the mysteries in each novel are ultimately explained in rational terms, neither one fully disavows the supernatural. This makes them unique: most examples of Gothic or fantastic writing that emphasize doubt end by clearly resolving any mysterious occurrences in the text,[17] whereas works that do feature the supernatural rarely interrogate it in depth. Although *Melmoth the Wanderer* is centered on a clearly supernatural character, every other mysterious occurrence is relentlessly interrogated (though not necessarily resolved). The narrator seems oddly fascinated with the literary mechanics of suspense, examining how an accumulation of effects produces a sense of terror—even absent any real cause. *Rękopis znaleziony w Saragossie* does the opposite: although the main events that had seemed supernatural are given rational explanations, the world is not entirely disenchanted at the novel's end. Instead, the novel reflects on the ways that a complex, unpredictable world can lead to mysterious tales that are, in fact, faithful records of human experience.

Notably, both authors also take on an aspect of the representation of the supernatural that critical accounts focused on fictionality rarely discuss, namely, its sociopolitical dimension, and the association of marvelous phenomena with "backward" or "uncivilized" cultures. Both texts push back against the association between the supernatural and a lack of sociocultural development that was typical of Gothic fiction. Initially drawing on the sense of exotic Otherness latent in the marvelous for the purposes of entertainment and suspense, both also contest this alleged Otherness, offering a more relativistic take on cultural difference. This critique opens onto the broader investigations of each text, into the nature of knowledge and world-building involved in fiction.

Thus, although the self-consciousness about the use of the supernatural that many theorists take to be the Gothic's signal contribution to the examination of fictionality is clearly manifested in both books, it is but a piece of a larger curiosity about whether fiction serves to educate or delude, how fictions transport their readers, and how such movement produces a sense of world. The centerpiece of this inquiry is in the form of both novels, in their complex architecture of interlaced and overlapping tales. Individually mysterious, when assembled into a larger whole the stories produce a different kind of effect, the image of a vast, interconnected realm, an intersubjective space that is cocreated by the various people within it, the things that happen to them, and the way they make sense of them.

I begin by discussing the way the supernatural is treated in each novel and how this connects to its broader explorations of fictionality before turning to an examination of the form of both texts together. Whereas Potocki is primarily interested in considering how fictions affect their audience—whether they inform or delude, and whether the entertainments they offer are useful or immoral—Maturin focuses on the relationship between fiction and history, examining how stories give readers knowledge about the world.

❧

Tzvetan Todorov described *Rękopis znaleziony w Saragossie* as one of the premier examples of the literary fantastic, a genre dwelling in the space of hesitation between the supernatural and the rational, with a main character who is in perpetual doubt as to whether his experiences are otherworldly in nature.[18] Indeed, throughout the text, Alfons vacillates between certainty that his cousins are human, and lingering doubt that they may not be. But recurring though this question may be, it is also insistently localized and separated from the larger question of how the world works. In Todorov's argument, the inexplicable events at the heart of fantastic fiction open onto the question of the nature of reality: "The person who experiences the event must opt for one of two possible solutions: either he is the victim of an illusion of the senses, of a product of the imagination—and the laws of the world then remain what they are; or else the event has indeed taken place, it is an integral part of reality—but then this reality is controlled by laws unknown to us."[19] But, as I show, Alfons's questions regarding his cousins are not connected to a broader existential fear; they are far more specific in nature. He wants to understand the things happening to *him*—the nature of reality as such does not seem to trouble him. The focus of the novel thus shifts from an inquiry into the nature of reality to an investigation of how people make sense of the world around them.

Notably, when questioned as to whether he believes in demons, Alfons repeatedly demurs. "Co się tyczy tych rzeczy, zwracam się zawsze do ludzi, którzy więcej imieją ode mnie. Dość dla mnie, że nie lękam się żadnych widm ani upiorów" ("I defer on such matters as these to those who know more about them than I. It is enough for me to show no fear of ghosts or vampires").[20] He is perfectly willing to countenance the existence of supernatural forces—his central concern is how he ought to respond to them. As he explains from the outset, this approach to the world emerges from his own set of avowed beliefs, a commitment to a particular notion of honor that does not preclude a belief in the supernatural: "nie dlatego, abym nie był przekonany o istnieniu duchów, ale dlatego, jak dalszy ciąg tej historii pokaże, że w całym moim wychowaniu najwięcej zwrócono uwagi na wyrobienie we mnie poczucia honoru, a honor, jak sądziłem, polegał na tym, ażeby nigdy nie okazywać trwogi" ("It was not that I did not believe in ghosts, but, as will subsequently become clear, honor had been the focal point of my whole upbringing, and I took honor to mean that one should never show any signs of fear").[21] Alfons seems to take it as a given that the world he has found himself in is controlled by unknown forces: he wants only to understand how to comport himself accordingly.

Right away, then, the traditional ground of the fantastic begins to shift, and the uniqueness of the novel starts to emerge. Typically, refutations of the supernatural offer the competing image of a rationally grounded, empiricist conception of the world. As hinted already by Alfons's avowed allegiance to a code of honor, *Rękopis znaleziony w Saragossie* does nothing of the kind; indeed, even as it refutes some of the ostensibly supernatural aspects of the story, it also points out the limits of empiricism, and illuminates the marvelous nature of the everyday world. Rather than juxtaposing a rational perspective to an enchanted one, Potocki sketches a worldview that is provisional, assembled from an assortment of sources, some of which are fictional. The stories Alfons hears become as much a part of the action of the novel as his actual experiences do, a bewildering doubling of diegesis that collapses the borders between this story-world and the "real" world of Saragossa. The question of belief that Todorov sees as Alfons's central concern increasingly recedes from view, as his attention, and the reader's, shifts instead to the various stories he hears. The novel thereby stages an inquiry into the effects of stories on their audience, as a way of exploring the status of fiction and how it works.

At first glance, Potocki seems to produce an ethos of the otherworldly only to disenchant it, but a more careful reading reveals that the novel's stance on the supernatural is far more open-ended. Although the book closes by explaining that most of Alfons's mysterious experiences were staged, this finale does not serve as conclusive proof against the existence of supernatural phenomena. The Sheikh Gomelez explains that Alfons's suspicions were correct: he was indeed carried to the gallows in his sleep, and two of the storytellers that he met—the possessed man Paszeko and the Wandering Jew—were actors.[22] But while the stories may have been told for the purpose of entertainment, this does not mean that they were all untrue. Although the cabbalist Uzeda and his sister Rebeka are connected to the Gomelez family, it does not seem that their stories, or experiences, were orchestrated, nor is an explanation given for Uzeda's ability to make a letter appear out of thin air.[23]

What is more, the Sheikh says that the Wandering Jew's story was taken from family chronicles, and while listening to it, the geometer Velásquez repeatedly mentions having read similar accounts in historical texts.[24] This information makes it harder to altogether dismiss these tales: they are supported by other sources. The ghost stories that Alfons hears at the home of the cabbalist Uzeda are likewise taken from reputable authors such as Pliny or Philostratus. In this way, the novel subtly raises the problem of the historical supernatural, which was a recurring question in Gothic fiction.

In his first preface to *Castle of Otranto*, Horace Walpole famously presented the text as a found document, justifying the presentation of unreal phenomena with claims of historical fidelity: "Belief in every kind of prodigy was so established in those dark ages, that an author would not be faithful to the manners of the times, who should omit all mention of them. He is not bound to believe them himself, but must represent his actors as believing them."[25] This position, what E. J. Clery calls exemplary historicism, makes the portrayal of what is manifestly false acceptable on ethnographic grounds.[26] As Clery points out, however, this same argument makes superstitious material unacceptable in modern literature, where it could be mistaken as representing modern views. Potocki's characters live these contradictions, balancing their skepticism with obeisance to the wisdom of the past. The tension is made explicit in a scene from Alfons's childhood: his father relates a story that involves ghosts, and the family priest suggests that it may console the frightened child to know that ghosts do not exist. Alfons's father responds by asking if the priest is therefore claiming that the story, written by his ancestor, is a lie.[27] The novel repeatedly stages a confrontation between the credulous past and the apparently enlightened present, but it remains agnostic on the question of how the contradiction should be resolved. By leaving the tension unresolved, the novel seems to be training its readers to follow Alfons's example and defer judgment.

This sense of suspended judgment has sociocultural implications as well. Although the novel initially seems to rely on a hypersexualized Orientalism that aligns the terror of the supernatural with the threat of Islamic and Jewish Otherness, the gradual domestication of the supernatural works against this logic. The Otherness of the non-Christian characters is diminished, or rather (partly) assimilated, as Rebeka decides to give up her studies of the *Cabbala*, and, despite her distaste for Christians, ultimately marries the geometer Velásquez. Although Alfons never converts to Islam, he does fall in love with Emina and Zubeida, and later spends six months secretly living with them. At the end of the novel, Alfons is sent on a peacekeeping mission to the Barbary Coast. Upon arrival, he meets the Bey of Tunis—who turns out to be his son. He is reunited with Emina, Zubeida, and a second child, a daughter. Alfons's feelings are divided between the sorrow that his children are devotees of a faith "nieprzyjazna mojej" ("hostile to mine")²⁸ and the strong sense of paternal tenderness. A compromise is reached: although his son is deeply attached to Islam, his daughter is happy to become a Christian, and she will be her father's heiress (and marry the son of Rebeka and Velásquez). While this ending is not without its problems, and the novel's work in contesting Orientalized representations of its non-Christian characters, particularly the female ones, should not be overstated, these intimate connections are nonetheless notable, promoting a vision of pluralism and peaceful coexistence that sets the novel apart from other works of the Gothic.²⁹

Indeed, *Rękopis znaleziony w Saragossie* directly challenges the idea of mystical beliefs as remnants of an obsolete worldview by suggesting that even the realm of the supernatural can undergo processes of modernization. The cabbalist at one point remarks that "wielkie zmiany zaszły w świecie duchów. Tak na przykład upiory, jeżeli śmiem tak wyrazić się, należą do nowych odkryć" ("there have been great changes in the world of demons. Vampires, if I may put it this way, can be considered a new invention").³⁰ He goes on to distinguish between the vampires found in Spain and those from Poland and Hungary. Tellingly, this is the only time that Poland is mentioned specifically in the text. The mention of Polish and Hungarian undead is particularly notable, suggesting a connection between political oppression and spectrality, given that both Hungarians and many Poles were then living under the rule of the Habsburgs.³¹ Potocki wrote the novel in the aftermath of the third and final Partition of Poland, the one that wiped it off the map entirely.³² Maria Janion noted that Poland was frequently represented as a corpse after the Partitions,³³ but what is of specific relevance here is the notion of a modernized supernatural, which implies that the historical changes in certain parts of the world, many of which were undertaken under the auspices of an Enlightenment program of civilizing the benighted, have reinvigorated the otherworldly rather than laying it to rest. Ghosts, in other words, are not the archaic remnants of a past that has not been properly left behind but are actively produced by ostensibly modernizing processes.

Thus, though it is apparently centered on a supernatural mystery, *Rękopis znaleziony w Saragossie* repeatedly contests the logic that undergirds most of the Gothic fictions of the time, particularly the association between the supernatural and a barbaric Other. Rather than staging the victory of an enlightened empiricism over premodern belief, the novel offers a curiously open-ended perspective on the spectral, one that dovetails with a broader set of reflections on the nature of the world and how it is represented in stories. It is this broader set of reflections, to which I now turn, that is the true focus of the novel, for it is here that we find a more extensive examination of the workings of fiction.

Ultimately, the most mysterious phenomenon in the novel is not that of ghosts or demons, but the intricate architecture of the many stories Alfons hears, and the astonishing connections between them.[34] Seemingly following the logic of the explained supernatural, where what had appeared to be various forms of haunting or spectral torment are revealed not to be, the effect of these revelations is far more complex. Rather than presenting characters as gullible, or deluded, the occurrences narrated are so wildly improbable that they suggest that a belief in the supernatural is quite justified: all evidence suggests it as the most likely explanation. At the same time, these explanations redirect the sense of the marvelous away from the question of the supernatural and into an appreciation of the world itself, and of the stories told about it.

Throughout the course of the book, a number of stories describe what appear to be supernatural phenomena but turn out not to be. The explanation, however, is rarely provided within the story itself—more typically, it emerges in the course of another, entirely separate tale. The clearest example of this is in a story told by the Knight of Toledo, in a scene where his friend, the Knight of Aguilar, tries to convert him to a virtuous existence by attempting to prove to him that the afterlife exists.[35] He tells the Knight of Toledo that he is to fight a duel at midnight, and if he dies he will come to the Knight's house and describe the afterworld. Sure enough, after midnight, there is a knock on the window and a "sepulchral" voice confirms the existence of Purgatory. The Knight of Toledo rushes to the site of the duel and learns that his friend is indeed dead. Thus, the scene appears to offer proof of the afterlife. It is only many pages later, in the story of another character, Lope Soarez, that one learns the true explanation—a rather coincidental series of events that landed another man under the Knight's window, wounded, terrified, and perfectly ready to attest that he himself was dead.[36]

This explanation is itself a kind of marvel. Indeed, it is so improbable that the Knight of Toledo would hardly seem more justified were he to have assumed it. Notably, it does not conclusively disprove the existence of the afterlife; rather, it offers a striking example of how limited an individual's perspective is. *Rękopis znaleziony w Saragossie* thereby suggests that belief in the marvelous is a natural human impulse serving to supplement the gaps in knowledge that are inevitable in a massive, complex world. Pandesowna speaks to this directly: later in the book, encountering a young woman who has awoken beneath the gallows, Alfons assumes that she too must be the victim of demonic visitations and asks Pandesowna if he knows her story. The Gypsy Chief smilingly corrects him, explaining that it is mere coincidence: the young woman was wandering in the night and happened to fall asleep there. But, he notes, it is not surprising that Alfons had assumed something more sinister, for "taka jest natura ludzka, że raz zasmakowszy w cudowności, rada by najprostsze wypadki życia pod nią podciągać" ("such is human nature that once one has had a taste of the marvelous, it will come to encompass even the most ordinary of events").[37]

Unlike works of the explained supernatural that juxtapose a rational, empirical worldview with a marvelous one, Potocki's novel playfully re-enchants the world by repeatedly showing the truth to be stranger than fiction, filled with startling coincidences, unexpected connections, and everyday occurrences that produce marvelous effects. These interconnected stories and the revelations they provide not only serve to justify the character's beliefs in the supernatural; by demonstrating how such beliefs can seem like reasonable explanations for genuinely mystifying occurrences, they also implicitly produce a sense of wonder in the nature of the world itself and the unlikely events that take place in it. At the same time, the novel draws attention to its own artistry, soliciting admiration for the dazzling interconnectedness of the many complex tales. The arrangement of the stories delays the explanations of various mysteries, thereby indulging the possibility of the supernatural, and producing a pleasurable sense of suspense. Whether a rational explanation is found is of lesser concern: the focus is on how the way that the stories are told makes them more entertaining. Thus, the representation of the supernatural becomes an entry point into an examination of literary technique.

Sarah Tindal Kareem has recently argued that, despite its reputation for realism and increased probability, eighteenth-century fiction was suffused with a sense of wonder, as authors sought to find ways of producing a sense of the marvelous that did not rely on the supernatural.[38] One of the transitions that she charts in this process is a shift from soliciting wonder at their content to an admiration for the work of fiction itself—for the careful composition of the text's plot, or its production of suspense, for instance. Although Potocki does draw on the supernatural, the novel's primary bid to solicit wonder from the reader is to represent how a sense of the marvelous emerges from an unlikely, but rationally explicable, array of coincidences, skillfully arranged into a series of stories. In Kareem's account, this process of rechanneling wonder also trains the audience in the cognitive skills required for enjoying fiction, modeling the balance between absorption and reflection, thereby teaching them to be engrossed without being deluded—in other words, how to suspend disbelief. This process frequently involves a kind of metafictional play, where the novel strives to give the reader the same experiences as the character, even as it makes explicit that it is doing so. Thus "dramatizing their own reception," the novels enthrall the reader by mirroring the experiences of the character, but they simultaneously provide the critical distance to reflect on how such experiences are produced.[39] *Rękopis znaleziony w Saragossie* offers a similar pedagogy. Although the stories-within-stories structure of the novel produces many scenes of characters engaging with various tales, Potocki thematizes this engagement in a more extensive fashion, using it to model different ways of thinking about how fictions influence their audience.

To explain the complexities of Potocki's inquiry into fiction's effects, I draw on Joshua Landy's elucidation of the various ways that the benefits of reading fiction have been theorized throughout history. Landy divides these different schools of thought into three main branches: the exemplary, the affective, and the cognitive.[40] The exemplary branch, the dominant view in the eighteenth century, sees fiction as a model that is to be either imitated or avoided. The affective branch, more prevalent in our own historical moment, examines the emotional effects of fiction, arguing, for instance, that fiction trains readers in empathy, thereby making them more moral.[41] Finally, the cognitive branch sees literature as a repository of information, which teaches the reader something about the world. Landy also proposes a fourth branch, a pragmatic account of what he terms "formative" fictions: works that train readers in particular skills, rather than providing them with beliefs or information—a description that aligns with the kind of pedagogy that Sarah Tindal Kareem identifies in eighteenth-century fiction.[42] There is no need, I think, for these categories to be mutually exclusive; some seem rather to be overlapping. For instance, Landy places the idea of fiction as a simulation space to test out one's responses to hypothetical circumstances in the cognitive category, but it arguably partakes of the affective as well. One can readily conceive of a text that embodies several different approaches at once, striving, for instance, to provide an example of moral behavior even as it encourages empathy for a less sympathetic position. Nonetheless, these categories offer helpful distinctions between different facets of the way stories are understood to affect readers, which help elucidate the myriad ways in which *Rękopis znaleziony w Saragossie* contemplates the status of fiction. Potocki's novel offers examples of each of the first three approaches and demonstrates the limitations of all of them. It is through these critiques, and by modeling the process of suspending disbelief, as described above, that the novel can be seen as training its audience to read it, thereby serving as a formative fiction in the way that Landy (and Kareem) describe. I discuss each of these approaches, and Potocki's take on them, in turn.

The exemplary branch was the most dominant model of the late eighteenth century. The notion that fiction provided a model of ideals to be emulated, the epicenter of Samuel Johnson's reflections on fiction in *Rambler* No. 4, was also at the heart of debates between the so-called romantic and novelistic, and discussions of Gothic fiction, which seemed particularly problematic in this regard, as offering examples rather of immoral or lascivious behavior.[43] Johnson worried that "the best examples only should be exhibited; and that which is likely to operate so strongly should not be mischievous or uncertain in its effects," a sentiment shared by Clara Reeve in *The Progress of Romance*, which similarly defended romances on the grounds that they could offer persuasive examples of virtue.[44] The sense of fiction as providing a powerful stimulus to moral behavior seemed to depend on its ability to compel readers to imitate, but this opened onto the dangers of delusion and quixotism, as attested to by multiple examples of literary characters suffering from such a disorder in eighteenth- and nineteenth-century writing.[45] Tellingly, Potocki sets his story in the heart of Cervantes's landscape, in the mountains of the Sierra Morena, "to pasmo, które oddziela Andaluzję od Manszy" ("the mountain range . . . which separates the provinces of Andalusia and La Mancha").[46] Although the emphasis of such arguments about fiction's referential status seemed to be the insistence that fiction only contain material that passed muster of morality, as Michael Gamer points out, these concerns about romance are "linked less to its content than to the reading experience that they reportedly produced."[47] At the heart of such exemplary accounts is an anxiety about the powers of fiction: that, like a dangerous drug, it could utterly confuse a person's sense of reality, actively deluding its readers.[48]

Potocki seized upon this threat of delusion, gleefully presenting myriad cases of readers misled by unreal worlds or struggling to resist the powers of fiction's persuasion. *Rękopis znaleziony w Saragossie* abounds with examples of characters imitating novels in the very ways that critics feared. When Emina and Zubeida tell Alfons the story of their childhood, for instance, the story is of two young girls who become so drawn into romantic literature that they begin to imitate it, reenacting the erotic scenes with each other and yearning for a male on whom to ply their sexual arts.[49] Multiple characters report becoming so absorbed by stories that they set off to live them, or begin to see the world through the lens of expectations shaped by novels they have read.[50] These cases are frequently erotic in nature, sexualized examples of literature's didactic potential to model moral behavior, and playfully cautionary tales about literature's engrossing powers.

These scenes not only testify to the more erotic possibilities of fiction's powers of example; they also speak to the anxiety that a compelling tale is powerful enough to actively transform the reader's sense of reality. As *Rękopis znaleziony w Saragossie* makes clear, stories do not need to be true, or even probable, in order to exert an influence. Pandesowna speaks to this notion explicitly: describing the "good old days" when travelers gathered at roadside inns and swapped stories of their adventures, he relates the tale of a man named Giulio Romati, whose wanderings take him to an enchanted castle where he battles skeletons (he shows his listeners his wounds as evidence). Alfons interrupts to say that he has read this very same account in a collection of curious stories. Pandesowna is unfazed: "To być może . . . że Romati nauczył się swojej historii z tej książki, a nawet że całkiem ją zmyślił. Wszelako opowiadanie jego wielce przyczyniło się do podniecenia we mnie chęci do podróży" ("Perhaps that is so . . . . Perhaps Romati took his story from that book. He may have made it up. But what is certain is that his tale contributed greatly to giving me a taste for travel").[51] This example attests to the powerful effects that literature has on its readers, and makes clear that they do not depend upon a story being truthful or even probable. Pandesowna's cheerful indifference when confronted with the possibility that the story was invented, or borrowed, suggests a different set of priorities, and a calm acceptance of the threat of delusion.

Indeed, although Pandesowna himself offers many examples of people being tricked or misled by seductive stories, which can be seen as humorous warnings against excessive credulousness, he is clearly not advocating for a position of extreme skepticism. When Pandesowna is relating the tale of a cuckolded husband, Cornádez, who meets a Reprobate Pilgrim named Blas Hervas, and Rebeka repeatedly interjects, assuming that the purpose of the tale is to mislead Cornádez, and that the story must therefore be false, Pandesowna insists that she is jumping to conclusions.[52] This admonishment is puzzling, for an earlier tale has already established that Cornádez's wife and her lover have been plotting an elaborate deception to coax him into leaving on a pilgrimage.[53] Admittedly, the appearance of Blas Hervas may be an unrelated coincidence, but given that he concludes with an explanation of why Cornádez is being haunted by the Conde de Peña Flor, a being invented by Cornádez's wife in order to make him believe he was being haunted, Blas Hervas's tale seems suspect. The point of Pandesowna's rebukes therefore does not seem to be that Rebeka is misinterpreting this particular story, but rather that her mode of engaging the tales is misguided. To treat these stories as conspiracies or puzzles and look for the solution or hidden motives of the characters is to miss the point. In this way, the novel models the process of suspending disbelief and withholding judgment—not to such an extent that one is entirely carried away, perhaps, though such flights of fancy have their pleasures,[54] but at least enough to properly appreciate the story.

Indeed, Alfons himself offers a more compelling example of such a critical reading practice and of the potential benefits of imitating fictions. At the novel's opening, we learn that the commitment to honor that is his defining characteristic is one that he has been trained in through stories. Describing his education, Alfons relates a series of tests administered by his father, whereby the young boy was told various stories, which his father interrupted at crucial moments to ask his son how he would feel in a given situation. He fails one trial—his father asks him if he would be afraid if he were in that position, and he responds that he would—but quickly learns what is expected, and confidently responds to later tales with pledges of courage. Thus, Alfons is trained in a form of reading that treats the material as a virtual reality that serves as a testing ground, training him in the correct responses to various situations, no matter how unlikely. Crucially, however, the training Alfons undergoes includes a component of critical reflection—the moment of pausing the story to consider one's own responses to it. This is precisely the delicate balance Kareem describes, a negotiation between the pleasures of immersion and the powers of detached contemplation. Alfons is being taught to suspend disbelief while remaining critical in particular ways.

The benefits of such a pedagogy are manifested in a few scenes in which the stories that Alfons hears provide him with an effective model for conduct. Soon after describing his childhood education, Alfons listens to tales told by a possessed man named Paszeko, describing his encounters with demons. Directly after hearing each story, something happens to Alfons that seems to mirror the events described, and, mindful of the resemblance, Alfons knows how to respond. For instance, Paszeko says that he heard a goat bleating at the door—a goat that later turned out to be a demon—and that evening as Alfons lies in bed, he too hears a goat bleating at the door. Sword in hand, he tells the goat that the door is locked, and he goes back to sleep,[55] apparently having learned from the example offered. Although scenes like this one seem to exemplify the merits of good reading, as it were, they also undeniably contribute to the uncanny feeling of the text—an unsettling repetition, and a moment where fiction seems to threateningly encroach upon reality.

Potocki offers a similarly ambivalent portrayal of another one of the powers ascribed to fiction, what Joshua Landy terms the affective branch of engagement: the claim that fiction trains readers in empathy, thereby making them more moral. Alfons initially appears to serve as the sterling example of how stories can lead a person to question and reconsider their own beliefs as a result of learning more about how other people see the world. His somewhat dogmatic commitment to ideals of honor, and hostility toward those who he believes do not respect it sufficiently, abates as the novel progresses. But a careful reading reveals just as many moments where he remains entrenched in his views, and suspicious of any attempts to change them.

From the outset, the people Alfons encounters tell him that his chivalric worldview is obsolete.[56] Furthermore, the stories he hears from others give him insight into what life is like for the "dishonorable," suggesting they may not be as villainous as he had once thought. These new revelations throw Alfons into disarray, leading him to question his own beliefs: "Dziwiło mnie, że ciągle wychwalał honor, subtelność i nieposzlakowaną uczciwość ludzi, którzy powinni byli za łaskę uważać, gdyby ich tylko powieszono. Nadużycie tych słów, którymi szastał z taką pewnością siebie, pomieszało wszystkie moje myśli" ("He had repeatedly praised the honor, delicacy, and integrity of people for whom hanging was not a severe enough punishment. His misuse of these words, which he uttered with such conviction, completely bewildered me").⁵⁷ Although there is no clear moment of conversion where Alfons explicitly disavows his former ways of seeing the world, there is evidence that he becomes at least slightly more reflexive about his posturing. Initially telling Pandesowna that, as a member of the Walloon Guards, he needs no protection other than his sword, he then repents somewhat, accepting assistance and saying, "zawstydziłem się niepotrzebnego junactwa" ("I felt somewhat ashamed of my excessive bravado").⁵⁸ Although it is a minor adjustment, it is a notable one, given that up to this point, the young man's hubris is one of his defining characteristics.

But Alfons also offers plenty of resistance to the stories he hears, particularly those of the cabbalist and the Wandering Jew, put off by their sacrilegious content, or by the suspicion that they are intended to convert him—or simply out of boredom. Although the novel gestures toward a more relativistic sense of cultural and religious difference, the compromise is but a tenuous one. There are clear limits to Alfons's willingness to entertain alternate value systems and ideas, subtly pointing to the inconsistencies in such theories of empathetic education.⁵⁹

The novel's most explicit discussion of the kind of knowledge that fictions offer is to be found in the theories of Velásquez, a mathematician who struggles to transform the tales into data, and an organized system of information—what Landy calls the cognitive approach. Velásquez's passion for seeing the world in mathematical terms initially seems like a quirk designed to add humor to the text. When he earnestly explains how love can be expressed in algebraic terms, for example, Rebeka comments that she is is "przekonana, że nie ma kobiety, która by nie uległa podobnemu rozumowaniu" ("convinced that there is not a woman alive who would not yield when faced with such arguments"),⁶⁰ a response that seems intended to point to the gap between theory and practice. However, the reading of Velásquez as mere comic relief is complicated by the sheer amount of space that the novel devotes to his theories. He delivers several lengthy disquisitions on his "system," which are much more nuanced than his earlier calculations may lead one to expect, and which speak to the limitations of reason and the moral imperative of religious tolerance. For Velásquez, intelligence is the ability to combine ideas, and the more ideas a man has, the more combinations he can make.⁶¹ Notably, these ideas do not need to emerge from experience, but can also come from books. Thus, he says, that "człowiek, który obejrzał całą ziemię oczami podróżników, który widział w dziejach wszystkie ważne wypadki, rzeczywiście ma w głowie mnóstwo obrazów . . . jeżeli zaś kombinuje swoje pojęcia, zestawia je i porównywa, natenczas mówimy, że ma wiedzę i rozum" ("the man who has seen the whole world through the eyes of travellers and has seen all the events of history really has an infinity of images in his head . . . , and if he combines ideas, associates them and compares them, then this man really has knowledge and intellect").⁶² This is precisely the cognitive argument, in concrete terms: that fictions educate their readers by giving them information and knowledge about the world.

Despite this apparent endorsement of literature, however, Pandesowna's stories frustrate and flummox the geometer, particularly because of their embeddedness and the confusion of chronological order. He has always believed, he says, "że romanse i inne dzieła podobnego rodzaju winny być pisane w kilku kolumnach, na kształt tablic chronologicznych" ("that novels and other works of that kind should be written in several columns like chronological tables").⁶³ Rebeka offers a sarcastic rejoinder about the role of surprises in sustaining interest, a critique that speaks to literature's dual purpose of education and entertainment. One could add, however, a second critique, one that the text itself elegantly models: that form, too, holds meaning, and the way a story is told is part of what it has to say, without, however, being something that can be directly distilled and extracted as information.

This brings us to Landy's fourth category, the idea of "formative fictions," whose purpose is to train its readers in a particular skill: "what they give us is *know-how*; rather than transmitting beliefs, what they equip us with are *skills*; rather than teaching, what they do is *train* . . . . They present themselves as spiritual exercises (whether sacred or profane), spaces for prolonged and active encounters that serve, over time, to hone our abilities."⁶⁴ In Sarah Tindal Kareem's historical account of this process, a series of texts serve as formative fictions in a similar (albeit more restricted, because limited to reading) way in the eighteenth century, training readers in the balance of absorption and credulity that the conceptual category of fiction requires. The emergence of fictionality in the modern sense is facilitated by books that offer new strategies for soliciting wonder, doing so in explicit ways that make the reader appreciate how the text produces such effects: "By triggering readers' recognition of their own susceptibility to illusion, eighteenth-century fiction makes readers' first-person experiences the basis for their critical awakening, encouraging them to engage with the world both admiringly and critically."⁶⁵ *Rękopis znaleziony w Saragossie* engages in such training in a number of interrelated ways: repeatedly demonstrating how perfectly rational events produce mysterious, quasi-supernatural effects, without, however, fully disavowing the possibility of the supernatural. Potocki reframes the question of belief, imbuing the world with a sense of wonder. Simultaneously, the way this sense emerges from an intricate architecture of overlapping stories draws attention to the work of narrative, encouraging the reader to notice how skillful storytelling can change one's perspective on the world. Finally, modeling different approaches to making sense of stories, the novel reflects on how fictions produce knowledge, and trains readers to be mindful of the way they read.

Thus, the strangeness of *Rękopis znaleziony w Saragossie*, its curious combination of philosophical skepticism and delight in spooky tales, its tangled web of stories-within-stories, its balancing act between multiculturalism and Orientalized exoticism, are all components of an active interrogation of form and meaning—of ways of reading, and the sociocultural assumptions underpinning them. Although seemingly far removed from the realist fictions of its time, Potocki's novel investigates the mechanics that they too, depend on.

↝

If *Rękopis znaleziony w Saragossie* seems contradictory in the way it portrays the status of the supernatural, vacillating between skepticism and credulity, *Melmoth the Wanderer* is downright paradoxical. Indeed, the novel is centered on a paradox, being the story of how, even at moments of utter desperation, no person would ever trade or sell their soul to the devil, yet following the exploits of a protagonist who has done just that and now seeks to convert someone else. Much like *Rękopis znaleziony w Saragossie*, the novel flirts with the boundaries between illusion and demystification, playfully striving to have it both ways. Although *Melmoth the Wanderer* is emphatically a work in which the supernatural *is* possible (despite some initial skepticism, by the end of the book it is clear that the Wanderer is in fact a being with supernatural powers), the narration is always given in such a way as to cast doubt on what is happening. As with *Rękopis*, however, the novel's highly self-conscious use of the supernatural is but a piece in a larger puzzle investigating the status of fiction. But, as I will explain, where Potocki's novel is concentrated on exploring fiction's effects on readers, *Melmoth the Wanderer* is more interested in the nature of fiction itself and its relationship to history: how pieces of reality become enfolded into fictional narratives, what this process of transportation means for the truth-status of such scenes, and how techniques associated with documentary reference, such as footnotes, are changed when incorporated into invented stories.

Melmoth the Wanderer seesaws between eerie descriptions of mysterious events and interludes that seem to admonish the reader for being taken in by them, thereby creating a dynamic of contestation that offers a self-conscious reflection on techniques for producing illusion. Thus, for instance, the narrator describes the weather in portentous terms and then notes that "terror is very fond of associations, we love to connect the agitation of the elements with the agitated life of man; and never did a blast roar, or a gleam of lightning flash, that was not connected in the imagination of some one, with a calamity that was to be dreaded, deprecated, or endured, - with the fate of the living, or the destination of the dead."[66] As in *Rękopis znaleziony w Saragossie*, the narrator speaks to the allure of the mystical—the tendency to seek out supernatural explanations for otherwise inexplicable events. Notably, however, this observation does not discredit such associations, and indeed, in this particular case the storm described presages a disaster at sea where many lives are lost. But the narratorial intrusion invites meta-reflection on the reader's part; a moment to pause and observe one's own responses to the text's narrative stimulus—and to question them.

The main character, John Melmoth, is subjected to similar treatment, as his assessments of a given situation are continuously challenged and revised, particularly in the beginning of the novel, as he gradually becomes acquainted with his ancestor's story. When John first arrives at his uncle's home, he is portrayed as a wholly rational young man, highly skeptical of anything suggestive of superstitious beliefs. But soon enough the gloom of the old house seems to work its effects, and upon a first sighting of what appears to be Melmoth, we are told:

> His first impulse was to utter an exclamation of terror, but his breath felt stopped. He was then rising to pursue the figure, but a moment's reflection checked him. What could be more absurd, than to be alarmed or amazed at the resemblance between a living man and the portrait of a dead one! The likeness was doubtless strong enough to strike him even in that darkened room, but it was doubtless only a likeness; and though it might be imposing enough to terrify an old man of gloomy and retired habits, and with a broken constitution, John resolved it should not produce the same effect on him.[67] (20)

John's rationality now becomes a matter of self-control, a struggle to resist the influence of the irrational. This is, of course, a commonplace of Gothic fiction—the notion of the supernatural as preying on a normally rational mind that is rendered particularly vulnerable by shock, exhaustion, or an unfamiliar environment.[68] As the reader may already suspect, however, John's skepticism is incorrect: the figure is indeed the mysterious Melmoth, whose appearance fully warrants terror. In fact, John almost always ends up being incorrect, whether he believes events to be supernatural or not, ironically gesturing to the difficulty of correctly understanding such encounters, and removing any simple explanations (such as being overly impressionable or unduly skeptical) for the mistake. Such dramatic irony renders the central character of the novel unreliable as a witness, but the narrator's coy commentary does not provide a more stable ground of knowledge. There is a perpetual sense of doubt about any given event in the story, and a question of whether its eerie atmosphere is genuinely meaningful, or mere literary effect.

A particularly vivid example of this fascination with narrative technique can be found in a scene where two characters, Donna Clara and Father Jose, read a letter from Donna Clara's husband, Don Francisco (381–384). The letter recounts a strange series of events, featuring the arrival of the specter of his daughter, Isidora, to warn him of impending danger, then reappearing to inform him that "it is too late" to save her (383). Don Francisco emphasizes that he is never sure whether these appearances are dream or reality, though he "has ever been a hearty contemner of your tales of spectres and visions," but he does recall that after the second appearance (which foretold doom), he heard the clock strike three (383). As Donna Clara and Father Jose read these lines, the clock strikes three. The coincidence terrifies Donna Clara, who then thinks she hears a sound in the house. Father Jose says he hears nothing, but he mentions having heard a sound earlier. They notice the candles flickering and, realizing that another window must be open in the house, discover Isidora's empty room, whereupon Father Jose echoes the specter's words from the letter: "it is too late" (384).

What is striking about this scene is that while it has all the trappings of the supernatural—spectral visitors, portentous clocks striking, mysterious noises, and danger to an innocent young woman—the crucial details are actually rather meaningless. The strangest aspect is the matter of the overheard sound: the striking of the clock, which is completely coincidental, leads Donna Clara to think that she has heard something, but the event (which had indeed been Melmoth's arrival) that would have produced a sound relevant to this situation actually occurred several hours earlier, when it was in fact overheard by Father Jose, who thought nothing of it at the time. The sound Donna Clara hears is never explained—and could easily be a product of her frenzied imagination. What is the purpose of this episode? It would be just as simple—simpler even— to have these eerie effects linked to the concrete event (Melmoth absconding with Isidora) that they seem to portend. Instead, they are bizarrely separated, rendering all of the "clues" in the scene meaningless, while nonetheless retaining the ominous occurrence they seemingly refer to. The result of such narrative strategies is an unstable and somewhat contradictory combination of the "explained supernatural" and the supernatural itself that leaves the reader in a continuous state of suspense, often without any real resolution.

Although *Melmoth the Wanderer* may appear to rely on the connection between the Gaelic and the supernatural, transporting its protagonist from Dublin to the West, the logic of the novel's overall approach to the supernatural belies this link, presenting the mystical beliefs of the Catholic peasantry as superficial trappings. Although Ireland does provide a suitably atmospheric setting, decked in its stereotypical gloomy grandeur, this is precisely the kind of eerie effect that the novel repeatedly calls into question. Indeed, Biddy Brannigan, the primary authority of those local beliefs, particularly as regards the supernatural, is described as a fraud, "a withered Sybil who prolonged [sic] her squalid existence by practicing on the fears, the ignorance, and the sufferings of beings as miserable as herself" (10). Her words do excite "involuntary awe" (13) in John, but this is clearly due more to her theatrics than the validity of her views. Jim Kelly argues that Brannigan "practices a form of spiritual enslavement," and thereby indexes a broader problem related to the class dynamics underlying the conscious deployment of "authentic" tradition.[69] As he further points out, the description of Brannigan's powers is not especially linked to Irish culture but is "a straightforward prose rendition of folk customs mentioned in Robert Burns' poem 'Halloween.'"[70] This problematizes readings such as the recent one by Laura Doyle, which takes Brannigan as an example of subaltern speech. Doyle notes John's condemnation of Brannigan, but adds: "And yet . . . John himself depends on Biddy Brannigan to make sense of his uncle's death and his family history. . . . Although the novel does not actually record her version of the tale, John himself has heard the subaltern speak, and he cannot 'conquer' the power of her story over him, which he transfers, in effect, to the reader."[71]

To say that Brannigan's story helps John to "make sense" of events is overstating the case: her narrative certainly makes a strong impression on him—a "folly he could not conquer"—but "the result of these impressions was, a resolution to visit the closet, and examine the manuscript that very night" (24–25). In other words, Brannigan's account is a further piece of evidence, one that John initially doubts (making it all the more likely to be true, in keeping with the book's narrative logic)—"He recapitulated the Sybil's story word by word, with the air of a man who is cross-examining an evidence, and trying to make him contradict himself" (26)—but it is hardly the final word. Although Brannigan presents what turns out to be genuine information, her authenticity is resolutely intertwined with a theatricality that is deeply suspect, a pleasure in terrorizing others. This complicates any straightforward claims of supernatural belief as a marker of backwardness, suggesting that the supernatural is less a matter of belief or folk wisdom than it is a canny performance of power.

Indeed, tellers of supernatural tales are regularly regarded with great suspicion in this novel—an obvious irony in a book of supernatural horror. As critics such as Syndy Conger, Terry Eagleton, and Regina Oost have discussed, this is a recurring theme in the text, one that serves as an underlying inquiry into its own moral status. We see another example of it later, when the Parricide says that the same impulse that makes him interested in hearing the death throes of two young lovers is "that curiosity that brings thousands to witness a tragedy, and makes the most delicate female feast on groans and tragedies" (211), a blatant critique of the consumers of terrifying tales and dramas.[72] These moments of irony index a broader set of questions about the morality of storytelling and its entertainment value, an ambivalence that echoes the structure of the novel's representation of the supernatural. Both contribute to a larger dynamic of interrogation running through the book, insistently probing at the ethics and epistemology at work in Gothic literature. It is an unstable, almost self-sabotaging effect, as the narrator investigates the very grounds that the story is built upon, without seeming fully in control of the effects produced. In this way, *Melmoth the Wanderer* offers a prime example of an explicitly Gothic exploration of fictionality and its effects, examining how representations of the supernatural illuminate a larger problematic of fiction: its referential status, its moral status, and its effects on readers. Maturin's novel is a particularly intriguing model of this kind of play, precisely because it is such a messy and convoluted one: the mechanics of the process are more readily apparent.

But this sense of restless inquiry is not limited to the supernatural elements of the novel; it is part of a larger investigation of the effects of fiction. As with Potocki, the experimentation with forms of storytelling goes much deeper. The most interesting aspect of *Melmoth the Wanderer* and its exploration of fictionality is not particularly tied to its representations of the supernatural—it is its use of footnotes, which raise an entirely different set of issues, offering reflections on the functioning of fictionality that are, I believe, unique to this novel.

We frequently think of fiction in terms of transport, as a process of taking a reader on a journey to a new place, and Maturin investigates the possibility that specific kinds of metaphors can produce such travel. But his primary focus is instead an examination of the movements of the materials from which stories are formed—how incidents or ideas venture from the real world to the pages of fiction, and what this voyage means for their truth value. Making this movement visible, I argue, Maturin models fictionality in action, illuminating the process of creating verisimilar stories, in order to investigate the kind of information they provide to their readers.

Where Gothic authors such as Horace Walpole frequently relied on psychological realism to claim credibility for their supernatural tales, Maturin relies on an authenticating paratext—which is then also called into question. The novel is heavily bolstered with footnotes, many of which serve explicitly to anchor the story in fact. These frequently take the form of personal anecdote, where the narrator mentions having heard someone relate a similar story (56), or simply states that the event is true: "Fact, - me ipso teste" (200), "This is a fact well established" (218), or "Fact, - it occurred in a French family not many years ago" (425). At first glance this might appear to be a fairly standard tactic, a pseudofictional pretense common in works of the time and arguably similar to the "based on a true story" tagline we see even today. But a closer look reveals that the effects of the paratext are decidedly more complex, likewise participating in the novel's meta-reflection on itself, in a sustained—but also highly contradictory—investigation of the relationship between fiction and reality, and of the way that a given scene or detail moves from one place, or text, to another.

While the footnotes often link the story to factual discourses such as history or travel literature,[73] they also more frequently cite literature or drama.[74] The claim in such cases, it would seem, is not that an event is strictly *true*, but rather that it is *conceivable*, having (presumably) already been accepted as credible in another text. For the narrator to use a play of Shakespeare as documentary evidence of a historical fact is to accord the drama an authenticating power, and to retroactively project expectations of credibility onto the earlier text. But it is also a reminder that much of what readers know of the past does, in fact, come from fictional works, which are often read as historical documents of its mores, bringing the texture of reality to life.

Theorists of fictionality have pondered how the novel developed a notion of verisimilitude as opposed to literal truth. The process is frequently linked to the rise of realism: in order to make the case that they were presenting something true about the world, novels needed to be seen as believable, which they did by portraying everyday life rather than marvelous occurrences, or, in the case of the Gothic, by claiming to present how real people would behave in extraordinary circumstances. As Catherine Gallagher noted, by a curious sort of paradox, at the same moment in which eighteenth-century novels seem to have freed themselves from the pretense of literal truth, they developed a normative sense of probability, limiting fictionality "by locking it inside the confines of the credible."[75] We see clear evidence of this pressure in *Melmoth the Wanderer*, which responds with a bizarre sort of compromise. Clearly attempting to capitalize on the shock or thrill of the uncommon or supernatural, the novel also struggles to maintain a (tenuous) claim to probability.

The footnotes function to reassure the reader that the kinds of things being described in the novel can actually happen, because they have already happened before, in other places. Yet in opposition to this dynamic of recurrence as verifiability and therefore truth, events are repeatedly described as "singular." The word is repeated more than forty times over the course of the book, and what is most amusing, often at moments that are not properly singular at all. The word is frequently used synonymously with strange or eerie, at times retaining its root of unique, one-of-a-kind. It regularly appears whenever a new character first meets Melmoth and is struck by his particular qualities. The sheer repetition of these encounters in the novel, however, defies this very singularity. If, as Marthe Robert writes, "the truth of the novelistic narrative resides not in the singularity but in the statistical frequency of the events described,"[76] then the similarity between the episodes is precisely what establishes them as "truthful," while allowing each to retain, individually, a sense of the marvelous, albeit one that is challenged by the barrage of footnotes attesting to its truth value. This is a paradoxical—and highly unstable—compromise, testifying to an internal conflict between two competing notions of the pleasure and the utility of fiction.

But the work of the paratext is even more complex. Upon initial reading, the footnotes appear to be a tether, however tenuous, between the real world and the body of the novel. Thus, they seem to be in a stable and dependable realm of the documentary, anchored in the reality we know—and indeed, this is how they are read by many critics: Christina Morin, for example, says that the footnotes "vitally link fictional and factual narratives."[77] This idea is thrown into disarray, however, when the footnotes begin providing documentation for aspects of the story that are obviously invented, as when a description of one of the characters mentions a book that she is fond of, and a footnote helpfully informs the reader that the text was Taylor's *Book of Martyrs* (452). Another such case occurs when a footnote explains that a woman whose sedan Stanton sees at the theater is "Mrs. Marshall, the original Roxanna in Lee's Alexander, and the only virtuous woman then on the stage" (271). This trick of planting real people and objects into the book via the footnotes destabilizes their authenticating function, letting them in on the fictional fun. This is only exacerbated when they offer meta-textual commentary, as when the Inquisitors holding Immalee prisoner say that they have never heard of a case of Melmoth tempting a woman, and a footnote suggests that "From this it should seem that they were unacquainted with the story of Elinor Mortimer" (525). Implying that the story of Elinor Mortimer is one that other characters ought to be familiar with, as though it were common knowledge, not only creates a presumption of interconnection between the characters, calling for and thereby implying a sense of completeness in the fictional world of the text; it also makes clear that the paratext is not a stable realm of the factual, as opposed to the fictional.

Even more baffling in this regard is a curious instance where a footnote *refutes* the narrative. It is in the Spaniard's story, when he becomes a prisoner of the Inquisition. A stranger visits him and begins to tell stories of various historical events that occurred so long before that he could not possibly have witnessed them, describing them in explicit detail. Monçada is increasingly terrified, and the mood grows more and more ominous: as he says, the account "was interspersed with such reiterated mention of the dead, that I might be pardoned for feeling as if the speaker was one of them" (228). The suspense mounts, with Monçada (and the reader) wondering whether the stranger is a supernatural being or simply a gifted storyteller, and then the truth is revealed: describing Queen Henriette, the stranger says that he was "beside her carriage, *it was the only one then in London*" (228, all italics author's). This climactic moment, when the reader is confronted with the fact that this mysterious person was apparently an eyewitness to the events he describes, meaning that he is over 150 years old, is interrupted with a footnote: "I have read this somewhere, but cannot believe it. Coaches are mentioned by Beaumont and Fletcher, and even glass coaches by [Samuel] Butler in his 'Remains'" (228). The authorial voice of the footnotes (let us call him the editor) here takes umbrage with the claim that the Queen's coach was the only one in the city, casting doubt upon Melmoth's reliability as witness (for the stranger is, of course, Melmoth). The footnote seems, oddly, to reassure Monçada as well, for he allows the stranger to continue his tale, and it is only two paragraphs later, when the stranger again makes reference to being present at a past event, that Monçada finally asks him outright whether he was actually there—and does not receive a reply. It is a strange scene, one where the story is seemingly held in abeyance by the demands of the real world. This limitation only serves to accentuate the novel's claim to realism, implying that any tendency toward imaginative invention is checked by a careful editor, but also puzzlingly implying that this editor is confused when the characters say something untrue.

One might be tempted to explain this by seeing the editor as another character in the text, or at least as grounded in its fictional universe, but this view is challenged by other footnotes where he casually notes an anachronism and then blithely dismisses it with a simple "n'importe" (457), or says that it is an "*anachronism prepense*" (91–92), making it clear that the editor knows that the story is not true (and doesn't necessarily mind). In fact, in one footnote Maturin himself steps forward to announce himself as the author, interrupting one of the Wanderer's speeches to say that he does not personally share his views: "As, by a mode of criticism equally false and unjust, the worst sentiments of my worst characters (from the ravings of Bertram to the blasphemies of Cardonneau), have been represented as *my own*, I must here trespass so far on the patience of the reader as to assure him, that the sentiments ascribed to the stranger are diametrically opposite to mine, and that I have purposely put them into the mouth of an agent of the enemy of mankind" (303). Here he makes explicit his own authorship of both the novel and the footnotes. This does not, however, resolve the problem; it simply indicates an inconsistency in the way the footnotes construe the text, a further confusion in the boundaries between fact and fiction. Maturin can confidently clarify that the character's views are not his own, or make clear that he knows that something is anachronistic but has chosen to leave it that way, but he can also seem puzzled when Melmoth testifies to there being only one carriage in London, as if he had no control over Melmoth's words, or express that certain characters aren't aware of each other, as if they ought to be.

This confusion between fiction and reality is what distinguishes Maturin's use of footnotes from that of his most famous contemporaries, Maria Edgeworth, Lady Morgan, and Walter Scott. Although they all use extensive footnotes in their works, as critics such as Ina Ferris and Fiona Robertson have discussed, none of them approaches Maturin's daring in blurring fact and fiction. Lady Morgan bolsters her novel, *The Wild Irish Girl* (1806), with a veritable barrage of paratext, but her footnotes are grounded in antiquarian works and empirical observation of the real world, while the body of the text is clearly fiction. Maria Edgeworth's footnotes (and glossary) in *Castle Rackrent* (1800), on the other hand, construe the story as literally true, but they are presented as written by the alleged editor of the work, in an extension of the book's pseudo-factual pretense as a "found" manuscript. The pretense of truth is also offset by the editor's careful claim at the end of the preface that "these are 'tales of other times,'"[78] ensuring that the world of the story is clearly demarcated as separate, and at a safe remove from that of the reader. Walter Scott's novels offer more complex examples of a slippage between fiction and documentation, most obviously with the editor characters who frame his tales. In *The Monastery*, for instance, there is an Introductory Epistle from a Captain Clutterbuck to the Author of *Waverley*, recounting how he came to possess a manuscript that he hopes *Waverley*'s author will edit and present to the public. This is followed by a letter from the author that teases Clutterbuck for being a fictional character. In the midst of this letter, however, is a footnote from Clutterbuck clarifying one of the author's points.[79] Although such examples certainly demonstrate a slippage between fiction and reality, they are localized, and seem more connected to the aura of playful mystery surrounding the authorship of the novels. Scott is very interested in the interplay between fiction and reality, but rarely does he genuinely attempt to confuse the distinction between the two.[80] What is more, in the Magnum Opus editions of the novels, Scott took pains to elaborate on the relationship between his novels and the history they were based on, identifying his sources and clarifying how he had used them. This is quite different from the willful blurring of *Melmoth the Wanderer*, where the relationship between the story and the documentary material that it draws on is far more convoluted.

Maturin's insistence that various features of the novel are "true" when they are part of a story that is obviously invented scrambles any simple notion of truth. Any authenticating device in the text—the footnotes, the intrusions of the narrator, or even the moments that seems to reassert the laws of the empirical world we know in defiance of what appear to be supernatural occurrences— is ultimately folded back into the fictional world being created, or called into question, rendering it unreliable.

Maturin is not simply engaging in a kind of postmodern play avant la lettre: *Melmoth the Wanderer* represents a complex inquiry into the ways in which fiction represents the past. Blurring the lines between documentary and imaginative writing, Maturin explores fiction's ability to create an immersive virtual reality, raising questions about the kinds of knowledge that fictional representations provide when they create scenes that seemingly transport the reader into the moment. This claim may seem surprising: despite studies by scholars such as James Watt, Toni Wein, and Ian Duncan, which probe the ways in which Gothic writing engaged with history, and Fiona Robertson's impressive work documenting Walter Scott's indebtedness to the formal strategies of Gothic novels, Lukács's view that Gothic novels treat history as "mere costumery" is oddly persistent.[81]

The Gothic has an intriguing, multifaceted relationship to history and its writing. Not only did many Gothic authors frame their stories as historical or ethnographic fictions in an attempt to capitalize on that mode's propriety, but the particular form of the Gothic is also frequently perceived as symptomatic of historical pressures. More centrally to my argument, however, the relationship between fiction and history was a key component of a broader set of negotiations with fictionality, as *Melmoth the Wanderer* makes clear. The novel illuminates the way in which fiction offers a resource in helping readers understand other places and times, not only by telling them what happened, but also what it felt like. Strikingly, Maturin seems to suggest that the "when and where," the meat of history, may be less important than accurately portraying the emotional effects of a given occurrence.

Notably, even when the footnotes seem to be anchoring the story in fact by reference to history, it is almost always to the history of another place. For instance, when Melmoth is describing religion to Immalee, a footnote appears that cites historical fact, then explains that "this circumstance, though long antedated, is therefore imaginable" (291). What counts in this case is not veracity, but plausibility—if an event has happened at any time or place, it is suggested, then it could just as easily have happened at the moment in the narrative that Maturin has chosen. This stands in contradistinction to the kind of approach seen in the preface of *Ivanhoe*, for instance, where Scott explicitly condemns anachronism. For Maturin, it seems, the temporal sequence or geographic location of particular events is not a constitutive feature: they can be rearranged and moved around if the occasion suits.

Most fascinating in this respect are the footnotes that inform the reader that the events described did in fact happen, but in Ireland. The first moment is when Monçada is told that he is presumed to have perished in a fire that killed a number of people whose cinders filled but a single coffin. This gruesome detail is supported by a footnote that tells the reader that "this extraordinary fact occurred after the dreadful fire which consumed sixteen persons in one house, in Stephen's Green, Dublin, 1816. The writer of this heard the screams of sufferers whom it was impossible to save, for an hour and a half" (251). The second is but a few pages later; after the Parricide is murdered by a mob, we are told that "this circumstance occurred in Ireland in 1797," and given a brief gloss of that event (256). Many commentators have convincingly discussed these moments as eruptions of historical trauma,[82] but my focus is rather on the portability of "facts" and "occurrences" from one place and time to another.

This movement blurs the lines between fiction and reality, giving novels the stamp of documentary authenticity if the events described in them have some basis in historical fact. The context in which they occurred is seemingly irrelevant; it is enough that they are represented in "truthful" detail. This documentation serves to validate the marvelous aspects of the text, rooting them in a more factual discourse as parts of history, not products of imagination. It also transforms the novel into a species of historical document, creating a kind of realism of sentiment that strives to depict real-world events in a different setting. Absorbed in the story, the reader is meant to experience emotions akin to those of the people who were there, thus placing him or her into the position of the historical protagonists. Maturin thereby aims to give the reader a kind of knowledge about actual occurrences in the real world: he tries to show them what it would feel like to experience a given event. The reader is thus taken on a kind of sentimental journey, "moved" via fiction to the scene of historical tragedy—even as that scene of tragedy is itself moved from one context into another.

This, I argue, is the development of fictionality in action: the novel marks an important step in a process of seeing invented stories as conveying information about the world. If, as Catherine Gallagher writes, the rise of the novel as a genre is "part of a larger epistemological shift from a narrow construction of truth as historical accuracy to a more capacious understanding that could include truth conceived as mimetic simulation,"[83] Maturin's novel explicitly performs this shift, providing footnotes that insist on the referential nature of the scenes, not as literal truth, but as a transplanted copy of it. Maturin seems to be asking whether a text that can convey the experience of events that are based in history, and that can virtually place the reader in a fully realized world and allow them to feel the emotions associated with a given event, can make a claim to truth.

An intriguing part of this dynamic, one that makes its problematic aspects more apparent, is that the novel also stages this process of transplantation and use of virtuality as a form of knowledge in another way, through metaphors and images clearly marked as "foreign." In the most generous interpretation, this process can be seen as an effort to transport readers, not only in space, but also in perspective, striving to imagine both what happens in other places and how the people in those places perceive those events. Trapped in the Inquisition, for instance, Monçada says he felt himself "tottering on a narrow ridge,—an Al-araf" (233), a reference to the *Qu'ran* that is noticeably odd, given the Christian setting. In fact, descriptions of Catholic strongholds such as the monastery and Inquisition are particularly weighted with "Eastern" metaphor: Monçada is "suspended like Mahomet's tomb between heaven and earth" (181), or reprimanded for being "the Upas, under whose poisonous droppings all living things perished" (221)—a footnote clarifies that this is a reference to Javanese myth—and the Inquisition is described in terms of the "genii, or the demons of the place" (235). One could read this as an effort to enact a form of mediation coupled with translation, an attempt to convey to English readers a sense of how people in other places see the world.

A metaphor as a descriptive device does not only ornament a text; it can also serve to explicate, or translate, relating something unknown to something familiar. It is along these lines that Wayne Booth argues that a metaphor must be "accommodated to the audience."[84] In *Melmoth the Wanderer*, however, the effect seems to be quite the opposite: the already strange scenes are compared to things that are equally removed from the day-to-day life of its readers. It is in this vein that Massimiliano Demata has suggested that the purpose of such metaphors is to compound the horror, further distancing readers from the events described and aligning them with the darker places of the Earth.[85] But one could also argue the exact opposite—that such metaphors serve as an effort to bridge the space between East and West, or rather, between the Oriental Tale and the novel as forms of representation. While some of the metaphors may have served to present new ideas to readers (such as an Al-araf or Upas), many of the references would have been familiar to an audience fond of oriental tales. As Srinivas Aravamudan has argued, such transcultural metaphors served as important techniques of immersiveness, offering ways of introducing readers to foreign cultures.[86] While these techniques were typical in texts such as *Lalla Rookh* (1817) or *Vathek* (1786), which were seen as providing detailed information about the culture of distant locales, Maturin is unique for the way he transplants these metaphors, resolutely connecting them to more local contexts.[87] The use of "foreign" metaphors lends exoticism to the text, but also implicitly denies their difference, or rather, renders them fungible—they are brought home for the readers, who learn to deploy them in their own comparisons.

What makes this problematic, however, is the fact that the language used to mark this translation is one drawn from representations of the Eastern world that are deeply intertwined with orientalist discourses. Whether one should read Maturin as a cultural imperialist, an avid admirer acting in good faith, or as engaged in an effort to forge some kind of transnational solidarity among victims of colonial violence, is an open question, one that I do not pursue here. But there are clear links between these experiments with various kinds of transpositions and the exploration of fiction's educational potential through the creation of a virtual reality. Once again, however, the lines between invention and documentation are blurred, for the sources alluded to in these metaphors or footnotes are more commonly literary than historical. The entanglement of fictional and empirical descriptions becomes all the more difficult to sort out when the subject is the "exotic" Orient, an area that many readers would only encounter through texts, most of which were fictional (or fictionalized). This undecidability also makes clear how fictions can be mistaken for reality to such an extent that for many readers the two become indistinguishable.

This type of reading practice, fiction as a form of travel, is illustrated most strikingly when Monçada, getting stuck while attempting to make his escape through the underground passages of the monastery, says that he "could not help recollecting and *applying* a story I had once read of some travellers who attempted to explore the vaults of the Egyptian pyramids" (192, author's italics). This movement is crucial, emphasizing as it does the way in which travel narratives have not only made people aware of different parts of the world, but have also come to form a frame of reference. By doing so, the novel illustrates the way that perception itself is conditioned by literature: Monçada's relationship to reality is framed by the stories he has read. In this way, literature becomes a kind of alternate reality, one that the characters experience as relevant in the same way that the actual world is. This does not require seeing it as true—one can apply a story even if one sees it as wholly fictional.

We are accustomed to thinking of fiction as moving the reader by whisking him or her off to a different place, but what Maturin's novel shows us is that the stories are moved as well, as various events are taken from their own contexts and inserted into new stories—from whence a reader may pluck them and apply them anew. Monçada's application of the story is but another example of what the narrator has been doing all along, transplanting events, stories, metaphors, from one location to another, occasionally signaling their original provenance in the footnotes. Where and when an event happened, or if it actually happened at all, has little bearing on its potential applicability to a new context. In this way, fictions take on a life of their own, becoming subtly interwoven into the texture of the reader's experience, gaining a kind of reality in the process.

This scene dramatizes the action of the entire novel—Monçada's application of the story parallels John Melmoth's process of compiling stories about his ancestor before finally confronting him. It also recalls Alfons van Worden's efforts to collate a series of stories into an understanding of a foreign context, as clues to solve various supernatural mysteries he is confronted with.[88] Thus Maturin's novel, like Potocki's, speaks to the ways in which fiction permeates reality, serving as a kind of virtual experience that has tangible effects on the characters, in both positive and negative ways. Even if they are not strictly true, it is suggested, stories can teach us something, help us make sense of the world.

In other words, we live our lives partly with reference to the fictions we have encountered, which shape our perspective, whether or not we believe them. Both novels thus illustrate the very powers of fiction that critics of romances had ascribed to them, and worried over—their ability to shape the way readers view the world.

In both books, the power of fiction is of an ambiguous nature. Stories may benefit the characters by giving them information or helping them negotiate a foreign environment, but they also serve to deceive or terrify. These novels are not only collections of tales that are being presented to the reader, but also scenes of listening, or transcribing—scenes where we witness others reacting to stories and making use of them, or being changed by them. Both works are thus a sustained reflection on literature and the act of reading. As I have shown, both engage in extensive inquiries into the workings of fiction and its effects, considering what, exactly, novels teach their readers, and how.

But they also take this reflection a step further, in ways that implicate us as modern-day readers, examining how fiction produces a persuasive image of a full-fledged reality. Through their intricate structure of interconnected tales, these novels model the way that the accumulation of stories serves to generate the sense of a world, thereby illuminating how our conceptions of world are underwritten by techniques specific to fictions.

The emergence of World Literature Studies as a field, and increasing critical reflection on climate change, have transformed the idea of a world from an apparently straightforward object into a question, inviting us to reflect on what, exactly, constitutes a world, or to ponder the differences between world, globe, and planet. In a recent contribution to these conversations, Debjani Ganguly has raised the question of the specific value of the *literary* in understanding the idea of world: to think of what "the work of genre, rhetoric, trope, and narrative . . . have to offer in understanding the complex relationship between the globe and the world."[89] These novels, I argue, indirectly offer an answer, demonstrating the intimate, and inevitable, links between storytelling and world-building, the fictive underpinnings of any sense of worldedness. In these two texts, the elaborate formal structure that produces the sense of an autonomous world, collapsing the distinctions between fiction and reality in ways that terrify the protagonists, offers a different way of conceiving of *the* world, upending binaries of East-West, domestic and foreign, by modeling a space that is densely interconnected.

To explain how they do so, I draw on Eric Hayot's work, which proposes a number of variables that are useful in examining literary worlding: amplitude, completeness, meta-diegetic structure, connectedness, character-system, and dynamism.[90] The two most applicable to Maturin's and Potocki's novels are connectedness, or how the text theorizes the set of relationships between its characters, and completeness, how it handles the question of totality and the text's ability to encompass the entire world. From this perspective, what *Melmoth the Wanderer* and *Rękopis znaleziony w Saragossie* share is a highly interconnected character structure, where people who seemingly have nothing to do with each other are shown as related in various ways. This would seem to be a small-world effect, except for the second variable, the way both works keep pointing out their own incompleteness, alluding to a vast realm of other, similarly connected stories that remain untold. They thus produce the sense of a world that exists independently of the particular story they are telling—one where the multiple connections between the characters exceed the narrator's awareness or control.

In each of these books, the main character is faced with a mystery, then exposed to a large collection of stories told by different people, which gradually become interconnected. The case of *Melmoth the Wanderer* is fairly obvious; completely unrelated people tell apparently different stories that all turn out to be about the same person, thus not only giving more information about that one mysterious person, Melmoth, but also creating the unsettling sense of a relationship among groups of strangers. *Rękopis znaleziony w Saragossie* is slightly different, because there is no single link between the tales, but rather a series of coincidental ties. As discussed above, there are numerous examples where information from one story is found to be integral to the understanding of another one, as in the case of the Knight of Toledo and Lope Soarez, where the key to an apparently supernatural occurrence is found in a completely unrelated tale.

Both Alfons, the central character of *Rękopis*, and Monçada, the main storyteller in *Melmoth*, note the eerie sense of a connection with others. Alfons remarks to himself that "Nie ma wątpliwości, że sam jestem jednym z ogniw tego niewidzialnego łańcucha, który coraz ciaśniej mnie krępuje" ("It is obvious that I myself form part of this invisible chain, which binds me ever tighter").[91] When Monçada hesitates to transcribe the story of a woman named Immalee, another character rebukes him, saying "and dost thou still hesitate to record the story of those whose destiny a link, wondrous, invisible, and indissoluble, has bound to thine" (271). The "link" between these various characters is that of story: the novels are the collections of those tales, along with the description of their collation.

This technique appears similar to the densely interconnected character structures typical of realist fictions of the Victorian period, but these two novels go further, creating the sense of an endless profusion of such stories and the connections between them. In *Melmoth*, for instance, an innkeeper tells one of the characters, Don Francisco, that "your worship must needs be a stranger in this part of Spain not to have heard the name of Melmoth the Wanderer" (396), gesturing toward a vast collection of stories, an oral realm of myth and legend. Each new character in *Rękopis znaleziony w Saragossie* has their own tale to tell, and given the connections between other stories, it seems only reasonable to assume that new ones will offer similar links. These connections distinguish both texts from other story collections such as *The Canterbury Tales*, *The Decameron*, or *1,001 Nights*, where the stories may be many, but they remain isolated from each other.[92]

What is more, as the above line from the innkeeper suggests, although both texts are organized around one main character compiling the stories into a comprehensible whole, it is clear that other combinations are possible, and could reveal different connections or concerns. We see this in *Melmoth the Wanderer*, where we learn early on that it is not only John Melmoth who seeks to learn more about his mysterious ancestor, but also the shipwrecked sailor Monçada, and a man named John Stanton. Similarly, although the tales in *Rękopis znaleziony w Saragossie* are filtered through the perspective of Alfons van Worden, and his specific interests in understanding who his cousins are and what kind of place he has found himself in, we also see the transmission of tales affecting the lives of other characters. As described above, for instance, when Pandesowna the Gypsy Chief hears Lope Soarez's story, he immediately runs to tell the Knight of Toledo the truth, leading the Knight to abandon his prayers and the monastery he had intended to settle in. Other characters are also transformed by the tales in various ways, such as Rebeka, who forgoes the study of the *Cabbala* and falls in love with Velásquez, the geometer. In both books, we have an overall sense of different people interacting with sets of stories that change them, and those sets of stories are in some ways overlapping (in others not).

How this sense of a broader world emerges from networks of interlaced stories in both texts also has implications for the image of the (reader's) world, and the sociocultural relationships in it. The tales in *Rękopis znaleziony w Saragossie* reconfigure the terms of an apparent clash of civilizations between an exoticized East and allegedly empirical West, calling both characterizations into question. Likewise, the massive geographical sprawl of Maturin's novel, which moves from Ireland to Spain to an island in the Indian Ocean, decenters the action, granting different places equal status, and relativizing them by setting them alongside each other. This transnational perspective is further developed by Maturin's footnotes, which relate events in one location to those of another, noting, for instance, that similar things have occurred in other places, or in other fictional works. The sprawling and capacious nature of the stories in both books creates a greatly expanded image of their world, which in turn produces an expanded image of *the* world, a transnational perspective crisscrossed with surprising links and similarities.

Alexander Beecroft has recently described this kind of story as a "plot of globalization": stories that use multi-strand narration (*entrelacement*) as a technique for representing the experience of life in our expanded, globalized world. He argues that while *entrelacement* is a well-established technique, its use in the twenty-first-century novels and films that he examines is distinctive, representing the emergence of a new form. These more recent works, he argues, offer the key innovation of using *entrelacement* "to project onto the level of form the paranoiac interconnectedness of life in a globalized era and the expansion of the scale on which these narratives are interwoven to the level of the planet itself."[93] But Maturin and Potocki, writing roughly two hundred years earlier, do something quite similar with their interconnected tales. While their scale may not be truly global, both expand the geographies of their time period in important ways. What we see, in other words, is that these two novels, coming from seemingly peripheral and "backward" regions, offer a strikingly modern—or even postmodern—image of the world, as an interconnected space of cultural multiplicity and dialogue.

They also illuminate the link between this kind of world image and the act of storytelling. In recent, separate works, Debjani Ganguly and Pheng Cheah have considered the specific resources offered by the literary in understanding the idea of the "world" in world literature, and its relationship to the globe. Both argue against the notion of the world in literature as mere extension, spatial category, or secondary reproduction of our physical world: "The 'world' in the contemporary world novel is not the literary analogue of our current geopolitical world order nor is it bound to any serial, sequential, or compressed space-time of a single world like the nation or the globe."[94] In different ways, both scholars emphasize, instead, the constitutive property of the literary, its ability to "world" particular kinds of worlds, to imagine new chronotopes of world and to contain many different kinds at once. What is more, both see this property of the literary as offering a crucial contribution to the process of worlding our own reality, as "something that can play a fundamental role and be a force in the ongoing cartography and creation of the world."[95] Citing Hannah Arendt, Cheah writes of the world as being formed by telling stories, and describes the shared mixed ontological status of both literature and world as being neither object nor subjective. This theorization aptly captures the way that Maturin's and Potocki's novels illuminate the peculiarly literary quality of their universes, which are an intersubjective realm of shared stories, endlessly multiplying, that enfold geographically distant locales and overlapping temporalities. In both texts, the main character collates a series of stories into an understanding of a foreign context or as clues to the various supernatural mysteries he confronts.

Notably, both characters initially respond to these stories as fictions, only gradually realizing that these tales are describing their own reality, for in both novels the stories the protagonists collect have a frightening way of exceeding their narrative boundaries and coming directly into contact with their own lives. Deidre Lynch notes, for example, a particularly ironic moment when a character named Stanton visits a mental asylum and becomes so engrossed in a patient's memoir that he fails to notice when someone locks him in, making him a patient as well.[96] *Rękopis znaleziony w Saragossie* offers an even more explicit example, when Alfons's own father makes an appearance in the tales.[97] What makes it so terrifying for the protagonists is not the possibility of an endless chain of stories, but rather that they initially encounter these tales as fictions which are then gradually incorporated into reality, thereby melting the barriers between the two.

The process gives that reality an oddly fictional texture, a sense of the story stepping off the page, which gradually melds into an implicit awareness of the way that stories, whether fictional or not, become part of someone's worldview. Monçada, John Melmoth, Alfons, and others are continually contemplating and reapplying the stories they hear, assembling them into new worldviews, thereby blurring the boundaries between fiction and reality. These are worlds made of stories, and a unique commonality of these two texts is the vivid way in which they model that truth.

Until recently, the prevailing critical narrative of the Gothic saw it as developing in parallel, or even opposition, to the rise of realism, and suggested it was a mode governed by a set of conventions so stable as to be cliché.[98] I share, instead, Sarah Kareem's view that although in content the Gothic may be the night to realism's day, their formal mechanics are of a piece with each other.[99] Indeed, as I have shown, although they do so in a particularly Gothic way, the central questions of *Rękopis znaleziony w Saragossie* and *Melmoth the Wanderer* engage a problematic more generally relevant to fictionality: questions of fiction's referential status, and of its effects on its readers. While they stand out as particularly self-conscious (and admittedly, somewhat convoluted) examples of this kind of inquiry, this is precisely because of the lengths they are willing to go in order to explore these problems in detail—and, perhaps, because of the gleeful pleasure they take in these inquiries.[100] Rather than excluding them from consideration in examinations of the novel's rise, then, this ostensible oddness is the reason that these two books deserve particular attention, for the way they illuminate the complexities of literary mechanics. This is particularly the case with the features of these novels that seem to set them most starkly apart and mark them as trafficking in obsolete and outmoded forms: their elaborate construction of multiple intertwined tales. Far from being an archaic or regressive use of literary form, these carefully networked stories are striking models of literary worlding that anticipate the (post)modern architectures of today's globalized fictions. Without being realist, *Rękopis znaleziony w Saragossie* and *Melmoth the Wanderer* explore the nature of reality and its relationship to both fiction and form.

CHAPTER THREE

Queer Tales and Seductive Paintings
Żmichowska and Wilde

The two novels that I discuss in this chapter, Narcyza Żmichowska's *Poganka* (*The Heathen*) (1846/1861) and Oscar Wilde's *The Picture of Dorian Gray* (1890), are queer stories, texts that seem both old-fashioned and hypermodern, at odds with the literary trends of their time.[1] Both books are considered outliers in terms of the novelistic genre; some would even go so far as to call them antinovels, or argue that they are not novels at all. The resemblances between them, at first glance slight, multiply with closer observation. Both stories revolve around portraits with an eerie, difficult-to-describe power; to say magical seems to put it too strongly, and this ambivalent attitude to what would seem to be the central, animating force of both books is one of their striking similarities. Both are also clearly in thrall to a Hellenistic vision of beauty, pleasure, and love, with clear echoes, especially, of Plato's *Symposium*. And both are generic hybrids, uneasy compilations of disparate material that barely holds together: lengthy scenes of drawing-room dialogue compete with lyrical, ornate descriptions that are equally at odds with the sensational drive of the plot.

The critical responses to these works have often circled back to the same-sex desires of their authors, seeing them as somehow central, although the question of exactly how those desires manifest in the texts is less clear. Such readings are more explicit in Wilde's case, both because of his notorious trial, and because those desires are more visibly present in *The Picture of Dorian Gray* (although their status is ambiguous). Żmichowska's attraction to women is less firmly established, and its manifestation in the novel is also more opaque: the central love story is between a man and a woman, but critics have argued both that the female narrator seems as fascinated by the heroine as by the male lead, and that the male protagonist is clearly a stand-in for the author herself, who was rumored to be in love with a woman.[2] Certainly, the two novels feature a highly complex interplay of repulsion and desire, narrating the ways that love both enraptures and destroys.

So when I call these novels queer, I mean, in part, that they are texts that arguably belong in a canon of gay writing, and that they are written by authors with same-sex desires. But I also mean the term in the broader sense, as works that seem fundamentally strange, not only falling outside the norm, but also as questioning or deconstructing that norm in the process. Part of the work of this chapter is to examine the many meanings of the term "queer" in the context of these novels, and their connection to each other, and to examine the resources queer theory offers for understanding them. As I discuss, queer theory conjoins historicist and formalist methods, tracing manifestations of particular forms of desire within literary works, grounding abstract questions of technique in a material history of sexuality and sociopolitical institutions. But it also, more abstractly, models an affective mode of reading that invites a different kind of engagement with the text, a creative response to the erotic play of its form and the ideas it generates.[3]

Research on both *Poganka* and *Dorian Gray* has focused primarily on their content, their representations of sexuality, or of women, but curiously, the scholarship has largely overlooked their central component, namely, the mysterious paintings. Reading the two works alongside each other brings those artworks into sharper focus, illuminating their pivotal role in the formal dynamics of both novels. Those paintings are not merely devices that serve to motivate the plots, a necessary ingredient that sets into motion the events of the stories; they are also at the center of the reflections of both novels, an interrogation of the nature of painting and its relationship to prose fiction.

The notion that nineteenth-century realism was influenced by painting is well established: Ruth Yeazell has documented in detail how prevalent the idea was among authors and critics of the period.[4] But painting, in these accounts, typically signifies vivid detail, and visuality—realism, in other words.[5] Wilde and Żmichowska, however, figure painting very differently, as idealism made tangible, while remaining not-quite-real, not of this world. As well, both authors are interested in the formal features of painting that are unavailable to narrative. Drawing on Lessing's famous theorization of the distinction between painting and poetry in *Laocoön*, I argue that understanding these texts as seeking to emulate the representational strategies of paintings gives us a new way to make sense of their odd formal features: their stylistic hybridity and peculiar play with time. For these authors, paintings are not inherently realistic—quite the opposite. These authors show us that the apparent referentiality of the visual is superficial, ultimately untethered to the vagaries of life in the world.

Peter Brooks tells us that plots are not only stories of desire, they are also structured by desire. Playfully expanding this idea, I suggest that these novels are not only stories of a protagonist who desires a painting, they are formally structured by that (queer) desire for the painting's form, thereby enacting an interrogation of the difference in the way paintings, as opposed to words, represent worlds. The queerness of these works, I argue, is an explicitly aestheticized one—a queer formalism. As I will show, in both texts, this examination of the status of paintings and fictions is aligned with an inquiry into the nature of morality, posited as a set of social norms that are presented as ideals. Seemingly focused on the power of paintings to seduce, both novels instead reveal the limits of their powers to make real, implicitly arguing for the world-building powers of non-mimetic fiction, and for a morality that is inherently entangled in the messiness of reality.

The story of *Dorian Gray* is well known: the eponymous Dorian, seeing a beautiful portrait of himself painted by the artist Basil Hallward, envies the artwork its power to remain forever young, while his own body will be subject to the ravages of time. But instead, the opposite comes to pass: Dorian remains permanently youthful, and the portrait gradually manifests signs of age, and more importantly, of Dorian's cruelty and extravagant lifestyle. This prodigal mode of living is at least in part a product of the influence of a third man, Lord Henry, whose droll and flippant philosophy seduces Dorian into a decadent life led in pursuit of sensation and beauty. Dorian ultimately murders Basil before killing himself (or rather, the painting). Upon its demise, he and the portrait again switch positions: the canvas is restored to its former beauty, and he becomes an aged corpse. The story is prefaced by a text from the author that articulates an Aestheticist philosophy, asserting that art is intended to be beautiful first and foremost, divorced from questions of truth or morality.

Less widely known, Żmichowska's text likewise opens with a kind of philosophical preface; a group of friends debate love, and whether it is a force for good or ruination. Asked for his opinion, one of them, Beniamin, offers instead the story of his own doomed love affair with a woman he calls Aspazja, a tale that makes up most of the text. Beniamin lives a simple life in the country with his family, until his brother Cyprian, an itinerant artist, returns home and, like Lord Henry in Wilde's book, inspires the young man with descriptions of an amoral philosophy of Aestheticism. Cyprian explains his ideas as he works on a painting of Beniamin as Alcibiades with his head in the lap of his lover, Aspazja; and based on his brother's words, Beniamin falls in love with the woman in the painting (who is, as far as he knows, an invented personage). One night, Beniamin gets lost while riding his horse and finds himself in a strange castle, where he meets a beautiful woman, a femme fatale who enthralls him. Upon his return home, he learns that Cyprian has died, and, seeing the painting for the first time, he recognizes the woman from the castle. He abandons his family to join her, and she accepts his love, although she also torments him with her cruel flippancy. Eventually growing disillusioned with their relationship and hedonistic lifestyle, Beniamin murders one of her lovers and returns home, only to find most of his family dead. He tries to reconcile with Aspazja (she is never given any other name), but she mocks him. In a rage, he burns the painting—and later learns that she died at the same time. The story concludes with the friends returning to their debate about love, and Beniamin departing quietly, never to be seen again.

The comparatively large chronological gap (nearly fifty years) between the two novels, and the significant differences in their historical milieu, are perhaps the most powerful argument this book can offer against the notion that the resemblances between the various works I discuss are to be attributed first and foremost to their sociohistorical contexts.[6] I offer, instead, an account of their peculiar resemblance rooted in the conviction that their odd forms stem from an inquiry into a specifically aesthetic question: an interest in the difference between painting and narrative, how each balances between virtual and tangible, and the repercussions of that slippage for their moral status. The kind of inquiry both texts launch into the matter of ethics is intimately connected to questions of social and collective life, and art's role in both posing and answering them, but their approach to these reflections is not in the mode of high realism. Yet this inquiry is very much connected to an investigation of the novel form and its capabilities, and as such, it deserves to be included in a broader history of the novel as a genre.

༄

The feature that most obviously sets both *Poganka* and *The Picture of Dorian Gray* apart from the kinds of fiction generally considered under the auspices of the development of the novel is their central conceit, the mysterious power that the paintings at their center possess. This use of magic reads initially as an attachment to fairy tale, folklore, or Romantic forms—in other words, as a continuation of older modes of writing, disqualifying them from consideration as serious works of formal innovation. Notably, however, in neither book is this quasi-magical nature of the painting registered in fantastic terms. Neither book, in other words, is set in a world that is imbued with magic, where such occurrences would be commonplace, but nor do the supernatural qualities of the paintings serve to make the protagonists question their understanding of reality. The world of both novels is, for the most part, a recognizable and familiar one—the magic is merely the means to an end.

When Dorian first notices a change in the painting, after he rejects Sibyl Vane's love, there is a sense of shock and wonder: "He had uttered a mad wish that he himself might remain young, and the portrait grow old. . . . Surely his wish had not been fulfilled? Such things were impossible. It seemed monstrous even to think of them. And, yet, there was the picture before him, with the touch of cruelty in the mouth."[7] A moment like this could, in another story, lead to a realization that the world is enchanted, or magical. But Dorian's thoughts quickly move elsewhere, to a defensive reaction that he has not been cruel, or rather, that his cruelty is Sibyl's fault, and though he tries once more to dismiss the change as "an illusion wrought on the troubled senses" (75), he quickly moves to acceptance, and does not question the painting's power again, though he will later ponder exactly how that power works (86). When Basil sees the picture, he similarly begins by doubting whether what he's seeing is real, but rapidly turns his attention instead to what the miraculous changes say about Dorian (129). The magical qualities of the painting, in other words, are registered as strange, but they do not occasion deeper debate or investigation. It is for this reason, perhaps, that critics largely ignore it, or even deny it entirely (though both *Dorian Gray* and *Poganka* are often acknowledged as having a Gothic ethos). Michal Peled Ginzburg, for instance, writes that the supernatural dynamic in *Dorian Gray* is "only the rhetorical effect of Wilde's deployment of his signature figure—the paradox," and Theodore Ziolkowski even goes so far as to argue that everything in the book can be explained in rational terms, as an effect of Dorian's imagination.[8] It is only in the final scene, when Dorian stabs the painting and the servants arrive to find his withered, almost unrecognizable body with a knife through the heart (183–184) that the truly mysterious nature of the relationship between painting and subject seems to be emphasized, as a kind of dramatic, cliff-hanger finale.

Similarly, in *Poganka*, the fact that the woman in the portrait turns out to be the very woman that Beniamin meets is noted with a sense of surprise and wonder: "wyraźnie ona, też same rysy, toż samo czoło wzniosłe i milczące, też samę usta namiętne . . . tak jest, to była ona" ("It was her! Clearly her—the same facial features, the same unruffled noble brow; the same passionate lips. . . . Yes, it was her!")[9] —but also as being almost unbelievable. Beniamin says, "nie mogłem rozczarować ułudzenia" (90), that he "cannot resist the charm of the delusion" (109), suggesting a psychological explanation, but whenever he looks at the painting, he insists that it *is* Aspazja, and it is impossible to determine whether he means this in a literal or metaphorical sense.[10] Both readings are equally available, but, as with Wilde's story, the conclusion seems to insist upon a supernatural view, as Beniamin relates to his friends that at the very moment when he threw the painting into the fire, Aspazja died in convulsions, and her body turned black. Anna's astonished, incomplete response—"więc naprawde ta kobieta była . . ." (121) ("So that woman really was . . .") (149)—and Beniamin's curious ending to the sentence, that she was "poganką" ("a Heathen"), produces "głuche milczenie" (a "hollow silence") in the room. As in *The Picture of Dorian Gray*, this moment suggests an insistence that the ostensibly magical quality of the portrait not be dismissed as metaphor or delusion—but this revelation cannot actually be incorporated into the text's worldview. The questions it raises are addressed only with a reverberating silence.

In both books, then, aside from a touch of dramatic fanfare at the conclusion, the supernatural is essentially a means to an end. It is a necessary component, in that it engineers the plot, but once set into motion it does not figure in any significant way (unlike the texts described in the previous chapter). The question is not whether magic exists, or whether the paintings truly have the otherworldly powers ascribed to them; it is instead an examination of the consequences of this magical power on the protagonists (for they are the only ones aware of the secret). Both texts, in other words, offer a kind of hypothetical case or philosophical experiment. What is this experiment seeking to understand? What questions are these texts asking?

❧

It would seem that the question at the heart of *Dorian Gray* is: What if a person did not age? In Wilde's hands (or in the warm waters of his Victorian milieu), this question becomes, what if the moral consequences of a person's actions were not visible on their face, or, what if a man were able to freely indulge his desires and avoid society's censure? Similarly, in *Poganka*, we could say that the question is: What if a young man completely neglected his duties toward family and nation in order to pursue a romantic passion? Or, as the narrative frame puts it, is love a force for good, or not?

Thus, both texts present themselves as being moral fables with a kind of fairy-tale logic, where the use of enchantment both adds an atmospheric charm and bends the rules of reality so as to set up the philosophical experiment. Both works explore the possibility of an amoral (or immoral) life, one lived in the pursuit of beauty, in defiance of social convention. And, despite Wilde's aestheticizing frame, both end unhappily, suggesting that such an existence is, in fact, untenable, that morality will exact its revenge.

It is not far to go from this premise to a queer reading: the story of a protagonist who pursues pleasure outside the confines of a heterosexual, reproductive marriage is already well on the way. But the queerness of these texts both eludes and exceeds this formulation: it is not enough to say that these are texts that depict illicit desires. Reading the two novels alongside each other illuminates the complexities of queer narratology: whether it addresses the content, the identity of the authors, the narrative form, or the relationship among all three of these things. In what follows, I take a detour through queer methodologies to draw on the resources they offer, and to better account for why the peculiarity of the forms of these novels is not reducible to the same-sex desire that animates them. As I will demonstrate, these are texts that pursue a queer formalism: not a representation of queer desire per se, but a manifestation of it in the erotics of their textual construction.

To begin with the matter of content: the question animating *Poganka*, of whether love is a moral force, takes on a new valence if we see the text as addressing same-sex desire. As well, reading it in these terms changes the way we see the failure of the relationship—Aspazja's narcissistic hedonism and refusal of Beniamin's exalted fantasy of love and union. Heather Love notes that "same-sex desire is marked by a long history of association with failure, impossibility, and loss . . . homosexual relations are often seen as marked by immaturity and selfishness, by the refusal to compromise (i.e., 'settle' for marriage or monogamy) or to give back to society (i.e. raise children)"[11]—a description that seems fitting for Aspazja's willful, cavalier attitude toward love.

Biographical interpretations of the text ground such readings in Żmichowska's documented passion for Paulina Zbyszewska. Maurycy Mann explains that Żmichowska creates Beniamin in her own image, including the love affair and its disappointments, because "w rzeczywistości panna Żmichowska kochała się . . . w drugiej pannie" ("because in reality, Miss Żmichowska was in love with . . . another young lady").[12] Ursula Phillips, though ambivalent about such interpretations, points out that Aspazja "occupies the most emotionally charged and compelling passages in the entire novel," suggesting that it is not only Beniamin who is in her thrall.[13] These readings are not unpersuasive, but they can seem more like a suggestive wink to a knowing audience than an engagement demanded by the text: without the biographical information about Żmichowska's amours, the romance in the novel seems rather less queer. Certainly, Aspazja is more femme fatale than loving wife, but the intimations of specifically same-sex passion are faint, at best.

Efforts to find a representation of queer desire in the content of *Dorian Gray* are similarly troubled: homoeroticism is everywhere suggested but nowhere made plain. Basil desires Dorian, certainly, and perhaps Dorian desires Henry, who may desire him as well (and whose wife practically calls herself a beard), and there is the matter of Dorian's later dalliances with both women and men, so shocking that they cannot be described—but to actually sort out who wants whom and what it really means is more complicated. Thus, for instance, although Jeff Nunokawa declares that "homosexual desire spills out into the wider boulevards of the novel's plot, taking the prouder place of explicit topic," he also notes that "Wilde's text declines to cooperate wholeheartedly with its *après-coup* canonization as an old testament version of the exodus from the closet."[14] Similarly, Valerie Rohy writes of "the possibility of a homosexuality that remains ineffable"; Elisa Glick describes homosexuality in the book as "ephemeral, variable, and elusive"; and William Cohen, noting the way the text both expresses and conceals homoerotic themes, cautions that "Wilde's energetic denial of precisely the kinds of readings that latter-day gay-affirmative critics propose, however, needs to be taken seriously, not written off as self-delusion."[15]

Of course, there *are* readings of gay male desire and sociality in the text: Eve Sedgwick, for instance, says that the novel "takes a plot that is distinctively one of male-male desire . . . and condenses it into the plot of the mysterious bond of figural likeness and figural expiation between Dorian Gray and his own portrait."[16] Jed Esty sees the resistance to aging and development as a resistance to heterosexual institutions;[17] Jeff Nunokawa argues that the love of an older man for a younger one is the only enduring form of passion in the text, though with the caveat that the body that is the image of that desire will ultimately become a spectacle of decay;[18] and Ed Cohen sees the painting, which cannot be captured in language, as the metonymic representation of male-male desire.[19] As Valerie Rohy points out, however, such readings frequently seem to work backward from Wilde's own trial to the text; the modern reader cannot ignore her knowledge of Wilde's personal life, which inevitably shapes her view of the story.[20] Thus, although *Dorian Gray* does invite the question of same-sex desire on its own, the answer within the text is curiously strained, and frequently linked, if only implicitly, to supplementary evidence from the author's biography.

To compare Żmichowska and Wilde as queer authors in a biographical sense, meanwhile, suggests an equivalency in their particular forms of sexual identity—a problematic assumption, not only because one is male and the other female, but also because of their different cultural and historical milieus. There is a long-standing debate over the position of historicism in queer studies: whether it is de-historicizing to use a term like "queer" in a trans-historical way; whether homosexuality is truly "invented," pace Foucault, in the late nineteenth century; whether the claim that same-sex desire is meaningfully different at different moments of history reifies the past as Other, and on and on.[21] I do not wish to take up this debate here, though I believe it is an important one. As is the case elsewhere in this book, I am resistant to the impulse to read these novels first and foremost in relation to their sociohistorical context, and this kind of biographical approach is a species of that, fraught though its relationship to historicism may be. To argue that the same-sex desires of their authors provide the missing link between the novels not only suggests a trans-historical sameness of queer experience across extremely different cultural and historical milieus, but also, paradoxically, simultaneously disavows and reaffirms the significance of sociohistorical context as the fundamental basis from which to understand aesthetic production.

What interests me, instead, in the resources that queer studies offer for an understanding of these texts is a formal dimension: how we gain a better purchase on the form of these novels by seeing it in terms of desire. Queerness is often associated with a deconstruction of form, or even a refusal of it.[22] But, bracing though the negativity of such accounts may be, it does not always do justice to the work of construction in a text—to the fact that something is produced.[23] To read that labor of production as queer is not necessarily to align it with specifically sexual content,[24] or to see it as analogizing sexuality within the social order, but rather, to attend to the desires that drive it. As I will explain, these two novels model a queer formalism: a desire not for a body, but for a form—a desire that shapes the way they are themselves constructed.

For indeed, formally speaking, these two works are markedly odd. Both novels have a curiously fragmentary quality. They seem to be a mélange of three different styles, or three different areas of narrative interest: rapturous descriptions of nature; lengthy scenes of dialogue; and the storyline, that is, the plot itself, which is a kind of sensationalistic thriller.[25] Of course, fiction frequently combines a variety of elements, but in these texts, the distinction between the different kinds of material is particularly visible, the connections especially tenuous.[26] The moments of description do not advance the plot, but on the contrary, seem to stall it, digressing into rapturous accounts of scenery or decor as though this were the real focus of its interest. In *Dorian Gray* they are entirely separate from Wilde's trademark scenes of witty repartee, which, in turn, are largely divorced from the drama of Dorian's increasingly wicked ways, which are kept carefully sequestered from the eyes of society, but gradually build up to a suspenseful murder-mystery plot. Similarly, in *Poganka*, Beniamin's family life seems to be a different order of reality, and narrative, from his existence with Aspazja, and the two are completely incompatible. Where his family life is described in pastoral, sentimental terms, his interactions with Aspazja have a surreal, dreamy quality. Both, of course, are completely distinct from the conversation that frames the text, with the occasional interjected bit of dialogue serving to remind readers of this other time and place, creating a vivid juxtaposition.[27] In both books, then, there is a clear sense of distinct, competing parts.

By making those various pieces of the text visible, the authors remind us that the work of narrative is precisely the arrangement of motley materials into a smooth form. In these two texts, that process is strained, thereby highlighting the labor of plotting them, and their resistance to assembly. As against the notion of plot as a static structure, Peter Brooks has emphasized its active nature, defining it as a "structuring operation," an "interpretive activity," "the active process of sjuzet working on fabula, the dynamic of its apparent ordering."[28] In other words, the plot is not a given arrangement of events, but rather, the process of arranging them. Brooks links the labor of plotting to desire: on the one hand, novels are typically stories of desire, of characters who want something and pursue it. But they are also fueled by desire; they "arouse and make use of desire as a dynamic of signification."[29] This is a manifestly erotic procedure, a yearning for satisfaction that can never be fully satisfied (for that would mean the end of narrative). Leo Bersani also describes the work of plotting in such terms: as that of fantasizing, conjuring an image of fulfilled desire, which binds together various moments, "inventing a dramatic logic for unexpected relations among things."[30] He offers an idea of how this process could be queered in his account of a disruptive desire, one that threatens both the social order of its world and the narrative logic of the novel. "In formal terms, disruptive desire could be thought of as a disease of disconnectedness in a part of the structure which rejects being defined by its relations to other parts and asserts, as it were, a scandalous affinity with elements alien to that structure."[31] This idea of disruptive desire gives us a way to read the blatant disconnection between different pieces of these novels as the manifestation of a scandalous desire that unites disparate material that nonetheless remains stubbornly separate. If the work of textual assemblage is an erotic one, these texts, I argue, queer that desire, calling the normativity of the procedure into question, seeking a way to do it differently, by pursuing a different kind of form.

But again, crucially, this is not a negation of form altogether: despite their fragmentary nature, neither *Dorian Gray* nor *Poganka* seems truly like an anti-novel, or a refusal. Their collation of different modes—which includes a use of magic we could consider embarrassing, or pastoral scenes of rural life that represent fantasies of national belonging, or lengthy descriptions evincing a decadent and shallow worship of commodities—is acquisitive rather than parodic.[32] As against accounts of queerness as a species of negation, neither of these novels seems committed to formlessness or even disruption; rather, they resolutely attempt to connect their disparate parts, to insist that they do belong together.

Yet if queer form is an analogue, or metonym, of a longing articulated in the text, the peculiar contortions required for a concrete reading of same-sex desire in these novels similarly scramble this more abstract approach. To call these texts queer is to name the peculiarity of their form, and to give it an erotic cast, but to link it specifically to a representation of same-sex desire is more difficult, and risks reductiveness. I argue that this desire needs to be framed differently, that to better understand these texts, we must look elsewhere, to what was directly in front of us all along: to painting.

Earlier, I described the central question of both texts as an inquiry into the moral status of a life lived in pursuit of beauty or love. But it is significant that in both books, these questions are channeled through paintings. Both texts, alternatively, could be seen as posing an altogether different kind of question: What if a person fell in love with a painting? Or, more simply: What if a painting was real? This becomes a formal question: What do paintings do, and how can a novel represent that process? Which is to say: What kind of novelistic form can represent—or recreate—the work of a painting? It is this inquiry, I argue, that is at the heart of these two texts and their peculiar formal dynamics. One can argue that the painting is a figure of same-sex desire[33]—it may well be. But it is not merely a figure. The painting is a central component of both novels, not only because it engineers the mechanics of the plot, but because it is integral to the peculiar construction of both texts. The longing for form—what I term their queer formalism—is the yearning that is shared by their protagonists, which is embodied, as well, in the form of the texts: a longing for a painting.[34]

The question of how words represent as opposed to images was famously taken up by G. E. Lessing in his *Laocoön*.[35] "Painting and poetry," he said, "should be like two just and friendly neighbors, neither of whom indeed is allowed to take unseemly liberties in the heart of the other's domain, but who exercise mutual forbearance on the borders, and effect a peaceful settlement for all the petty encroachments which circumstance may compel either to make in haste on the rights of the other."[36] As Lessing explains, the difference between the two is that painting depicts objects in space, side by side, whereas poetry depicts objects through time, one after another. For this reason, paintings portray bodies, whereas poetry portrays actions.

We obtain an idea of an object in space by observing its parts, then the union of its parts, and finally, the whole object, but we do so, he says, with such speed that these separate operations seem like one. Poetry cannot do this. The poet "enumerates slowly one by one,"[37] and the various details are lost in the process. "And if they be so retained, what pains and efforts it costs to recall their impressions in the proper order and with even the moderate degree of rapidity necessary to the obtaining of a tolerable idea of the whole."[38] One of the crucial aspects of looking at a painting, then, is that "the various parts are always present to the eye";[39] although complex and composed of multiple pieces, there is an all-at-once-ness to visual art that poetry, which unfolds over time, cannot replicate.[40] Poetry, instead, can represent action, change over time, a slow unfolding, a process of creation.

The difference between verbal and visual is thus, according to Lessing, first a matter of content—actions as opposed to bodies—and second, a matter of the different relationship between parts and wholes, a different approach to totality, which both requires and produces a different sense of time.

As I show, these two concepts are central to the peculiar forms of *Poganka* and *The Picture of Dorian Gray*, giving us a way to understand the work they do. Both texts produce the notion of a distinct totality precisely by refusing to unite their materials into a smooth form, creating the sense of a whole by making us aware of the parts that compose it. And both disorder time in ways that suggest an effort to mimic the particular temporality of a painting, and explicitly contrast it to the affordances of narrative chronology.[41]

In the case of the visual object, we always have the totality before us, and though we may focus on one particular piece at a time, the whole is always immediately graspable, and any piece is implicitly in relation to it.[42] In the verbal description, though, the whole is always a process of accumulation, and is always tenuous, a flawed labor of organization. We can add, too, that the totality in a written work is virtual: it is the sum total of the words, but practically speaking, it is result of the reader's individual construction as they read of an idea of the whole and its meaning. Anna Kornbluh has recently described the work of critique in the novel as a process of assemblage, arguing that the "novel's conceptuality is neither linear nor logical but contrastive and accretive; when novels think they do not iterate evaluative judgments (child labor is bad, patriarchy sucks) but mobilize ideas in a sensuous, plastic synthesis (the problem of child labor is inseparable from first-person narration and bildungsroman plotting). This special mode of conceptuality inheres in the novel's assembly of sometimes complementary, sometimes contrastive strata of representation."[43] This is to say that the work of plotting is the way novels think, and the totality, always configured anew, is an effort to draw conclusions. These two texts, both by virtue of their particularly convoluted process of assemblage, and because of their open-ended nature, producing questions rather than answers, make this labor particularly visible. Their contrasting strata are so extreme as to force a confrontation with the question of how a totality is constructed and its role in the production of meaning.

Whereas in painting the relationship between parts is a matter of space, in writing it is necessarily a matter of time. Similarly, as Brooks points out, following Genette, although a plot is fundamentally a spatial arrangement, it is experienced through time, and the production of meaning depends on temporal succession and sequence.[44] Time is the medium through which meaning in narrative is created, but it is itself also created by the text, through various temporal indicators, either concrete or implicit, which indicate when the events take place. The time in which meaning unfolds for the reader is tethered to the time lived by the characters, the sense of diegetic duration. The sense of development is thus subtly linked to the delicate parallel between two modes of time; the way the story occupies time is what enables the illusion of watching events unfold chronologically. By occupying the reader's time, the novel creates the illusion of time passing: a paragraph becomes a day, a page becomes a year. The affordance of narrative is its ability to emulate time in a way that a painting cannot, by narrating the passing of time as it occurs. We accept this convention almost without noticing it. This is precisely what a painting cannot do: it must capture time in other ways. Instead, paintings aspire to a timeless present that is simultaneously an accumulation of both past and future, grasped at a particular moment.

This is especially true of portraits. Discussing the specificity of portrait stories (as opposed to other ekphrastic novels), Michal Peled Ginsburg notes that a portrait is "an attempt to transcend the merely physical, ephemeral aspect of the subject (by summing up a whole life or bringing out the subject's essence)."[45] I will return to this idea of "transcendence" later, but here I wish to note how this description figures a portrait in relation to time. The portrait is not only an image of the subject at a given moment, but is also a summing-up that aspires to also capture the past, and perhaps even the future.[46] This gives us a way to understand the odd layering of temporalities in these novels—as an effort to emulate the painting's ability to be both a specific moment in the present, a summation of the past, and a prognostication of the future.

We see this approach to time most clearly in the frame narrative of *Poganka*, which opens with a series of character descriptions that are distinctly portrait-like. Each of the characters is defined as a type—Leon the Methodist, Edmund the Mystic, Teofil the Kid—or, capriciously, as people who are types despite failing to instantiate them:

> Obok tych czterech kobiet, ze stale określonymi charakterami, wyobraźcie sobie trzy inne jeszcze, które nie były tym, czym je Pan Bóg stworzył. Jadwiga nie była poetką. Augusta nie była artystką. Anna nie była matką. Jednak pewna jestem, że nim przyszły na świat, ich przedchrzestne imiona w niebie były: poetka, artystka, matka. Do urzeczywistniena owych imion na ziemi Jadwidze brakło pisarskiego talentu, Auguście pracowitości, a Annie dziecięcia. (10)

> Alongside these four women with fixed and well-defined characters, imagine three others who were not that, which God made them. Jadwiga was not a poet. Augusta was not an artist. Anna was not a mother. Yet I am convinced that before they entered the world, their pre-baptismal names in heaven were: poet,

artist, mother. Lacking, for the realization of these names on earth, was a writer's talent, in Jadwiga, diligence in Augusta, and children, in Anna. (10, translation modified)

The opening offers a series of "sylwetki" (14) ("silhouettes") (14), that describe each character in terms that strive to sum up their biographies—"Jej życie całe było czyste i tylko ciągle z niższej do wyższej przechodząc piękności, rozwijało się niby dzieło muzyczne według praw rytmu i harmonii" (7) ("Her whole life was pure and moved from lesser to ever greater beauty, developing like a musical composition according to the rules of rhythm and harmony") (6)—and distill them into an essential being. "Dla mnie wyobrażała ona jakąś zasadę przykrej rzeczywistości, objawianą miłosierdziem chrześcijańskiego serca i wspartą przykładem chrześcijańskich uczynków" (10) ("For me she represented a kind of principle of unsavoury reality manifested through the mercy of a Christian heart and bolstered by the example of Christian deeds") (9). Yet the narrator insists, as well, that these are people captured at a particular moment, frozen in the past in a perfected form: "O! jak to dobrze, Henryku. Może później byłbyś się zmienił . . . jak to dobrze, Henryku, że my się już nie spotykamy z sobą!" (18) ("Oh! What a good thing it is that we shall never meet again, Henryk! Perhaps later you would have changed . . . . What a good thing is it, Henryk, that we shall never meet again!") (19, translation modified). Thus, we see a quintessentially portrait-like approach to character in this opening, one that aims to portray a total person, a cumulative effect of experience over time, captured at a specific moment, and immobilized there.

This approach to temporality pervades the entire text. The novel begins with a narrator explicitly situating the entire story as a retrospective account, with a melancholic nostalgia that clearly sets this narrated past apart from the time of writing/recollection: "bo wtedy się kochaliśmy tak szczerze. . . . Dzisiaj? Los nas rozwiał po szerokiej ziemi" (5) ("how well we all got on in those days. . . . And today? Fate has scattered us across the wide earth") (3). There is a gesture to a possible future, as well, though one that would also be a return to the past—"Gdyby nam znów gościnne kto rozniecił ognisko, gdybyśmy się tak wszyscy dokoła zgromadzili" (5) ("If someone were to kindle again the welcoming fire, were we all to gather round it once more")—but it is immediately denied, as the narrator warns, "nie próbujcie nigdy powtórzenia przeszłości waszej" ("my advice is never to attempt to relive your past") (4). Thus, we have a time of writing coupled with a remembered moment among friends, and a fraught vacillation between them, as the effort to cross the gap of time is both made and refused.

Disorientingly, there are no clear indicators of when either of these moments is actually happening, and how far apart they are (ten years? fifty?). Although each of the people in the fireside chat is described, there are no explicit indicators of their age, for instance. One might guess that they are in their twenties or early thirties: although they have clearly defined interests and occupations, they are also dreaming of their futures, still planning to get married and have children, and Beniamin is described as "already" bald, "już wyłysiał okropnie" (21), suggesting that he has lost his hair prematurely. The scene thus seems to float outside of time, concrete and yet somehow ineffable. And then a third layer of time is added, a memory within a memory, as Beniamin begins to tell his story, which will become the bulk of the novel. Although his account is obviously far lengthier than the briefly sketched descriptions of characters, it too can be seen as aspiring to the affordances of the sense of totality offered by painting by virtue of the way that it is presented as an exemplum, an answer to a question. It is proffered in static terms—as an object to be scrutinized—in part because of how the tale summarizes or condenses an expanse of time.

The novel thus offers something like a series of images—Beniamin's story, offered as anecdote, and the fireside chat, likewise a frozen moment—and a movement between them, both retrospective and anticipatory. The way these different moments are jammed together becomes dizzying, a sense of both simultaneity and collapse. So, for instance, as Beniamin finishes his tale, we are brought rapidly back to a different present, the moment of conversation between friends, and then the narrator, recounting the dialogue, abruptly reminds us that this, too, is a memory: "jak dziś pamiętam jeszcze" (121–122) ("I can still remember how . . .") (149). Instead of the gradual unfolding seemingly available to narrative, we have the abrupt leap from one static frame to another, an effort to bind still images into a greater totality, to let us see them all at once, as if they were one large painting. As I will show, the actual reckoning of time within these various moments is curiously uneven —occasionally quite exact, but often hazy, further challenging the ostensible difference between the representational strategies of word and image. But first, let us return to Wilde and his narrative framing.

Readers of *Dorian Gray* may be surprised to remember that it, too, is a retrospective account. On the first page, the narrator introduces Basil Hallward by mentioning his "sudden disappearance some years ago" (1)—a disappearance that occurs, of course, when Dorian murders him, as described toward the end of the text. This sets up the story as a straightforward recollection of a past event,[47] but also makes it circular, delineating the contours of a fixed expanse of time.

We find, too, a number of peculiar sentences scattered throughout the book, subtly playing with its temporal frame. For instance, describing his time in the country to Lord Henry, Dorian says, "All during this wonderful May we have been having, I used to run down and see her two or three times a week" (173).

This is a singularly bizarre construction: a combination of the present perfect progressive (we have been having) and the past habitual (I used to), puzzlingly conflating two different orders of time. Likewise, the opening of the twelfth chapter tells us that it is the ninth of November, the eve of Dorian's thirty-eighth birthday: the chapter then adds "as he often remembered afterwards" (120), signaling to a future that will hearken back, repeatedly, to this moment. The habitual aspect suggests duration, a lengthy future, but in fact, Dorian will be dead less than a year later. These are small, barely noticeable markers, but they disrupt what might otherwise seem to be a straightforward, unidirectional flow of time.

The way the two books both define and collapse a collection of temporal frames is, I suggest, specifically portrait-like in its combined insistence on a particular moment, a here-and-now akin to the portrait's present, while also spooling out both past and future, in the way a painting aspires to. We could say, then, that these are novels striving to be paintings that aspire to be novels . . . They aim to replicate the way a painting presents time, which is itself, one could argue, an attempt to capture development in the way that a narrative can. The masterful twist in these two texts is to show us the contrast by ostentatiously deploying narrative markers of time and decoupling them from development—by showing us what prose could do but refusing to do it.

If, according to Lessing's account, narrative can track development because it has the affordance of duration, these novels play with this idea by marking time most clearly when nothing is really happening. At the very moments when there is change, time seems to vanish or become impossible to calculate. Stephanie Insley Hershinow has recently illuminated the way that our conception of character is based on the idea of development over time by examining characters in early novels who fail to develop;[48] Dorian and Beniamin, too, seem to accrue experience without being meaningfully changed by it, and this is in part, perhaps, because they do so in the interstices of time. If there is indeed any significant development in the characters, it happens precisely when time seems to disappear. This is all the more noticeable because both novels are otherwise so very adamant about marking time in concrete ways that prove both strange, and, upon reflection, strangely meaningless.

Caroline Levine, who shares my view that Wilde is purposefully evoking Lessing—or, as she puts it, "fully intending to wreak havoc" with his theory[49]—points out that the opening page of *Dorian Gray* neatly evokes and subverts the terms of Lessing's argument. As the shadows of birds on the curtains remind Lord Henry of Asian art, the real becomes reminiscent of a painting that strives to imitate reality; a creature in motion recollects a static image that strives to depict movement. Levine builds this into a reading of how the painting of Dorian makes difference visible, and therefore creates a sense of time. When the painting and subject are self-identical, she argues, the text is static; difference produces narrative, but it depends upon moments of stasis to mark the change. Thus, she argues, Wilde inverts Lessing, making painting the mode that can track change: "If pictures rely on narrative, narrative is dependent on the static frames of visual representation, which, thanks to their very stasis, provide not only the stimulus to narrative knowledge, inviting readers to put their faith in the truth-telling powers of the plotted text, but also the static moments necessary to the apprehension of discursive time."[50] What this reading neglects, however, is the curious way in which Wilde obsessively marks time in these ostensibly static moments, thus setting up an odd tension between clock time and discursive time. We find a similar dynamic in *Poganka*: time is both carefully reckoned and utterly dissolved, progressing in a stilted, leapfrogging fashion that abnegates the very kind of work that written narratives seemingly excel at. Even as the texts evoke the differences between painting and narrative, they also seem to opt for the techniques of painting instead.

Examined carefully, the action of *Dorian Gray* essentially falls into four (or five) clusters of time: the opening of the novel, when the painting is completed and Dorian meets Harry (and the following day, when Harry goes to his uncle's house to learn more about this new acquaintance); then another several days, occurring some time later, when Dorian is engaged to Sibyl Vane, then breaks off the engagement, after which Sibyl dies. Another length of time passes, and then, over several days, Dorian murders Basil, persuades Alan Campbell to dispose of the body, and confront James Vane. A week goes by, and then Dorian spends several days in the countryside, where James is accidentally killed. Another lapse, and we read of a final evening that Dorian and Harry spend together, after which Dorian goes home, stabs the painting, and dies. Thus, the novel proceeds in a hop-skip rhythm—a few days described with some level of exactitude, then a jump whose length can be curiously difficult to ascertain, then another few days, scrupulously accounted for.

These jumps in time are notable because so much of the novel is so precise: events are regularly described with reference to particular hours of the day: "at half past twelve the next day" (25); "when he arrived home, about half-past twelve o'clock" (49); "on reaching the library he found that it was just after five o'clock" (101); "That evening, at eight-thirty" (143). Furthermore, pauses are calculated: "For nearly ten minutes he stood there" (15); "A quarter of an hour afterwards" (67); "An hour later he was at the Opera" (87); "In two or three minutes there was another knock" (98); "For nearly twenty minutes, neither of the men spoke" (141); "After about ten minutes a knock came to the door" (141). Nine of the book's twenty chapters begin with sentences that explicitly state the time of day. Wilde keeps a scrupulous eye on the clock, situating events as if on a daily planner, emphatically displaying narrative's power to clearly mark time.

This exactitude is contrasted with the gaps that divide these scenes of action, gaps where it is sometimes genuinely difficult to be certain of how much time has passed. The first one is relatively straightforward: the fourth chapter opens with "One afternoon, a month later" (36), and Dorian tells Harry that he first met Sibyl three weeks earlier (39). What is slightly disorienting is that this burgeoning love for Sibyl is occurring at the same time as Dorian's growing friendship with Lord Henry, yet it is also implied that Dorian's attachment to Sibyl occasions a change in that relationship: "That is the reason, I suppose, that you never dine with me now," chides Harry (44). Levine describes this segment as "a state of stasis, marked by Dorian's perfect identification with his portrait,"[51] but I would suggest, rather, that this gap of one month seems rather too short for all that is meant to have happened in it: a cooling of Dorian's friendship with Basil, an established intimacy with Lord Henry, and Dorian's falling in love. Thus, clock time and discursive time begin, subtly, to part ways; the ability of prose to chart progression begins to seem shakier.

That night, Dorian asks for Sibyl's hand, and the next day, the three men go to see her at the theater. Her disastrous appearance (which, too, suggests that she has changed) leads Dorian to break off their relationship, and she dies during the night afterward, probably around the same time as when Dorian is first noticing the change in his portrait. The next two chapters take place the following day and the one thereafter, describing Dorian's conversations with Lord Henry and Basil, noting the time throughout: "Three o'clock struck, and four, and the half-hour rang its double chime, but Dorian Gray did not stir" (78). The meticulous accounting of time serves only to mark its passing—there are no major developments taking place. Finally, Dorian begins reading the yellow book from Lord Henry, which "so fascinated me that I forgot how the time was going" (103). Then, another massive jump, of indeterminate length, as the novel seems to forgo its interest in progression altogether, instead evoking a timeless present.

The following chapter, chapter 11, chronicles the passage of time in ways that are both specific and vague. So, for instance, a sentence like "Once or twice every month during the winter, and on each Wednesday evening while the season lasted, he would throw open to the world his beautiful house" (105), which gives reasonably specific coordinates within a broader time span that is unknown. We learn that "for a whole year" (114) Dorian is fascinated with Eastern textiles, and that "after a few years" (115) he cannot stand to leave England and risk being away from the portrait, but there is no larger frame of reference to know how much time is passing. This vagueness, of course, mirrors Dorian's own mysterious agelessness. On the one hand, it seems, nothing really happens during this interval. He reads books, he collects beautiful objects, he studies jewels and embroideries, he attends parties—but the chapter is curiously dull, a collection of musings and description.⁵² On the other hand, this is precisely when the seemingly crucial action of the book is taking place: Dorian is becoming an increasingly vile person and a toxic influence on those around him. Yet little is said of these changes; there is but one paragraph that mentions the rumors swirling around him, the growing suspicion and notoriety. A much longer paragraph is devoted to a stroll through Dorian's portrait gallery, as each painting is brought to life, a description of the canvas blending seamlessly with an account of the subject's life, and a musing on the person's legacy. This period of Dorian's life would seem to be the critical moment regarding character development, the very kernel of the novel's philosophical reflections, but the narrator is completely uninterested in recounting it, basking, instead, in a seemingly endless present.

The opening sentence of the twelfth chapter begins with a specific moment in time: "It was on the ninth of November, the eve of his own thirty-eighth birthday" (120). The reader may recall that Dorian was not yet of age in the opening pages, so this information serves as one clue of how much time has elapsed, but the more explicit moment comes later, in his confrontation with James Vane. Attacked by the young man outside an opium den, Dorian uses his own face as an alibi, proof that he could not be the man who undid Sibyl Vane, who died, her brother says, eighteen years earlier (157). The relationship between alibi, crime, and the exact recording of time pervades this cluster, for the description of Basil's murder involves not only charting the specific hours of his coming and going, but also the ways in which Dorian strives to evade this reckoning, by sneaking out of the house, returning, and asking his servant what time it is, for instance (132). Action is carefully plotted in relation to time, in the mode of detective fiction, but there is no real development; the change in our hero is a fait accompli, and we merely chart the minutiae of his coming and going, which has little to do with any significant change.

A week later Dorian is in the countryside, where James Vane appears as a threatening possibility of consequences of his actions and is soon (within three days) vanquished. This jump can be counted as a meaningful one or not (hence my saying above that there are either four or five total clusters). Also, although it does not seem terribly important, there may be an error in this jump. The murder takes place on the ninth of November; the next day, Dorian and Harry discuss the Duchess of Monmouth's plans to come down to Selby on the twentieth (148). But it is only a week later (the seventeenth) that we find Dorian, Lord Henry, and the Duchess at Selby in conversation (158). It may appear pedantic to point out this discrepancy, but given the narrator's scrupulous attention to time, it seems notable.

Then, a final jump, as we come upon Dorian in conversation with Harry, discussing Basil's disappearance, Alan Campbell's suicide, and his own resolution to be henceforth good. The only clue we have as to the passage of time is when Dorian mentions the "wonderful May we've been having" (173), establishing that it is some six months later. He leaves for home—"it is nearly eleven" (179)—where he thinks over his life, deciding "not to think of the past" (181). Resolving to focus, instead, on the future, he stabs the portrait—and brings life to an end.

So what we have is a series of scenes that reckon time fairly exactly, separated by intervals of various lengths, and a crucial central segment that seems to float apart. Levine compares this rendering of time to stop-animation of cinema,[53] and indeed, it is precisely an odd concatenation of verbal and visual, of images lashed together with narrative, but without the gradual development over time that a written work could offer.

Poganka does something similar. After the opening brings us into a past whose distance from the time of writing is unclear, Beniamin begins to relate his story, taking us into a further past, to relate an event that took place three years earlier.[54] But he begins even further back, with his own birth. He narrates his early childhood, then brings us to his seventeenth year, which is where his tale truly begins, on Christmas Eve. He and his brother Cyprian are reunited in their parents' home after a long absence. For a week, Cyprian will talk to Beniamin about love, and beauty, and the painting that he is working on, a portrait of Alcibiades and Aspazja, and his realization that in Beniamin he has finally found his Alcibiades. Over the next six months, Beniamin tells us, as he rides alone through the forests, he falls in love with the woman his brother describes—with his brother's words, and with the woman in the painting (though he has never seen it).[55] As with *Dorian Gray*, we begin in a relatively familiar rhythm of novelistic time, speeding up through some phases, lingering over others, within a defined span.

"Jednego dnia, był to dzień lipca," (64) ("One day, it was a day in July") (76, translation modified), he meets a mysterious woman while on a horseback ride and ends up attending a ball in her castle. Returning home the next morning, he finds a letter informing him of Cyprian's death, enclosed with the painting—which depicts the very woman he has just met. He falls into a fever, flees his lodgings, and meets the woman once again. Time becomes hazy: he relates how the relationship changes him, tells of travels the two of them take together, and mentions letters from home begging him to return, all of which suggest a passage of years. As their relationship sours, he chronicles events sequentially, but without reference to time: "Najpierw oddałem jej wspomnienie umarłego brata. . . . Potem oddałem jej wszystkie moje upodobania. . . . Potem jednego wieczora. . . . Potem —już nie wiem, gdzie to było . . ." (100–101) ("First of all I surrendered to her the memory of my dead brother. . . . Then I relinquished all the things I liked. . . . Then one evening. . . . Then . . . I can no longer remember where it was . . .") (121–122). Although there is mention of a particular evening, events are described only in relation to each other, or to location, but there is no external, calendrical measure of time, and no way for the reader to gauge it. Halfway through he notes that "kilka lat" (103) ("several years") (124) have passed—and carries on narrating. He finds himself wishing he had killed her "dawniej, och! dawniej, kiedy ją kochałem jeszcze" (105) ("long ago, when I still loved her") (127). Later, when he writes a letter to Aspazja, we learn that it has been six years. As with Dorian's story, during this stretch when time becomes hazy and diffuse, one has the simultaneous sense that nothing is really happening (one party after another, various travels or adventures that are merely listed, but seem meaningless) and that the most significant developments of the entire story are taking place. If the purpose of Beniamin's story is to answer a question about love, wouldn't this expanse, where love is being most thoroughly tested, be the most relevant? But we do not receive a careful account of the metamorphosis, only a hazy recollection of scattered moments, and the statement of its conclusion.

The letter Beniamin writes to Aspazja after returning home occasions a more strict reckoning with time, as we are told that he waited "dni trzydzieści; bez zmyłki pamiętam, bo pilnie liczyłem" (118) ("exactly 30 days; I am certain of the number, because I counted closely") for a response (144, translation modified). The answer he receives brings about the story's grim finale—Beniamin's burning of the painting. Then, suddenly, we are brought back to the opening scene of the fireside chat with friends, and, in another bit of temporal weirdness, we are told that two weeks prior to relating this story, he received a letter—which had been sitting on his desk, unopened, for two years. This letter tells him of Aspazja's death, which he realizes must have occurred at the very moment that the painting was burned. This simultaneity is in striking contrast to the odd dilation—two years, plus two weeks. Moreover, we may recall that Beniamin began by saying that the events he will describe took place three years earlier; either this is an error, or it makes no sense. Again, as with Wilde's story, it may seem punctilious to note the discrepancy, but at the very least it evinces how slippery the sense of time is in both books, despite their apparent pains to calculate it. The scrupulousness of the chronology in this conclusion seems almost absurd, not least because we have no idea what happened in the intervening period. It tells us that time has passed, with such exactitude that it seems as though it *must* matter—but it really doesn't. It is completely beside the point. At the same time, it *does* matter, but in a very different way: it is integral to the reflection happening on the formal level, on the difference between painting and prose.

In both novels, the kind of slow development over time that is ostensibly the provenance of written work is replaced with a series of scenes, with the crucial moments of change happening in sequences where time notably seems to dissolve. The contrast between these competing modes of reckoning duration highlights the difference between the way a portrait figures time and the way a narrative does. Both books strive to emulate a painterly sense of time, but they make us conscious of that decision by interlacing moments of carefully charted "novelistic" time, while rendering them, as it were, merely decorative, thereby insisting that we notice the specific capabilities of both modes.

This play of time is echoed, in both novels, by the peculiar disjointedness of generic mode. Not only do the novels awkwardly stitch together various moments of time, they also create a ragged whole out of various genres, binding them together without unifying them. Both of these qualities, I have argued, are the results of a strategy of representation that draws from painting, rather than narrative: an effort to replicate the effects of looking at a canvas, taking in the different pieces and seeing them as part of a larger whole. Striving to emulate this effect, these novels simultaneously show us that they cannot do so, entirely—that narratives cannot fully do what paintings can. The painting shows us everything at once—the writer, as Lessing tells us, enumerates slowly, and the reader must labor to understand the pieces in relationship to the whole. Wilde and Żmichowska achieve some measure of success in creating a different sense of time, and a different kind of form, but it is necessarily incomplete. Yet even as the novels fail to do what paintings can, they also, curiously, seem to refuse to do what writing ostensibly can, surrendering their ability to carefully recount development and change. It is this simultaneous success and failure that produces the peculiar effect of these works: their strange hybrid forms are the manifestation of a reflection on differing strategies of representation, an attempt to emulate what their characters desire. Thus, I argue, to understand the queer play of form in these works, we must conceive of their particular desires differently, as a pursuit shared by protagonist and novel alike: not for a lover of the same sex, but for the kind of ideal beauty that can be found on a canvas, rather than a page.

At the beginning of this chapter, I described the question these novels ask as one of ethics, a consideration of what it would mean to forgo social strictures and lead a life in pursuit of beauty. I said that these texts are (also) asking a different question, about the relationship between narrative and painting. I have considered these facets separately, largely skirting the first question, noting only that the unhappy endings of both texts seem to represent a victory for moral norms. Focusing on the second question, I argued that it gives us a different way to understand some of the peculiarities of the construction of the two novels, desire thereby read as refracted through an investigation of artistic forms. Now the time has come to examine the relationship between these two sets of questions, and what it means for these books—to reconnect the more abstract matter of painting versus prose to the question of how one ought to live one's life. These questions are bound through the figure of the painting desired by the protagonists: what I have called their queer formalism, their desire for a painting's form, is also a desire for the painting's subject, or world, an idealized realm of beauty that is free of society's rules. By making the two desires into one, the novels invite us to think about the relationship between them: between the form of social norms, and the form of paintings.

Although they seem like very different matters, what these books reveal is the way they are structurally similar: each centers on a problem of fictionality, of how much something imaginary partakes of the real, and what effects it has on the world. Staging both questions at the same time, the novels invite us to consider why asking about what happens when paintings come to life entails asking about morality, thereby leading to a consideration of the relationship between imagination and reality, its relationship to moral life, and the particular purchase that painting and prose have on embodying it.

In the previous chapter, I described how eighteenth-century thinkers worried over the power of fiction, and I observed that they perceived its salutary effects as connected to its ability to inculcate proper notions of virtue. The realm of moral virtue was thus aligned with fiction's ability to instantiate an ideal, as a way to quell fears about the power of this form of invention, and attendant threats of delusion. To invent a story, it was suggested, was a risky endeavor, but it was made justifiable if the story represented a kind of imaginary realm that one believed *ought* to be real.

Wilde and Żmichowska turn this notion on its head, calling into question the desirability of that idealized realm of virtue. In each of these books, the protagonist investigates the possibility that the moral norms governing their lives are a fiction, a superficial web of appearances or a set of idealized fairy tales that can be replaced with other, more beautiful aims. The paintings they become devoted to represent a different dream, an aim just as worthy—or more so, because it is tangible, visible. Once the paintings come to life, once their beauty walks in the world, it becomes available as a graspable reality, an ideal one can actually live out. But the same move that makes the idealized beauty represented by the painting into a reality is one that pushes the virtual web of morality into the background, treating it as an autonomous fiction that can be discarded or ignored. What both men discover, through their unhappy endings, is that paintings never truly become real, and moral strictures are never entirely idealized. In the process, they probe the curious way that prose fictions are both: they demonstrate literature's particular power to build worlds that simultaneously instantiate ideas. Or rather, they show us that the way that novels think ideas is inextricable from thinking them in a world, rather than as an autonomous fantasy that floats free of consequences.

The fictionality of a painting is never entirely believable: a painting always seems to be a painting of something, or of someone, and that something *must*, it seems, exist. Consider, for instance, Descartes's observation in the *Meditations*, that

> the visions that come in sleep are like paintings: they must have been made as copies of real things; so at least these general *kinds* of things—eyes, head, hands and the body as a whole—must be real and not imaginary. For even when painters try to depict sirens and satyrs with the most extraordinary bodies, they simply jumble up the limbs of different kinds of real animals, rather than inventing natures that are entirely new. If they do succeed in thinking up something completely fictitious and unreal—not remotely like anything ever seen before—at least the colours used in the picture must be real.[56]

Although a painting may be an effort to transcend its subject, to evoke an idea that is immanent in the subject's physical being, it nonetheless seems to be grounded in concrete reality, thereby reassuringly suggesting that it always retains some kind of truth.

But in a written description, even the words may be invented (heffalumps, houyhnhnms, supercalifragilisticexpialidocious). Although language exists, it is always troublingly tinged with unreality (Descartes worries in the second *Meditation*, for instance, that though he thinks with words, he is perpetually at risk of being deceived by them). Listening to Lord Henry, Dorian, too, notices this terrifying property of language: "But music was not articulate. It was not a new world, but rather another chaos, that it created in us. Words! Mere words! How terrible they were! . . . And yet what a subtle magic there was in them! They seemed to be able to give a plastic form to formless things, and to have a music of their own as sweet as that of a viol or of lute. Mere words! Was there anything so real as words!" (15). In typical Wildean fashion, the insight is inverted; words are described as troublingly real because they make tangible (or plastic) what does not exist. And indeed, what these novels show us, by making paintings real, is precisely that it is *words* that have this power to realize and shape worlds. The painting makes visible, but it is words that bring the immaterial to life. Similarly, Edmund Burke notes, in his *Philosophical Enquiry into the Origins of Our Ideas of the Sublime and the Beautiful*, that

> poetry and rhetoric do not succeed in exact description so well as painting does. . . . In painting we may represent any fine figure we please; but we can never give it those enlivening touches which it may receive from words. To rep-

resent an angel in a picture, you can only draw a beautiful young man winged; but what painting can furnish out any thing so grand as the addition of one word, "the angel of the *Lord*"? It is true, I have here no clear idea, but these words affect the mind more than the sensible image did, which is all I contend for.[57]

The painting can make visible, but it is through words, and their power to instantiate ideas, that invention takes life. The apparent truthfulness of a painting is illusory: though the paintings seem to become real, in these two books they never really do. They remain frozen, resistant to being incorporated into the worlds they have come to inhabit. The clearest evidence of this is their exemption from the social mores and moral strictures of their milieus; the living paintings are able to do whatever they want, without regard for the consequences. In *Poganka*, Beniamin's life with Aspazja always seems like a dream, a continuation of the masquerade ball where they first met. Dorian's charmed life, too, is a performance, his youthful face masking the activity occurring behind the scenes. Despite their physical existence, neither painting ever seems completely real.

In a similar way, idealized virtue does not ever completely exist. Virtue as an ideal is empty: it is meaningful only as action, in relation to other people. And this is Henryk's contention, in the opening conversation of *Poganka*—that the notion of virtue as an ideal is a sham.

> Co to są cnoty nadzwyczajne? Jeśli te, które się rzadko widują, to wszystko od razu—bo ja ani rzetelności w codziennych sprawach, ani wzajemnego przywiązania w rodzinach, ani przykładnego pożycia w małżeństwach, ani ładu i pilności w gospodarstwach nie spotykam dziś "zwyczajnie"—wszelkie dobro jest nadzwyczajnym—lecz jeśli przez nadzwyczajne cnoty chcesz jakieś "nadnaturalne" cnoty rozumieć, to się źle wyraziłaś, Emilio, takich cnot nie ma wcale, każda cnota jest naturalną każdemu człowiekowi, każda cnota jest powinnością każdego człowieka. (25)

> What are these extraordinary virtues? If you mean those that we rarely see, then all virtues are immediately extraordinary—for today I do not encounter "ordinarily" either straightforwardness in our daily affairs, or commitment in families, or exemplary living together in marriage, or orderliness and diligence in the running of our farms. Every good is extraordinary. But if by "extraordinary" you mean some kind of "supernatural" virtues, you have expressed yourself badly, Emilia. Such virtues do not exist; every virtue is natural to every human being and every virtue is the duty of every human being. (28, translation amended)

Virtue, Henryk tells us, may be extraordinary, but once idealized, it becomes meaningless. True moral life is precisely that which is lived, experienced, rather than set on a pedestal as a beautiful fiction.

In Wilde, of course, we find this insight inverted. As Dorian descends further into moral corruption, we learn that he has embarked on a pursuit of the real. His quest for beauty becomes, instead, a drive to ugliness, a movement that aligns the beauty of art with moral goodness, and that depicts both as imaginary: "Ugliness that had once been hateful to him because it made things real, became dear to him now for that very reason. Ugliness was the one reality. The coarse brawl, the loathsome den, the crude violence of disordered life, the very vileness of thief and outcast, were more vivid, in their intense actuality of impression, than all the gracious shapes of Art, the dreamy shadows of Song. They were what he needed for forgetfulness" (152–153). Seeking to live a beautiful life, he has, instead, found that to experience life to its fullest is to lose oneself in a coarse reality, rather than a reified world of drawing rooms and bon mots.[58] Lord Henry's philosophy of life is in fact a philosophy of art, of a beauty sealed off from existence.

In seeking idealized beauty, it would seem that both protagonists would be perfectly positioned to pursue virtuous lives. Holding in abeyance the question of whether beauty truly is moral,[59] the texts instead pursue the question of what it means to pursue an ideal. In showing us the incongruity of an ideal made real, they show us the meaninglessness of the proposition of ideal virtue.[60]

However, this is manifestly *not* an argument for a gritty realism: both authors remain, clearly, devoted to fiction's ability to enchant, and invent, as a vital aspect of its mode of thinking. Idealized virtues may be meaningless, but so too is a world entirely lacking in fantasy. Narrative fictions have the curious power of interweaving invention and reality, and thereby revealing the power that inventions have to shape reality. The ability of a painting to make visible is seductive, but it is also empty. It is narrative fiction that can build worlds that render ideals living and morality meaningful.

❦

Reading these two novels alongside each other brings the peculiarity of their formal construction into clearer view. Rather than asking about the similarities of their sociohistorical contexts, I argue, we should examine the resemblances between their aesthetic interests: what each work seeks from the novel form. Both texts evince a clear fascination in fiction's ability to bridge romance and realism, to tell stories of enchantment without retreating altogether from the world we know—indeed, while remaining preoccupied with the realities of contemporary society. Yet the questions they pursue are in some sense timeless; an inquiry into the relationship between invented stories and idealized virtues, a question of whether art, or beauty, is moral. Their mode of representation is not allegory, nor do they seek to mirror social divisions or trauma in their fractured forms. Rather, they attend to the conceptual labor of form, to the way that literary structures articulate ideas without making propositional claims.

Both are stories of illicit desire: for an idealized being, and the seeming promise of an existence removed from the dull obligations of real life—a promise that is bound up in the specific form of the painting as both virtual and tangible. The nature of this longing has much in common with the dynamics of same-sex desire during this period—that both authors were queer is not insignificant. In these texts, however, the object of desire is a specifically formal one. The desire for the subject of the canvas and the idealized world it represents, is echoed, on a formal level, by the peculiar contortions of both novels, their efforts to become like the paintings they describe. Combining the representational strategies of painting and prose, they illuminate the differences between them: narratives create totalities via accretion and assemblage, unable to replicate the illusion of simultaneity that an image can provide, and have the attendant ability (which these texts refuse) to track time, and therefore, potentially, development.

As they examine the relationship between paintings and novels, both texts also explore how social norms function to dictate morality, and what a life freed from such constrictions would be like. There is a subtle equation between such an amoral existence and the world of a painting: both protagonists, pursuing the latter, are inexorably drawn to the former. In this way, the narratives slyly suggest a parallel between them, demonstrating how they are, formally speaking, aligned: neither is real, and their exalted status as an ideal becomes meaningless when it is rendered living. Thus, both texts probe the moral status of art, demonstrating that its ethical power is not, as eighteenth-century thinkers had argued, in rendering ideals desirable, but in depicting the messiness of life in the world, in all its imperfections.

Thus, I argue, *Poganka* and *The Picture of Dorian Gray*, though anomalous in many ways, are vital to our understanding of the novel form. Bridging two lines of inquiry that have intrigued literary theory since antiquity—the relationship between painting and prose, and the nature of virtue as ideal embodied in action—these two books offer a unique perspective on the novel's fictionality and world-building powers.

CHAPTER FOUR

Impossibly Free
Gombrowicz and Beckett

The novels I have been discussing are all, in various ways, explorations of the space of fiction and its power to articulate ideas that are unavailable to a "realistic" mode of writing. Up to now, they have been novels that are set in worlds that are generally familiar but with meaningful divergences such as make-believe islands, or ghosts, that serve to demarcate an entry into more explicitly fictional territory. The fictionality of the works I discuss in this chapter, Samuel Beckett's Trilogy—especially *Molloy* (1955) and *Unnamable* (1958)—and Witold Gombrowicz's *Ferdydurke* (1938), is of a different kind. To be sure, there are plenty of strange occurrences in the books, surreal or illogical moments that give the characters pause, but they serve to redefine the worlds in which the books occur, trapping the protagonists in a kind of alternate fictional reality. These are novels that use form to dismantle standard modes of reference and meaning in narrative, serving as limit cases in the power of fictionality to construct worlds. They are works built out of irony, dizzying evocations of impossibility. They flout basic laws of narrative structure, wresting meaning out of configurations that insistently deny its very possibility.

Seen in the context of twentieth-century literature, the self-conscious approach to form in these works appears less anomalous than that of the texts discussed in the preceding chapters: literary modernism is after all characterized by a heightened interest in formal experiments. While they may share a general problematic common to many other artists of their time, the particular approach taken by these two authors is different from that of other modernist texts: it is a far more extreme undoing of narrative form. Thus, they too qualify for inclusion in my collection of anomalous pairs. Moreover, it is possible to trace a continuity between the formal questions they investigate and those of the novels discussed in the preceding chapters—a specific interest in exploring the contours of the space of fiction and what it makes possible. Hence, they serve as an apt finale.

To give a brief overview of Beckett's Trilogy—*Molloy, Malone Dies,* and *The Unnamable*—is no easy task. *Molloy* begins with a monologue from the titular character, telling us that he is in a room, writing. A man comes every week to collect his work and return what he has written the week prior. Molloy describes a journey through the countryside in search of his mother, and the various adventures that befall him along the way. The second part of the novel chronicles the travails of a detective, Moran, who is tracking Molloy and writing a report about his quest.[1] *Malone Dies* is similarly the story of Malone, describing his experience of writing, as he tells a story about a boy whom he initially calls Saposcat (the name will change as the story progresses). Crucially, he refers, in the course of his musings, to both Molloy and Moran, suggesting that he is the author of the previous novel. The third novel, *Unnamable*, offers the most heightened version of the anxiety about writing and creation, as the narrator (I will refer to him hereafter as Unnamable) agonizes over how to speak. Significantly, he likewise claims authorship of the previous novel, thereby positioning himself as the creator of the entire Trilogy.[2] Although each of the novels could technically stand alone, they are clearly intertwined in crucial ways that lead me to treat them, instead, as one three-part work.

Gombrowicz's *Ferdydurke* has a more traditional sense of plot: it is the story of a young man named Józio, who is kidnapped by a professor and sent back to school through the machinations of what he calls Form. The novel narrates his struggle to break free, following him as he becomes involved with a young woman named Zuta and then escapes into the countryside. Interspersed are reflections on the act of reading, and writing, and two short tales, each of which has a preface.

I read these novels in relation to the genre of the Bildungsroman, but here already we run into problems, for their approach to the form is so extreme as to render them, arguably, outside the category altogether. This, however, is precisely the point. Crucial to these novels is the fact that their formal experiments are framed as attempts of their own characters to find a unique mode of expression: in other words, their goal is to produce a Bildungsroman that is not a Bildungsroman. This is hardly the first such attempt: the appearance of what came to be called the anti-Bildungsroman on the literary stage was practically concurrent with the rise of the Bildungsroman itself, as exemplified by works such as Novalis's *Heinrich von Ofterdingen* (1802) or E. T. A. Hoffman's *The Life and Opinions of Tomcat Murr* (1820).³ The twentieth century produced many notable examples of works that, anti- or not, seemed written in response to the ideas enshrined in the Bildungsroman. But while novels such as James Joyce's *Portrait of the Artist as a Young Man* (1916), Robert Musil's *Confusions of Young Törless* (1906), Virginia Woolf's *Voyage Out* (1915), or Elizabeth Bowen's *Last September* (1929) depict stunted or incomplete developments, they are still relatively realistic works, albeit in a psychological vein: although they are formally experimental, they are nonetheless based in an empirical world, and generally function through a mechanism of identification. The works of Beckett and Gombrowicz are more radical in nature, focused more on the metafictional examination of the act of writing a novel than they are on the experiences of their protagonists in the world. As is typical of the Bildungsroman, these novels are doubled in structure: each is not only the story of a character, but also the story of the process of telling the story. *Ferdydurke* combines the two in one novel, with clearly delineated splits in which the narrator pauses the action to discuss the process of writing and digress into other subjects. In *Unnamable*, the narrator's anguished debate over how to tell his own story becomes the story itself, overshadowing most of what he actually says about himself, but we also learn that he has authored the other two novels of the Trilogy, which allows us to reread *Molloy* as a product of Unnamable's imagination. These novels make explicit the union between form and selfhood that has been seen as integral to the Bildungsroman, and make it a central dynamic of the text, as part of the attempt to find an original way of being.

    It may seem disingenuous to argue that Beckett and Gombrowicz are overlooked or peripheral authors, or even to describe them as Irish and Polish, respectively. Both writers famously left their home countries and spent most of their lives abroad, and furthermore, insisted that they were not to be seen as representative of their respective nations. The argument for considering these authors, respectively, as part of an Irish and Polish tradition is easier in the case of *Ferdydurke*, which was written before Gombrowicz left Poland for Argentina, and which is obviously set in Poland and dealing with Polish culture, than it is for Beckett's novels. Arguments linking Beckett's Trilogy to a specifically Irish context can seem rather strained, given how bare the landscapes within the text are. Certainly, one can point to the Irish-sounding names such as Malone, Macmann, or Bally as evidence of the author's Irish identity. Beyond that, the critical argument becomes more abstract: what is "Irish" about the novels, some have argued, is precisely their dismantling of national identity, or the sense of organically belonging to a given place.[4] To complicate matters further, Beckett wrote most of his works in French, though he was active in translating them back into English. This is particularly the case with the Trilogy, which Beckett not only translated into English, but also revised in the process. As a result, the English versions of the novels have a certain autonomy from their French versions. I have chosen to work with the English versions, and have not provided the French counterparts of the passages quoted because I do not believe them to be necessary: they do not, I think, represent a more accurate or faithful version of the texts.[5]

As regards their peripheral status, certainly one could not say that these are authors whose formal innovations have been overlooked in the longer history of the novel, or occluded by historicist readings, as I have argued of the texts discussed in other chapters. Nor are these texts that have been derided for departing from the realist tradition. With literary modernism, experiments with form become more commonplace, even characteristic of the time. What is more, this kind of experimentation is no longer ignored by critical histories of the novel: in fact, it moves to center stage. As discussed in the introduction, this shift paves the way for a kind of rehabilitation of Irish literary history, seeing the earlier works as anticipations of twentieth-century writing, a modernism avant la lettre. Modernism as a tradition, arguably, and modernist studies, certainly, have long been characterized by a greater interest in works from the margins.

But this interest is not as evenly distributed as it aspires to be. Thus, for instance, Chana Kronfeld notes that Deleuze and Guattari's celebrated account of "minor writing," which they suggest can be extended beyond literature written by marginalized populations within major traditions to encompass "the revolutionary conditions for every literature within the heart of what is called great (or established) literature,"[6] dehistoricizes both the minor and the modernist by rendering "minor" writing largely indistinguishable from modernism. Their framework also, paradoxically, manages to exclude most peripheral traditions by restricting minor writing to texts written in major languages.[7] Deleuze and Guattari write that "minor literature doesn't come from a minor language; it is rather that which a minority constructs within a major language."[8] As Kronfeld points out, this proviso undermines the possibility of any non-major language participating in international modernism, unless it serves in the background as a resource for destabilizing the dominant language. Although Beckett fits easily into this category—indeed, he is mentioned specifically—Gombrowicz, obviously, does not. Indeed, while Gombrowicz's importance to modernism is increasingly recognized, his status is nothing like that of Beckett's.[9] Of course, one could argue that Beckett is the superior writer, but the fact that Gombrowicz wrote in Polish is unavoidably a major factor in his lesser recognition. Milan Kundera is particularly eloquent on this point:

> There are as many Poles as there are Spaniards. But Spain is an old power whose existence has never been under threat, whereas History has taught Poles what it means not to exist. Deprived of their State, they lived for over a century on death row. "Poland has not yet perished" is the poignant first line of their national anthem and, in a letter to Czesław Miłosz, Gombrowicz wrote a sentence that could never have occurred to any Spaniard: "If, in a hundred years, our language still exists. . . ." . . .Gombrowicz's *Ferdydurke* was published in Polish in 1937. It had to wait fifteen years finally to be read, and rejected, by a French publisher. And it took a good many years more for the French to see him in their bookstores.[10]

I point this out to emphasize that while modernism and its critical reception did increase the access of peripheral writers to literary renown, there were—and remain—obstacles for those from the periphery, even in the realm of modernism, which is seemingly a more cosmopolitan, equitable playing field. As I will discuss in the conclusion, emerging frameworks in modernist studies seek to remedy these inequalities, and examining the ways they do so—the terms they challenge, and the assumptions they leave untouched—sheds light on how we think about literary history. But in this chapter, I focus instead on the textual mechanics of these particular novels.[11] Reading Beckett and Gombrowicz alongside each other we can see more clearly the similar strategies the two authors pursue in seeking a unique form of expression. As I explain, both authors discern the shared structure of metaphor, which Peter Brooks describes as the basis of novelistic form, and irony, or contradiction—its apparent antithesis. This discovery allows both to hover at the very limits of the form, producing texts that seem relentlessly negative, and yet remain, for all that, novels.[12] And in so doing, they show us fiction's power to express an idea seemingly unavailable to words.

☙❧

In his *Way of the World: The Bildungsroman in European Culture*, Franco Moretti argues that the central problem at the heart of the literature of modernity is how to reconcile freedom and happiness, which are reconfigured as individual uniqueness and social conformism: "How can the tendency towards individuality, which is the necessary fruit of a culture of self-determination, be made to co-exist with the opposing tendency to normalcy, the offspring, equally inevitable, of the mechanism of socialization?"[13] The struggle of the modern novel, according to Moretti, is to discover a synthesis, or at the very least, a compromise between these two principles: "Our world calls for their coexistence, however difficult; and it therefore also calls for a cultural mechanism capable of representing, exploring, and testing that coexistence."[14] Like Lukács before him, Moretti argues that realism is best suited to this task, and more specifically, that it is the Bildungsroman which will do so with an unparalleled "force of conviction and optimistic clarity."[15] The Bildungsroman orchestrates a compromise by depicting the individual's entry into society, modeling the internalization of social norms necessary to reconcile freedom and happiness.[16]

This compromise is echoed on the level of form as a reconciliation of the tension between two narrative principles—that of classification, and that of transformation. In the former, the meaning of events lies in their conclusion and fixity, in the latter, it is found in the process of narration, which resists finality.[17] The formal harmoniousness of the novel, therefore, is analogous to the compromise of the protagonist who learns to conform. Thus, the Bildungsroman unites form and the self in particularly complex ways: to be a person is to have a story, one that obeys certain generic conventions.

Although Moretti sees the Bildungsroman as gradually dying out over the course of the nineteenth century and ultimately vanishing altogether with the rise of modernism, Gregory Castle argues that it survives, and describes what he sees as a modernist project of critiquing and rehabilitating the form. When the spiritual and aesthetic ideals of the original process of *Bildung* are perceived as having been betrayed by the increasing bureaucratization of self-formation, modernist authors, he says, respond with a radical new mode of writing. Their failure to conform to generic expectation "signals a successful resistance to the institution of self-cultivation" and an attempt to restore "individual freedom within the process of self-development."[18] The solution is sought through the formal structures of art: Castle writes that "the failure of the modernist Bildungsroman is a complex and contradictory phenomenon, for where the Bildungsheld (hero of the Bildung plot) fails to achieve inner culture or harmonious socialization, the genre itself appears to assert its integrity in powerful new ways, to exploit the formative and transformative power of failure in order to effect a rehabilitation of the Bildungsroman genre and a justification of the raison d'être of the form, Bildung."[19] The struggle to discover a different kind of selfhood is synonymous with the attempt to find new ways of plotting the development of the self. In this reading, therefore, the anti-Bildungsroman becomes crucial to the rejuvenation of the form, rather than departing from it entirely.

Paul Sheehan, who likewise sees the Bildungsroman as fundamentally bound up with plotting the relationship between the human and the novel form, construes the modernist intervention differently, arguing that the modernist novel is the "antagonist" of the Bildungsroman, and that, rather than rejuvenating the form, it models an effort to "break free of narrative" altogether.[20] This more radical version is, as I will explain, a better characterization of the works of Beckett and Gombrowicz, which offer more extreme attempts to find a new form than the kinds of modernist Bildungromans I have mentioned above.[21]

There is, of course, a political dimension to these accounts of *Bildung*. The resistance to processes of socialization takes on a different valence for authors from politically marginalized countries, and part of the complexity of both Gombrowicz's and Beckett's novels is their sense of being caught between colonial or European discourses that would discredit them as subaltern or peripheral, and a homegrown nationalism that they find repulsive. This is particularly visible in the way they describe schools and processes of education as forms of institutionalized coercion. Patrick Bixby offers a detailed account of this dynamic in Beckett's Trilogy, and Anita Starosta offers a compelling reading of this aspect of Gombrowicz's work.[22] The argument that I track in these books is a broader one, however: in the novels of Beckett and Gombrowicz, what is generally the realm of society and its norms becomes expanded into language itself. Józio and the protagonist of Beckett's *Unnammable* seek a unique form of expression, words unencumbered by past usages and conventionality. Their struggle calls to mind Wittgenstein's well-known thought experiment, described in his *Philosophical Investigations*: "But could we also imagine a language in which a person could write down or give vocal expression to his inner experiences—his feelings, moods, and the rest—for his private use?—Well, can't we do so in ordinary language?—But that is not what I mean. The individual words of this language are to refer to what can only be known to the person speaking; to his immediate private sensations. So another person cannot understand the language."[23] This famous dilemma makes clear that language depends upon shared meanings in order to be understood. If one has a sensation or experience that cannot be encapsulated in the available words of a language, one can, of course, simply invent a new word (such as Ferdydurke!), but if it cannot be translated into terms others know, then how could anyone understand what this new word means? To take the problem a step further, how can a unique individual ever give voice to his or her uniqueness and make it comprehensible to others? This impossibility has profound implications for art, suggesting as it does that private or unique experience cannot be given expression. This is precisely the anxiety at the heart of both *Ferdydurke* and *Unnamable*, or rather, what defines their quest: the attempt to find a unique way of expressing the self.[24]

Both texts are centered on the struggle of the protagonists to speak, or write, as they will, to tell the story in their own way, in a kind of quest for freedom. As will be seen, in one sense these quests end in failure: both novels appear to assert the fundamental impossibility of an escape from the strictures of language. The quests conclude with a sense of helpless resignation and despair. As I stated earlier, however, these projects must be seen as doubled, for the characters are also authors, making their descriptions of their struggle a renewed continuation of the same battle, and it is on this secondary level that they achieve a tenuous form of success. I begin by delineating this first level, the failures, and then turn to the comparatively more complex successes, and to what they say about the novel form, and its ability to contain contradiction.

༄

Gombrowicz describes the problem of private language through what he calls Form, which is not to be confused with the form of the novel, though the concepts are related. To avoid confusion, when referring to the concept Gombrowicz describes, I will capitalize the term (as he typically does).[25] As Gombrowicz explains it, Form is the medium through which we communicate: "sprawa przedstawia się, jak następuje: że istota ludzka nie wyraża się w sposób bezpośredni i zgodny ze swoją naturą, ale zawsze w jakiejś określonej formie i że forma owa, ów styl, sposób bycia nie jest tylko z nas, lecz jest nam narzucony z zewnątrz" ("matters stand as follows: a human being does not express himself forthrightly and in keeping with his nature but always in some well-defined form, and this form, this style, this manner of being is not of our making but is thrust upon us from outside").[26] Notably, it is not only a style, but a manner of being, a way of life, and, as he says elsewhere, it comprises even the very words we use, which are never entirely our own. Central to this notion is the idea that it is interpersonal; Form shapes our modes of expression, which in turn defines and determines our relationships to others.

A useful model for the idea of Form is Wittgenstein's language games, described concisely by Lyotard in *The Postmodern Condition*. In a language game, every speech act is a move, the rules are contingent and determined by contract, and any utterance must comply with the rules in order to be understood. This notion has implications for the individuals involved as well: Lyotard points out that "each language partner, when a 'move' pertaining to him is made, undergoes a 'displacement,' an alteration of some kind that not only affects him in his capacity as addressee and referent, but also as a sender."[27] In *Ferdydurke*, this state of affairs is literalized to an extreme degree, whereby the player with the upper hand is able to completely define their opponent's identity through the words they use to describe him or her. This creation of identity by others is described in bodily terms in the text, as "przyprawienie gęby" ("putting a face on someone"), or alternately, "robić pupę" ("dealing someone the pupa").[28] The gęba is the identity given to one person by another, quite literally how one person is seen by another. It is precisely by putting a face on another that you determine yourself: defining the other, you create a self in opposition, but meanwhile both create and destroy the other. The pupa is likewise an intrusion into another's identity, but in a different way; the pupa is an infantilizing force, the belittling construction of the other person as a child, or as immature. Deploying Form, each character in the novel thus becomes a kind of author, using language to bring a reality into being, making the world itself a coauthored fiction.

At the opening of the text, Józio, the protagonist, is at odds with society. He is stranded between youth and adulthood, lacking a crystallized social identity: "sytuacja moja była niewyjaśniona i sam nie wiedziałem, czym człowiek, czym chłystek; i tak na przełomie lat nie byłem ani tym, ani owym—byłem niczym" (7) ("my status was not at all clear, and I myself did not know whether I was a mature man or a green youth; at this turning point in my life I was neither this or that—I was nothing") (3). Maturity in this context refers to a unified identity, in contrast to a more fragmented, "immature" self, symbolized by greenness and "parts," particularly parts of the body. The mature adult is something coherent and fixed, connected to society; thus his Aunties beg the young man to be something, anything, just *something*: "Jeżeli nie chcesz być lekarzem, bądźże przynajmniej kobieciarzem lub koniarzem, ale niech będzie wiadomo . . . niech będzie wiadomo . . ." (7) ("If you don't want to be a doctor, at least be a womanizer, or a fancier of horses, be something . . . be something definite . . .") (3). By contrast, the youth is a chaotic jumble of pieces, constantly in flux, and connected to the natural world:

> Gdy ostatnie zęby, zęby mądrości, mi wyrosły, należało sądzić—rozwój został dokonany, nadszedł czas nieuniknionego mordu, mężczyzna winien zabić nieutulone z żalu chłopie, jak motyl wyfrunąć, pozostawiając trupa poczwarki, która się skończyła. Z tumanu, z chaosu, z mętnych rozlewisk, wirów, szumów, nurtów, ze trzcin i szuwarów, z rechotu żabiego miałem się przenieść pomiędzy formy klarowne, skrytalizowane—przeczesać się, uporządkować, wejść w życie społeczne dorosłych i rajcować z nimi. (7)

> When I cut my last teeth, my wisdom teeth, my development was supposed to be complete, and it was time for the inevitable kill, for the man to kill the inconsolable little boy, to emerge like a butterfly and leave behind the remains of the chrysalis that had spent itself. I was supposed to lift myself out of the mists and chaos, out of the murky swamps, out of swirls and roars, out of reeds and rushes, out of the croaking of frogs, and emerge among clear and crystallized forms: run a comb through my hair, tidy up my affairs, enter the social life of adults and deliberate with them. (3)

Józio protests this idea of unified self, arguing that every individual is a sum of parts rather than a single whole. The problem, then, is twofold: Józio's unwillingness to sever ties with his childhood self means that he does not perceive himself as mature, for he lacks the sense of unified identity that he believes is necessary for adulthood, and secondarily, his inability to present himself as such leads others to perceive him as immature, thus trapping him within this (lack of) identity. He is therefore in a somewhat vulnerable position: without a clear identity of his own, he has nothing to oppose other players with.[29]

The seriousness of this position becomes clear with the arrival of Professor Pimko, who firmly establishes himself as a professor and Józio as a student, kidnapping the thirty-year-old man and placing him in high school. Here the sinister physical force of Form is most clearly in evidence:

> Co? Co? Chciałem krzyknąć, że nie jestem uczeń, że zaszła pomyłka, porwałem się do ucieczki, ale coś mnie z tyłu chwyciło jak w kleszcze i przygwoździło na miejscu—dzięcięca, infantylna pupa mnie chwyciła. Z pupą nie mogłem się ruszyć, belfer zaś wciąż siedział i siedząc wyrażał tak doskonałą belferskość, że zamiast krzyczeć, wystawiłem dwa palce do góry, jak to robią uczniowie w szkole, gdy chcą się odezwać. (21)

> What? What's this? I wanted to scream "I'm not a schoolboy, it's all a mistake!" I tried to run for it, but something caught me in its claws and riveted me to the spot—it was my puerile, infantile pupa. I was unable to move because of my pupa while the prof, still seated, and while sitting, projected such perfect prof-authority that instead of screaming I raised my hand to speak, like boys do in school. (18)

From here, the novel becomes increasingly surreal, venturing into the realm of the fantastic, as Form's power to shape reality becomes more and more visible. As Michał Paweł Markowski describes it: "świat albo jest światem (i wtedy Józio ma trzydzieści lat i do gimnazjum klasycznego pójść nie może), albo traci swą oczywistość i wtedy organizuje się, załamuje wedle woli innych, którzy Józia gwałcą" ("either the world is the world (and then Józio is thirty years old and cannot attend high school), or it loses its reality and organizes and breaks down according to the will of others, who rape Józio").[30] Unlike the typical fantastic narrative, which involves a confrontation between the supernatural and empirical reality, here the struggle is between empirical reality and Form, which is a kind of fiction within reality, defined by language. The disjunct between the two "realities" is repeatedly registered in the text—"Zbyt głupie! Zbyt głupie, aby być mogło! Niemożliwe, ponieważ zbyt głupie! Lecz zbyt głupie, abym mógł się opierać . . ." (22) ("This was ridiculous! Too ridiculous to be real! Impossible because it was so ridiculous! Too ridiculous even to fight back . . .") (19, translation modified)—but the feeling generated is more akin to depression than suspense, as Józio increasingly submits to Form, realizing that he cannot simply go back to the reality he thought he knew. What Józio must learn as the novel progresses is to make a countermove—to master language and become the author of his own reality.

In order to make a successful countermove, it is necessary to involve other people. The first attempt at a countermove in the text is made by the student Gałkiewicz, who stands up to the teachers and says that he finds Słowacki's poetry boring and Latin uninspiring.[31] He poses a threat because the other students agree with him, thus throwing a wrench into the professor's tautology that Słowacki's poetry is great because he is a great poet whom everyone admires. Such moves are threatening precisely because they occur within the system,[32] and yet they reveal its weaknesses, thus placing the entire system at risk. Alas, Gałkiewicz's efforts are in vain, for the student Pyłaszkiewicz saves the day by reciting the poem with such eloquence that none can resist him. The relationality of the game is key, for it is precisely from the collective failure that Pyłaszkiewicz draws his strength: defining the others as the ignorant masses, and himself as the top student, he recites so beautifully that the other students are reduced to a complete stupor, and the great poet, and culture along with him, triumphs again.

But already, the idea of a countermove has emerged. The weakness in Gałkiewicz's attempt is that, while exposing the weakness of one paradigm, it fails to provide an opposing ideology, a new game, as it were. In a later scene, Miss Zuta can disarm Professor Pimko because she is not simply a schoolgirl, but a modern schoolgirl, a creature that both fits into and subverts Pimko's model, and she can thus force him to conform to her rules: "podała mu lewą [rękę] z taką obojętnościa bezceremonialną, jakby to nie był Pimko. . . . Profesor zmieszał się i nie wiedział, co począć z tą lewą młodzięczą wyciągniętą ku niemu, wreszcie ścisnął ją obiema dłońmi" (103) ("she extended her left hand with an unceremonious indifference, as if he were not Pimko . . . this disconcerted the professor, he didn't know what to do with the youthful hand stretched out to him, so he finally clasped it in both his hands") (105–106). And poor Józio is forced as well, finding himself trapped within the schoolgirl until he can come up with a successful countermove. This countermove is Józio's first great success, where he learns to dominate the other by "putting a face" on someone else. He not only de-faces Zuta's "modern schoolgirl" persona but provides a new face to replace it with just one word: "Mommy." His comment at the dinner table elicits a giggle from Zuta's father, establishing a certain complicity, and thus, the new mask is fixed into place.

By the end of the text, Józio has so fully learned how to play the system that he has evolved from the kidnappee to the kidnapper, convincing his cousin Zosia to elope. Fashioning their flight into a romantic escapade and Zosia into his lover, however, he rapidly finds himself stuck in this new reality, forced to kiss her when she turns her face to him, and gaze into her eyes and tell her that he loves her, as the role requires.[33] He ends the text by praying for a third, someone to help him get away from Zosia. Józio has succeeded in that he has learned to mimic maturity, and can dominate others, assuming a position of power within the game, but it is not exactly a happily ever after, for it is a temporary victory within Form rather than an escape from it: "Gdyż nie ma ucieczki przed gębą, jak tylko w inną gębę, a przed człowiekiem schronić się można jedynie w objęcia innego człowieka" (264) ("Because there is no escape from the mug, other than into another mug, and from a human being one can only take shelter in the arms of another human being") (281).

This is the standard Bildungsroman ending: the successful incorporation of the individual into society. In this case, however, it is clearly a somewhat pessimistic conclusion, one that completely negates any possibility for true individual expression. The world of relational identity is portrayed as a constant power struggle, where who you are depends only upon what context you're in. Józio's countermoves are not expressions of his individuality but calculated moves that are made in order to gain the upper hand. More surprisingly, what had initially seemed a "farce," or a divergence from reality, has become reality itself: there is no escape from Form. In other words, to return to the formulation of the fantastic, what had earlier been cast as a surreal incursion into some kind of abstract realm turns out to be an illumination of forces at work in reality itself: Józio's encounter with the seeming unreality of Form is not resolved in a restoration of normalcy, but in a frustrated surrender to a higher power, that of Form, which governs society.

Beckett's Unnamable faces a similar dilemma, grappling with the impossibility of a private language, wanting to speak the self but having only "the words of others" (314). In his case, however, this results in a more radical overturning of subjectivity, and an utter detachment between self and voice. The voice "issues from me, it fills me, it clamours against my walls, it is not mine, I can't stop it, I can't prevent it, from tearing me, racking me, assailing me. It is not mine, I have none, I have no voice and must speak . . . with this voice that is not mine, but can only be mine, since there is no one but me" (307). This is a similar situation to Józio's entrapment in Form, albeit a heightened one. Unnamable attempts two different strategies to confront this dilemma: a retreat into other identities, and contradiction.

If Unnamable's voice cannot be his own, well then, let it be someone else's. He tries escaping into a series of fictional identities who speak through him, thereby disavowing his own speech. He gives these "speakers" names and ascribes separate identities to them: "I'll call him Mahood instead, I prefer that, I'm queer. It was he told me stories about me, lived in my stead, issued forth from me, came back to me, entered back into me, heaped stories on my head.

I don't know how it was done" (309). This is one way to cope with the impossibility of a speech that expresses one's unique self—to remove the self from the equation, existing instead as a plurality of fictional identities. He does occasionally claim these separate identities as himself, saying, for instance, "Perhaps all they have told me has reference to a single existence, the confusion of identities being merely apparent and due to my inaptitude to assume any" (330), or "For if I am Mahood, I am Worm too, plop. Or if I am not yet Worm, I shall be when I cease to be Mahood, plop" (338). The other identities are configured as forays into a kind of alternate realm, an attempt to get away from the self, which nevertheless is always waiting upon his return. For example, he attempts to stop using the first person, substituting the third instead (355), but gradually slips into "we," and then back into "I." The "we" appears when he finds himself commenting on his own narrative—"let's drive on now to the end of the joke, we must be nearly there"—and, catching himself, says "who, we? Don't all speak at once, there's no sense in that either," creating the impression that the other speakers have begun to clamor to be heard once more (360). Carrying on with his narration about Worm, he stops short: "But not too fast, it's too soon, to return, to where I am, empty-handed, in triumph, calm, passably calm, knowing, thinking I know, that nothing has befallen me" (363). And there is the self once more; nothing has befallen it. Indeed, as Gabriele Schwab notes, the reader intuitively—almost inadvertently—apprehends Unnamable as a single subjectivity, and Worm, or Mahood, as fictional projections.[34] This is, of course, challenged by the fact that one had seen the narrators of the previous two books in the Trilogy (Molloy, Moran, and Malone) as individuals, only later learning that all of them are Unnamable's creations. Certainly, one could imagine a subsequent work with a narrator who claimed Unnamable as an invented character. But lacking such a work, we are inclined to treat Unnamable as the final authority, or rather, to see Beckett himself as his creator, rather than another fictional entity. The attempt, then, is a failure: Unnamable cannot avoid being himself, and retaining authorship over his own words.

Unnamable's second strategy, contradiction, is also a failure. Much of Unnamable's monologue is, in essence, a cluster of contradictions, or as he puts it, "affirmations and negations invalidated as uttered, or sooner or later" (291). By denying every statement as soon as he says it, he seems to avoid ever actually saying anything, thereby seeking an escape from language.[35] But of course, this only doubles his output without invalidating it: as Sheehan points out, language "conveys an intrinsic positivity, it is always assertive,"[36] even when it asserts that it asserts nothing. Unnamable is therefore still always trapped within language, unable to remain silent or to fully assume his own voice and actually say something. A sense of panic begins to enter the text as the sentences grow longer and the pacing becomes more frenetic, culminating in the famous anguished inability to go on, itself immediately contradicted. The blank page that follows the final "I'll go on" can, in a way, be seen as a form of resolution, settling definitively on not going on. It does not provide a way to speak; rather, it suggests silence, and perhaps death, as the only escape.

Yet there is a kind of victory in these contradictions, and this is where the secondary level, Unnamable as author, comes into play. Critics writing on Beckett often describe the sense of another kind of value that emanates from his novels, something that "transcends" the worlds they describe.[37] The insistent negation of any affirmed statement encourages the reader to seek understanding on a meta-level, to surrender the literal meaning of the statements and search for a figurative one that would surmount the paradox. Beckett seemingly does not reward this movement with resolution, for the novels seem to emphatically deny any possibility of transcendence. On a formal level, however, Unnamable has succeeded in creating something completely original: he has authored a new kind of novel. As discussed earlier, the Bildungsroman aligns identity with narrative form in a particularly close way, making the process of narrative creation akin to the process of self-development. In this, it is similar to autobiography, where having a self appears to rely on the ability to successfully narrate one. The process of incessant contradiction does not win Unnamable a happier existence; it does, however, represent a fascinating exploration of the limits of narrative.

What Unnamable (and, as we shall soon see, Gombrowicz) do in these novels is attempt to create a narrative based on irony in its most extreme form. As described by Schlegel, it is an irony that is "an absolute synthesis of antithesis, the continual self-creating interchange of two conflicting thoughts."[38] This extreme form of irony, absolute antithesis, would seem to be a denial of meaning, an utter undoing of narrative, and yet . . . these works are recognizable as novels, and do create the sense of a meaning. What makes this possible is the shared structure of metaphor and irony, both of which are uniquely qualified to produce meanings that lie beyond language.

ಎ

Theorists of metaphor have sought what Paul Ricoeur calls a "semantic theory" of its functioning. Ricoeur explains: "By a semantic theory, I mean an inquiry into the capacity of metaphor to provide untranslatable information, and, accordingly, into metaphor's claim to yield some true insight about reality"[39]— untranslatable information, or, we might add, a private experience or sensation, that could not be encompassed in standard referential language. This suggests that it is in figurative language that one may seek the solution to Wittgenstein's dilemma.[40] In fact, Ricoeur argues that fiction has a unique power to generate such meanings: "Fiction addresses itself to deeply rooted potentialities of reality to the extent that they are absent from the actualities with which we deal in everyday life under the mode of empirical control and manipulation. . . . It is in fiction that the 'absence' proper to the power of suspending what we call 'reality' in ordinary language concretely coalesces and fuses with the positive insight into the potentialities of our being in the world which our everyday transactions with manipulatable objects tend to conceal."[41] He specifies that it is fiction of a particular kind: "This productive and projective power of fiction can only be acknowledged if one sharply distinguishes it from the reproductive role of the so-called mental image which merely provides us with a re-presentation of things already perceived."[42] It is important to note that in Ricoeur's account, this is a potentiality of fiction that is only available if one surrenders its claims to empirical realism: it is a quality that emerges from fiction's conceptual work, but not in the form of straightforward representation.

But this positive insight is precisely what seems to be denied by Beckett's Unnamable, despite the fact that the textual mechanics appear to be similar. What Unnamable is doing is actually the opposite of metaphor: it is irony.

A metaphor generates meanings through comparison: one object is called by another's name, and thereby likened to it.[43] As Stanley Corngold, following I. A. Richards, beautifully explains, however, the workings of metaphor involve a kind of dwelling in the (unstable) process of metamorphosis: if one simply sees the first object, call it A, as equivalent to the second one, call it B, this is not a metaphor, but a literal meaning, a new name.[44] One must, in other words, compare A to B, but simultaneously bear in mind the distinction between the two: "The object (B) is quite plainly unstable, and hence, so is (A); as literalization proceeds, as we attempt to experience in (B) more and more qualities that can be accommodated by (A), we metamorphose (A); but we must stop before the metamorphosis is complete, if the metaphor is to be preserved and (A) is to remain unlike (B)."[45] Ricoeur emphasizes two aspects to this process; the suspension of literal meaning, and the role of the imagination in "completing" the figurative meaning.[46] The shuttling between similarity and difference in the metaphoric process bears a clear resemblance to the structure of irony, where two contradictory elements are brought into a relationship. In both cases, the use of contradiction or paradox evokes, albeit fleetingly, a space of (temporary) transcendence—a meaning that is to be found in the movement between two claims that cannot be reconciled.

Unlike metaphor, which produces a positive meaning in this process, irony's claim is more tenuous, and is defined through negation. In this sense, it is the opposite of a metaphor. A clear example of this can be seen in the case of the Irish Bull, a form of verbal irony which consists, to cite Coleridge's apt description, "in the bringing together of two incompatible thoughts, with the sensation, but without the sense, of their connection."[47] In Beckett's *Molloy*, for instance, we find: "The soup before me had stopped steaming. Had it ever steamed?"[48] Where a metaphor illuminates likeness, the Bull reveals difference, or incompatibility. Sydney Smith sums it up nicely, comparing bulls to wit (by which he seems to mean something like metaphor): "[Bulls are] the very reverse of wit; for as wit discovers real relations that are not apparent, bulls admit apparent relations that are not real. The pleasure arising from wit proceeds from our surprise at suddenly discovering two things to be similar, in which we suspected no similarity. The pleasure arising from bulls proceeds from our discovering two things to be dissimilar, in which a resemblance might have been suspected."[49] In both of these cases, irony and metaphor, the possibility of new meaning comes from a certain blockage—an unresolvable contradiction, the collapse of literal meaning—that forces the reader to engage her or his imaginative faculties in order to understand the idea being evoked. In both cases, furthermore, the new, private meaning is not a fixed entity, but is something that can be gleaned only in the process of motion, a movement between contradictions or metaphoric objects. But where the process of metaphor yields a "positive insight," the work of irony seems to illuminate nothing more than a contradiction. What Unnamable (and, as we shall see in a moment, Józio) does is to place the reader in that ironic space, which simultaneously is and is not a space of transcendence. He brings about the process that would seem to generate a meaning outside of language, only to again call that meaning into question. Yet, because of the shared structure of irony and metaphor, and language's innate assertiveness, there is the sense of a transcendent meaning here, even if its content is always denied.[50] Rather than creating a metaphor, he crafts a work that manages to produce a meaning precisely where it would seem to be least possible, a work that breaks free of narrative entirely, but simultaneously is a narrative.

Unnamable repeats this process in a slightly different way in the work that he authors, *Molloy*, creating a novel that again tests the power of fiction to generate an ironic world. There are many sources of irony in the novel,[51] but the ones particularly relevant here are the moments of explicit impossibility, where the space of fiction is fully exploited. For example: "Then, nicely balanced on my crutches, I began to swing, backwards, forwards, feet pressed together, or rather legs pressed together, for how could I press my feet together, with my legs in the state they were? But how could I press my legs together, in the state they were? I pressed them together, that's all I can tell you. Take it or leave it."[52] Or: "I found my crutches, against an easy chair. It may seem strange that I was able to go through the motions I have described without their help. I find it strange" (38). This is, once again, a species of the fantastic—an event occurs that disrupts the logic of the world as we know it, calling into question whether the laws of the empirical world obtain in the space described. But in this case, though the discrepancy is noted, it does not seem to generate a profound uncertainty. Molloy notices the strangeness, thus establishing that it is strange, that we are not simply in a world where such things are to be expected, but the novel will at no point resolve the mystery. The novel is not using these moments to generate confusion in the reader; rather, these moments illuminate the contours of the world in which Molloy finds himself and make clear its fictional nature. Molloy's complacency in the face of paradox calls to mind Maria Edgeworth's formulation of the Irish Bull: "Reason condemns the contradiction but necessity has allowed it, and use has made it intelligible."[53] This is precisely the world Unnamable has created: a literal rendition of Edgeworth's account. The moments of impossibility in the text could be described as literalized Irish Bulls, obeying the same logic, but without the succinct formulation (though as Christopher Ricks points out, there are plenty of actual Bulls in the novel as well[54]).

Of course, one can simply argue that these moments are nothing more than symptoms of Molloy's unreliability as a narrator, examples of his faulty memory or confusion—after all, it is a retrospective account. But any work of fiction requires a suspension of disbelief, or rather, a willingness to enter into the text and accept its terms. What makes *Molloy* so interesting is that it stretches this willingness to its limits, making the terms literally impossible to accept, as a way of illustrating the capabilities of fictionality, that it alone can depict such a space. Indeed, once you start dismissing portions of the text as unreliable, it is hard to know when to stop. Certainly, the entire account can be seen as a figment of Molloy's imagination, but this rather impoverishes the novel. The second half of *Molloy*, Moran's report, is more challenging in this regard. Moran, after all, concludes by telling us that he began to write his report, and that what he wrote was untrue—"Then I went back into the house and wrote, It is midnight. The rain is beating on the windows. It was not midnight. It was not raining" (176)—thereby opening the possibility that his entire account was simply make-believe. Moran's case is comparatively simpler: it is a straightforward illustration of fiction's power to deceive. Molloy, however, offers no such revelation, and there is no reason to suspect him of it simply because of Moran's confession. This reading gains credibility when we see it as one of Unnamable's experiments, part of his broader project of finding a way to speak. The impossibility of Molloy's world mirrors the contradictions of Unnamable's monologue: both are examples of extreme irony, a space of utter contradiction that is given life.

Józio, in *Ferdydurke*, does something very similar. As we saw, Józio's attempt as a character to break free of Form was not a success. But Józio is not only the protagonist, he is also the narrator, and his struggle with Form is repeated on a meta-level in trying to pen the novel, albeit with more success. He interrupts his reminiscences with two parables (about Filidor and Filibert), each of which is accompanied by a preface. In the first of the prefaces Józio confronts the matter of Form directly, suggesting that it is the institution of art that is the problem (rather than language itself). Following this more positive formulation, Józio restates the relationship between humankind and Form, giving it an entirely different valence:

> Czyż nie jest prawdą, że wszelka istota dojrzalsza i wyższa, i starsza jest uzależniona na tysiąc rozmaitych sposobów od istot na niższym stopniu rozwojowym, i czyż owa zależność nie przenika nas na wskroś aż w samo sedno, tak dalece, iż wolno powiedzieć: starszy przez młodszego jest stwarzany? Czyż pisząc nie musimy przystosować się do czytelnika? Mówiąc—nie uzależniamy się od osoby, dla której mówimy? (81)

> Isn't it true that every being who is at a higher level of development, who is older and more mature, is dependent in a thousand different ways on beings who are less well developed, and doesn't this dependence permeate us through and through, to our very core and to the extent that we can say: the elder is created by the younger? When we write, don't we have to accommodate the reader? Just as when we speak—don't we depend upon the person we're addressing? (83)

The real target of this critique is the devaluation of youth by adults, their insistence on severing ties rather than perceiving continuities. However, it also suggests a broader notion of mutual interconnection and an acquiescence to the need for compromise.[55] This is a wholly different portrayal of the situation from the "farce" that Józio finds himself trapped in. These are the words of a narrator who has not only accepted the overriding power of Form, but has come to see it as an innate part of human nature:

> Jeśli robaki, owady cały dzień uganiają się za pożywieniem, my bez wytchnienia jesteśmy w pościgu za formą . . . zawsze, bez przerwy szukamy formy i rozkoszujemy się nią lub cierpimy przez nią i przystosowujemy się do niej lub gwałcimy i rozbijamy ją, lub pozwalamy, aby ona nas stwarzała, amen. (79)

> And just as beetles, insects chase after food all day, so do we tirelessly pursue form . . . we always, unceasingly, seek form, and we delight in it or suffer by it, and we conform to it or we violate and demolish it, or we let it create us, amen. (80)

Józio thus seems to have internalized the constraints required to exist in society, as in the standard Bildungsroman. Nonetheless, a sense of anxiety remains, as he wonders how much agency an individual really has:

> Czy wreszcie my stwarzamy formę, czy ona nas stwarza? Wydaje się nam, że to my konstruujemy—złudzenie, w równej mierze jesteśmy konstruowani przez

> konstrukcje. To, co napisałeś, dyktuje ci sens dalszy, dzieło się rodzi nie z ciebie, chciałeś napisać to, a napisałeś coś zupełnie odmiennego. (71)
>
> Do we create form or does form create us? We think we are the ones who construct it, but that's an illusion, because we are, in equal measure, constructed by the construction. Whatever you put down on paper dictates what comes next, because the work is not born of you—you want to write one thing, and something entirely different comes out. (72)

This again portrays the subject as passive and helpless in the face of a greater power. It is important, as well, that the novel offers this alternative account of Form in the first third of the text, but it does not grant Józio the character the clemency of this discovery. The knowledge is presumably acquired after his adventures have ended, but before he has written his memoirs—that is, the novel we are reading. The pessimism of the ending indicates an awareness that this solution is, in some ways, not fully satisfactory. By leaving both versions in the text, the novel ultimately rests in a kind of ironic juxtaposition between two impossible choices—to surrender to Form, or to struggle for a unique voice. The presence of Form is a necessary state of affairs,[56] forcing a continuous struggle on the part of the subject to find new modes of expression. Józio, as both character and narrator, is intellectually unable to break free of Form, offering at best the idea that Form permeates the individual, and is thus not wholly external.

But there is another way in which Józio argues with Form—not in the literal description of events, but figuratively, in the construction of the text. The novel as a form suffers the same problem as the individual: Józio's struggle to develop an identity is paralleled by his attempt to craft an original work of art, where he again finds himself constrained by certain laws. Józio departs from this convention, digressing into two (seemingly unrelated) stories. He willfully claims that these digressions are meaningless, saying that "kto by mniemał, że włączając w me dzieło opowiadanie Filidor dzieckiem podszyty nie miałem na celu jedynie pewnego zapełnienia miejsca na papierze . . . byłby w błędzie" (67–68) ("whoever thinks that by including this little story, 'The Child Runs Deep in Filidor,' my sole aim was not merely filling space on paper . . . is sorely mistaken"). But he then modifies this position, saying that in his opinion, "poszczególne części ciała oraz słowa stanowią wystarczającą więź konstrukcyjną estetyczno-artystyczną" ("individual body parts and words form an adequate aesthetic-artistic linkage of construction") (69, translation modified). A text, like an individual, may be made up of various parts; it does not have to be a fixed, single whole. Thus, he not only includes the stories themselves, but also two prefaces, the second of which contains a long list of the "torments" that the book confronts, and then a list of potential causes of these torments. Here too, however, Form's power asserts itself, most notably in the second preface, which opens with:

> I znowu przedmowa . . . zniewolony jestem do przedmowy, nie mogę być bez przedmowy i muszę przedmowę, gdyż prawo symetrii wymaga, aby Filidor dzieckiem podszytemu odpowiadał dzieckiem podszyty Filibert, przedmowie zaś do Filidora przedmowa do Filiberta dzieckiem podszytego. Choćbym chciał, nie mogę, nie mogę, i nie mogę uchylić się żelaznym prawom symetrii oraz analogii. (184)

> And again a preface . . . I'm captive to a preface, I can't do without a preface, I must have a preface, because the law of symmetry requires that the story in which the child runs deep in Filidor should have a corresponding story in which the child runs deep in Filibert, while the preface to Filidor requires a corresponding preface to Filibert. Even if I want to I can't, I can't, and I can't avoid the ironclad laws of symmetry and analogy. (193)

Despite the reappearance of Form, there is a partial triumph in these parables and prefaces, the stubborn inclusion of heterogenous material unrelated to the text itself that nonetheless belongs, if only because the author put it there.

The unity that Gombrowicz denies in this work is one that traditionally defines plot itself. Peter Brooks has argued that the unity of a novel's plot is governed by the structure of metaphor, which brings unrelated materials into relationship with each other, and also, it is assumed, excludes that which does not belong: "Narrative operates as a metaphor in its affirmation of resemblance, in that it brings into relation different actions, combines them through perceived similarities (Todorov's common predicate term), appropriates them to a common plot, which implies the rejection of merely contingent (or unassimilable) incident or action. Plot is the structure of action in closed and legible wholes, it thus must use metaphor as the trope of its achieved interrelations, and it must be metaphoric insofar as it is totalizing."[57] Brooks, in describing elements of plot as linked by metaphor, presumably does not mean that the events of the story are actually considered similar—boy meets girl, say, and she breaks his heart (surely two very different moments!)—but rather that there is a relationship between those two events that is analogous to the relationship between the two objects in a metaphor. The two moments are similar in that they are part of the same story; they are therefore related, despite their difference.[58] It is this relationship of similarity that Józio refuses, providing another example of the ironic side of the figurative process.[59] The addition of the stories of Filidor and Filibert force the reader to incorporate them somehow into the story, despite the fact that it seems as though one could simply remove them and allow Józio's adventures to stand alone.[60] The insistence that they belong—

and even more, that they bear the "ostateczny, sekretny sens dzieła" (189) ("the final, secret meaning of this work") (198)—shifts the grounds of meaning. Once the secret has been comprehended, he continues, "nic już nie przeszkodzi zapuścić się nieco głębiej w gąszcz pojedyńczych, monotonnych części" (189) ("there is nothing to stop one from venturing somewhat deeper, into the thicket of those separate and tedious parts") (198), suggesting a model of understanding that resists unity and coherence.[61]

The creation of this ironic totality, a whole composed of disparate parts that refuse to be united, is an elegant elaboration of the power of the novel, its capacity to contain its own antithesis. Bakhtin famously argued that the power of the novel was its ability to encompass, or "cannibalize," other genres.[62] Lloyd Bishop, elaborating on this idea, sees it as the novel's acknowledgment of the insufficiency of a monologic account: the novel is "conscious of the impossibility of achieving full meaning and exploits this lack."[63] Bishop links this to Schlegel's vision of irony, with the novel as "the best instrument for expressing the chaos of being as perceived by a finite consciousness . . . and for expressing the 'eternal mobility' of that consciousness itself."[64] Gombrowicz renders this power of fiction visible in a particularly vivid way, all the more so by contrasting it with its impossibility in the real world through the story of Józio the character. Józio's struggle for a mode of being that is made up of various contradictory parts rather than being a single unified whole proves impossible in the world he lives in, where he remains trapped in Form with no prospect of escape. It can, however, be achieved on the pages of his novel, and in this way, his text attests to the power of fictionality itself.

☙

I must reiterate, however, that this is not a complete victory. Neither Beckett nor Gombrowicz can be said to find a successful resolution to the problems they describe. Unnamable's contradictions may represent a new form of narrative, but he nonetheless remains in his room, endlessly speaking his contradictions. Józio may have penned a novel that presents a more daring compromise with Form, but it is still a compromise, not a victory. To use irony (or metaphor) is not to invent a new language, but to find a way to gesture toward a meaning outside of language, without, however, actually articulating it. In this sense, these are deeply pessimistic works, despite their partial triumphs.

It is worth noting, too, that these triumphs are not so easily replicated: both Beckett and Gombrowicz can well be considered as representing limit cases in this sort of experimentation. In his reading of Beckett, Paul Sheehan sees him as a "voice-machine," exploring the limits of the human by illuminating the mechanical tendencies of narrative.[65] Indeed, while conventional narrative can stultify into an automatic kind of process, resistance to it runs the same risk, becoming a mechanical response of opposition that simply produces not-*x* instead of *x* as an output. What is more, while these authors are exploring the limits of what is possible in a novel, those limits do exist for a reason.

To start with Gombrowicz; as stated earlier, part of the work of a novel, traditionally, is the exclusion of irrelevant material. If the narrative were completely assembled from such unrelated bits of narrative, it would become little more than formalistic exercise, and not particularly entertaining reading.[66] It must be acknowledged that *Ferdydurke* arguably pushes against that line. What makes the digressions compelling in this particular novel is their link to Józio's broader project of seeking a unique form of expression. His desire to do something original renders the parables and prefaces genuinely necessary to the text, not simply despite the fact that they are seemingly so unnecessary, but precisely because they are. To remove them would be to consign Józio the narrator to the same trap of Józio the character, to deny his freedom to innovate.

The same can be said of Unnamable's experiments: despite its moments of impossibility, Molloy's world does not seem wholly arbitrary. There is just enough impossibility to make the reader pause and wonder—or to ignore these moments, or write them off as errors—but not enough to completely sever the sense of being in an actual world, strange though it may seem. Likewise, Unnamable's contradictions would become unbearable if there was nothing else in the narrative, or, for that matter, if it went on much longer.[67]

Indeed, it is worth adding that two crucial features of these novels are, first, that in spite of their efforts to interrogate the self, a meta-inquiry that arguably works against an absorptive reading, one does warm to the sense of a recognizably human presence in the text. And second, and perhaps more important, is that both novels are, quite simply, very funny. The humor is complex and testifies to the workings of laughter in fascinating ways that I do not have the space to fully explore here. As Paul Sheehan has noted, some critics find in Beckett's humor an "affirmative humanist credo,"[68] thereby resolving the problems his texts raise with a kind of manufactured happy ending. Thus, for instance, Wayne Booth claims that Beckett's works are only harmful "when readers take the literature for philosophy and think that Beckett's marvelously funny and moving portraits of despair add real evidence to the case for nihilism, forgetting that the evidence before them paradoxically undermines its own claims."[69] This is, I think, putting the case too strongly, and risks laughing away what is a genuine anguish at the heart of these works, the sense of a very real despair. What is more, it overlooks the moments when the humor is ethically questionable, as when, for instance, Molloy describes beating his mother, or Józio slaps a valet.[70] Nonetheless, it is hard to disagree with Booth when he claims that "the overt position of infinite negativity is always qualified by the essential artistic drive of the creative act in all its richness. Instead of self-pity, the works convey a positively bouncy verve, a joyfully rich inventiveness that is an inseparable part of the ironic reconstructions we are invited to make."[71] The humor qualifies, rather than undermining, the negative ideas within the text, and it is undeniably crucial to the conceptual work of these novels.

That is what is ultimately so powerful about these books: the way in which they bring to life fictionality as such. Although these novels are making highly abstract and rather esoteric arguments about form and how meaning is produced, these arguments are housed in characters who are, for all their strangeness and occasionally reprehensible behavior, quite human.[72] Similarly to Swift and Krasicki, although these authors do engage in specific political critiques of their local contexts, their works are ultimately aiming to articulate a worldview grounded in irony, a mode of thought that can only be realized in a fictional space. Both Beckett and Gombrowicz, or rather, the characters they have created, use the space of fiction to articulate a certain paradox that cannot be otherwise expressed. They do not merely describe the contradiction; they bring it to life, forcing the reader into a position of attempting to reconcile competing claims that cannot be resolved. The worlds they create do not transcend these contradictions, they dwell in them, illuminating the power of fictionality itself, its ability to bring worlds into being that are experienced as real despite their impossibility. In this sense, there is a triumph in these texts, an affirmation of fiction's ability to depict a problem, despite an attendant pessimism about the possibility of its resolution. Fiction's "as if" opens a space beyond the reach of logic or empiricism, gesturing to a realm beyond language itself.

Conclusion
Toward a "Weak" Theory of the Novel

> All nations and traditions are invented
> but some are more invented than others.
> ~Pat Sheeran and Nina Witoszek, *Talking to the Dead*

This book began with a critique of the history of the novel, arguing that considering the genre from a global perspective required a more capacious sense of form and a shift away from accounts focused strictly on the rise of realism. I also critiqued the tendency, in work on literature from "non-major" traditions, to focus so strongly on sociohistorical context as to minimize literary innovation, reading it in symptomatic terms. The uptick of interest in texts from parts of the world outside of Western Europe has been fueled, at least in part, by a sense of the historical injustices that have contributed to the marginalization or devaluation of these traditions, and by a desire for a more diverse canon. This motivation is not in itself a problem, but that interest in history can shape the approach to the literature, leading to the selection of texts that vividly exemplify their own culture (or cultural difference), or speak specifically to their historical conditions, therefore ignoring works that do not fit readily into available categories.[1] This produces the dual result of scholarship that is skewed heavily toward contextualist readings, and a canon dominated by texts amenable to such readings.

Much of the research on the global novel retains a commitment to realism as the irreducible condition of the novel form, producing accounts that privilege history, modernity, and realism as the primary coordinates of interpretation. As I will explain, even the more radical contemporary efforts to rethink the categories of modernism and modernity, and their corollary attempts to rewrite literary history, produce frameworks that do little to incorporate the myriad faces of the novel form across time and space. I argue, instead, that a truly global theory of the novel needs a better account of the kinds of works that have been described as anomalous or strange, and a willingness to engage more closely with their contributions to the novel's development. A new global literary history demands a more rigorous formalism.

To be clear, in making this claim, I am not arguing against the critic's right to study the texts that they find more interesting than others. There is a strain of contemporary research that has called for a more accurate literary history, a better account of processes of influence and change,[2] and, perhaps, for scholarship that would not ignore the masses of books that people actually read in favor of what the critic considers a "true classic."[3] Claims that a new methodology is required to achieve a truer vision of literary history are, I think, absolutely correct. Although I am sympathetic to these aims, however, my complaint is not that critics select things they care about or find meaningful in the fiction they study, but rather, that the standards for selection that currently dominate the field give us an impoverished account of the novel form. Indeed, as Scott Black has argued, they may not even live up to their own promise of what they see as the novel's strength: its ability to represent history.[4] Redressing this lack requires more nuanced examinations of all kinds of fictions, even—or especially—those that have heretofore seemed insignificant. What I am calling for, then, is a global formalism that would not subsume the literary craftsmanship of various kinds of novels into sweeping historical narratives and that would willingly linger over texts that may not be particularly influential or particularly representative, but that estrange our sense of the novel as a form, offering new and interesting perspectives on what it can do. What I am calling for is a "weak theory" of the novel.

The chapters of this book have provided a stroll through a different kind of history: looking closely at a series of pairs of novels, I have argued that their offerings to the theory of the novel are found neither in their development of techniques central to realist fiction, nor in the way they figure or reflect upon their sociohistorical realities. Instead, I have shown them to be texts fundamentally interested in questions of literary form and epistemology: examinations of fictionality as theorization that ponder how narrative dynamics structure thought, and the affordances of fiction as a medium. Crucially, these reflections are not in the service of a more accurate representation of reality; rather, these are texts that engage in efforts to formally model abstract ideas—ideas about freedom, time, ethics, and worlding.

In the first chapter, Swift's *Gulliver's Travels* and Krasicki's *Mikołaja Doświadczyńskiego przypadki* appear as texts concerned with the problem of how to build societies for humans who are persistently irrational, a question that is harnessed, in both novels, to the problem of irony and sincerity, enjoining the reader to both identify with and coolly judge the protagonists. In the process, they show us the paradoxes inherent in fiction's efforts to educate or persuade. The novels of the second chapter, *Rękopis znaleziony w Saragossie* and *Melmoth the Wanderer*, extend questions about literature's pleasures and educational potential into an examination of world-building through their use of interlaced and nested stories. Illuminating the fictive quality of any concept of our reality, they invite us to question our ideas of Otherness. In the third chapter, *Poganka* and *The Picture of Dorian Gray* stage the relationship between painting and narrative, and ethics and idealism. As novels that strive to reproduce the effects of images, they slyly suggest that the seeming reality of paintings is superficial in the same way that the idealized status of virtue turns out to be. Finally, *Molloy*, *The Unnamable*, and *Ferdydurke* seek the limits of novelistic form as part of a quest for a unique self, creating books that are almost (but not quite) unreadable in their commitment to undo the basic fabric of the Bildungsroman. They thus return, from a very different direction, to the problem raised by the utopian musings of the first chapter, of how to think irrationality as a form of freedom. The texts I discuss are anomalous enough that the question regularly arises whether they are even novels. What else would they be? The account of the novel as a genre is an impoverished one if it cannot accommodate books like these, which clearly participate in the work of theorizing the form and exploring its capabilities. De-provincializing the novel entails giving such works their due.

As I discussed in the introduction, the apparently benighted state of nineteenth-century Polish and Irish letters is typically attributed to their sociohistorical backwardness, for the history of the novel as a genre is one that is intimately tied to the rise of modernity. I described contemporary critiques that sought to unsettle, on the one hand, the primacy of realism, and on the other, the centering of Western European fiction, in studies of the novel. Recent scholarship has also mounted another kind of critique, taking on the concept of modernity and its emergence, and questioning, in particular, the status it accords to Western Europe. As the epigraph above so cleverly puts it, some traditions are more invented than others. While the account of the novel has become increasingly messy and complex, so too have theories of modernity. Given the enduring link between the two, the question arises: How does a new account of modernity give us a new history of the novel (or vice versa)?

For the most part, surprisingly enough, the many interesting and original efforts to offer new theorizations of modernity by scholars such as Ning Ma and Susan Stanford Friedman leave the story of the novel largely unchanged. The idea of an enduring link between the novel and modernity depends upon an image of the novel as realist: its role in the process of history seems to depend upon it serving as a faithful mirror of society.[5] It seems inevitable that any effort to write a single history of the novel, particularly one that aligns it with the emergence of modernity, will end up replicating these conceptual frameworks, along with their attendant blind spots. Accordingly, recent work by Julie Orlemanski and Scott Black contests this relationship between fiction and modernity, critiquing both the proffered image of modernity and the implicit notion of fiction that this equation entails. Both argue for a different approach to conceptualizing the history of fiction, as recursive (Black), or as a hermeneutics (Orlemanski). I conclude, finally, with an account of an especially promising strand in modernist thought, Paul Saint-Amour's description of "weak theory," and an argument for bringing it to bear on the way we think of the novel in the age of world literature.

❦

A particularly striking argument for rethinking Eurocentric accounts of the emergence of modernity, and the novel's privileged role in the process, is Ning Ma's *Age of Silver*. Drawing on the work of East-West world-systems studies, Ma explains that the global silver trade produced the historical, economic, and cultural conditions of modernity's emergence in Asia even before it took place in Europe.[6] European modernity (which is further subdivided, following Enrique Dussel's account, into two: an Iberian colonial expansion, and then an Anglo-Germanic "second modernity"[7]) is a belated and local response to an already extant global system. Ma argues, in other words, that the history of modernity must be rewritten, because it is, quite simply, wrong. This is a dramatic shift in how we understand the emergence of the modern world, a decisive provincialization of Europe, to borrow Chakrabarty's phrase.

What remains unchanged in this account, surprisingly, is the literary side of the story, which is more or less an expanded Lukácsean history of the form. Not only does the novel retain its privileged relationship to the process of modernity's emergence, but, perhaps more surprisingly, it also retains its realist teleology. Ma argues that "the novel in the East and West coevolved toward a socioeconomically informed and nationally allegorical mode of 'realism' due to transregional conditions of cultural displacement."[8] Thus, the history of fiction is not altered so much as supplemented: alongside Defoe and *Don Quixote,* we now find *Plum in a Golden Vase* and Iharu Saikaku's "floating world" narratives, all texts that, Ma shows, examine shifting systems of value in growing market economies and emergent sub-state publics in an era of "transcendental homelessness."

A history of novels that examines how they respond to the changing material conditions attendant to the rise of modernity needs such comparisons—and a more precise way of describing their forms. Ma persuasively demonstrates that the texts engage similar questions as far as changing economic and sociohistorical realities, but she does not delve into the differences between the literary techniques used to do so. The intriguing way Saikaku's *Life of an Amorous Man* shifts in perspective, moving in and out of free indirect discourse,[9] for instance, does not seem to be of interest to such an account, though surely it should matter to an argument for the text's contributions to the larger history of the novel. The risk of focusing on content over form is that it can homogenize the literature being discussed. While Richardson's *Clarissa* is a very long text, for instance, it pales in comparison to *Plum in the Golden Vase,* whose five volumes span over three thousand pages: surely a significant difference between two works that are being compared, but one that goes entirely unmentioned. More tellingly, what Ma calls Richardson's "epistolary style" is also absent from Chinese fiction, which, she further notes, "did not witness the spread of first-person narrative until the early twentieth century under Western influences."[10] Considered in terms of their literary technique, these texts seem extremely different from each other, calling into question the category of "realism" that apparently binds them.

To be clear, the problem here is not that Ma is blurring the differences between the Chinese or Japanese texts and the British ones; as she notes, the notion of a radical difference between East and West is itself a product of West-centric traditions of thought that position the East as "Other."[11] Furthermore, the field of eighteenth-century British literature is a highly heterogeneous one, and Defoe and Fielding seem as different from each other, stylistically, as do Saikaku and Defoe. And it is clear that a comparative reading of Saikaku and Defoe has much to offer to an account of the novel's rise.[12] The issue is not that the texts from different parts of the world are too different to be meaningfully compared: rather, it is the category of "realism" that yokes all these works together that seems questionable.

This becomes even more problematic when, throughout the book, the designation of "realism" seems functionally equivalent to the term "novel," even as it privileges one specific aspect of the texts and overlooks others. The lack of a more sustained engagement with form enables the normative account of the novel as a genre, and simultaneously renders it curiously both open-ended and constricted. The focus on content exemplary of sociohistorical shifts serves to exclude many other novels from the same period, providing a narrowed sense of the literary field, despite being capacious enough to include works that are quite varied in other respects. As a result, the category is both too narrow and too broad, and highly normative, despite its apparent flexibility.

So: a new way of thinking modernity, perhaps, but the account of the novel seems much the same, albeit with an expanded archive, though one that remains quite restricted.

We see the same problem in Susan Stanford Friedman's *Planetary Modernisms*, which also offers a dramatic conceptual shift in its account of modernity, but a similarly narrow account of the novel. Sharing the view that modernity as a concept is inevitably organized around the premise that it is invented by the West, Friedman seeks to redefine it, instead, as plural, recurring, contradictory, and global. Thus, modernity becomes "the condition or sensibility of radical disruption and accelerating change wherever and whenever such a phenomenon appears, particularly if it manifests widely. What is modern or modernist gains its meaning through negation, as a rebellion against what once was or was presumed to be." And modernism is "the domain of creative expressivity *within* modernity's dynamic of rapid change."[13] Friedman offers examples such as China under the Tang and Song dynasties (618–1279), the Mongol Empire (1200–1400), or the postcolonial independence movements in 1960s Africa, thereby demonstrating how widely the net can be cast.

As a move to decenter the West and knock modernity off its pedestal, this is highly effective. Whatever one's feelings about this way of framing history,[14] *Planetary Modernisms* offers a bracing intellectual exercise, inviting us to consider what, exactly, is lost in such a proliferating view of modernity, and whether that loss is truly problematic. But what does it accomplish for our reading of the novel?

One potential objection to this account is the way it seems to lay claim to every other historical period: if every major moment of change is described as a moment of modernity, and every literary movement within it a modernism, what happens to Romanticism, the Victorian period, the Renaissance?[15] Certainly, this view threatens to strip other periods of their specificity. The danger is that if historical categories become meaningless (everything is modernity, and therefore nothing is modernity), then literature is rendered, blandly, a barometer (or engine) of change. Alternatively, however, an act of estrangement that loosens the conventions of traditional periodization may open the possibility of better appreciating the heterogeneity of a given moment, shaking off calcified conventions of reading.

Paradoxically, however, even as this perspective seems to open up the historical categories on which literary history is built, Friedman reinforces the historicist grounds of literary study. Texts are examined, and valued, in terms of their contribution to, or participation in, the process of modernization. A text from an overlooked tradition can become appreciated, the argument implies, because it, too, is participating in modernity, in ways that have not been sufficiently appreciated, rather than because of its particular formal features.

To observe that this ostensible prioritization of historical context, and content, over literary mechanics seems to be an inevitable feature of this type of historicist scholarship is not to advocate for ahistorical readings—clinical discussions of form that ignore any kind of context and overlook complex dynamics of power and position. I have no wish to steer us toward the Scylla of empty universals and willful ignorance of the lasting effects of historical violence. But the allure of history may be a Charybdis, where the sweeping force of recasting socioeconomic master narratives exerts such a powerful thrall that the specificities of literature are lost in the whirl. And the most seductive of these narratives, for novel studies, is the story of modernity's rise.

A recent article by Julie Orlemanski brilliantly summarizes these dilemmas, noting the continuous entanglement between accounts of fictionality's emergence and narratives of modernity, secularism, and disenchantment. Her critique is particularly crucial to novel studies, because it clearly demonstrates how the shift to examining the emergence of fictionality has largely reiterated the premises of the rise of realist fiction (and indeed, frequently takes the realist novel as the model for fictionality as such). Namely, accounts of fictionality remain yoked to narratives of secularism and disenchantment (which have themselves been repeatedly discredited), positing the medieval period as both credulous and unsophisticated. Revisionist efforts to backdate such theories, arguing for the "invention" of verisimilar fiction in the eleventh or twelfth century, leave such premises largely unchallenged.[16] As Orlemanski shows us, however, the medieval period contains a wide array of rich and complex imaginative writing that offers a much more expansive catalog of the various techniques and practices that are relevant to the study of fictionality. Thus, she argues for a hermeneutics that would not ask *who* has fiction, but rather, *how* they have it, seeking out the manifold ways in which fiction is defined, the kinds of practices it is located in, and the interpretive communities that form around it. The objective is not only a more accurate history, but also a more robust sense of literary practice and possibility, one enriched by a comparative reading across periods and places. Following Nicolette Zeeman, Orlemanski argues that the work of literary scholarship is in part to "produce new conditions of visibility and explicitness for the claims of literary practice"[17]—to attend to the way texts theorize through practice. This is precisely what I have tried to do throughout this book: to show how the novels I discuss articulate different ideas about the possibilities of novelistic form through their particular literary practices.

One final example of an alternative approach to modernity offers an image of what such a hermeneutics might look like, though it is a comparative poetics of worlding, rather than fictionality per se. Discussed already in the second chapter, Eric Hayot's *On Literary Worlds* is a crucial effort to stake out a position where the text itself comes to matter. Hayot's account is in some ways similar to Susan Stanford Friedman's, in that it seeks to decenter the West-centric model of modernity by devising a different kind of epistemological framework. But he makes the relationship between fiction and its context into a question, thereby potentially loosening the relationship between the two. Rather than a new approach to theorizing modernity, Hayot's intervention into Eurocentric accounts of both modernity and literary development argues that we need a better concept of world. A world is both a content and a form, "a container that is identical with its content and its containing," an idea and an example of that idea.[18] It is, of course, also what we inhabit, the thing we live in; it thus always combines material reality and abstraction, idea and experience.

A theory of modernity is grounded in a certain concept of world—a model of world-system—and, Hayot argues, the concept of modernity commits us to an image of world where the non-West can never be an equal partner, which in turn generates an account of literary history that necessarily devalues certain works.[19] But if we create a different account of world—a history of the concept of world—all kinds of new texts become not only valuable, but crucial, to the project, as examples (and theorizations) of different modes of worlding.[20] "Aesthetic worlds," he writes, "no matter how they form themselves, are among other things always a relation to and theory of the lived world, whether as a largely preconscious normative construct, a rearticulation, or even an active refusal of the world-norms of their age."[21] This way of describing the relationship between text and world notably grants the text a measure of autonomy, as a space of theorizing and building a world of its own.[22] This approach makes the aesthetic work of the text matter in crucial ways, and links it to a flexible conception of modernity that is not West-centric.

As Hayot returns to the question of a global literary history, however, he begins to group different approaches to worlding into a typology, arriving at three modes: Realist, Romantic, and Modernist. Although he clarifies that he uses the term "modes" as a way of designating an orientation or a particular approach to worlding rather than a specific historical practice, he acknowledges that there is a significant, if partial, overlap between the normative mode and the historical practice. The effort to systematize thereby risks reinstating the very kinds of categories that the critique had initially seemed to advocate breaking with (as Hayot acknowledges[23]). The very act of typologizing implicitly suggests a static category that belies the dynamism and heterogeneity of the literary field at any given moment.

Scott Black's recent work on romance helpfully points out yet another aspect of the novel's dynamism that such theorizations occlude: that the history of writing is entangled with individual instances of reading, which are fundamentally anachronistic and untimely. A given author is shaped by their sociohistorical conditions, yes, but also by their reading a variety of texts from other times and places, which provide unpredictable forms of inspiration and influence. In their insistent linearity, accounts of the novel's rise ignore the wonderfully weird loops and swirls of the novel's history, its fundamental untimeliness. Black shows us how centering romance, rather than the novel, gives us a new perspective on literary history (and a very different account of what reading is). Old forms persist and resurface; texts are read outside of their original contexts all the time, and new communities of readers find new meaning in them. "Strangely enough, historicist readings remove texts from history. Approaching texts exclusively as historical documents, using them as one-way mirrors through which to observe their original contexts, we restrict their future to their past, as if they speak to us, their future, only of their moments of production."[24] The story of the novel cannot be a straightforwardly progressive and linear history. It is recursive, palimpsestic, an effort to track individual points and their unexpected movements across multiple dimensions of time and space.

A comprehensive global history of the novel, a strong account of its evolution, can hardly hope to do justice to this dynamism and heterogeneity. The stubborn persistence of these kinds of categories seems to be an inevitable side effect of any effort to write a comprehensive global history of the novel, a strong account of its evolution. Perhaps, then, we must strive, at least occasionally, to break free of the impulse altogether.

※

It may seem almost boring, or pat, to once again turn to an account of the novel that, à la Bakhtin, celebrates its formal openness, its refusal to be any one kind of thing.[25] If it is not history that we seek, what is the theory appropriate for such a creature?

I draw inspiration from Paul Saint-Amour's elegant way of formulating a synthesis of the recent movements in modernist studies as a rise of "weak theory."[26] Modernism, Saint-Amour explains, has long been a muscular, iconoclastic, self-mythologizing sort of thing, "strong people exhibiting strength." Of late, this view has given way, and, Saint-Amour suggests, opens the possibility of, instead, embracing its obverse. The word "weak" carries a plethora of meanings: designating the kinds of subjects who have previously been marginalized (the female, queer, disabled, or subaltern); a mode that resists the imperious self-possession of a claim to intellectual mastery; the expansion and subsequent decentering of its object of study as it became diffuse across time and space. This critique beautifully parallels my own intervention into accounts of the novel, which likewise tend inexorably to mythologizing and vigorous visions. I, too, wish to make space for the "weak," the works of prose fiction that have been excluded in such visions, frequently the works of the subaltern or subordinated, often dismissed as inferior because of their difference. As the realist-centered account gives way, "novel," too, becomes a softer and more diffuse category, inviting a different, gentler engagement.

Following the work of Gianni Vattimo, Saint-Amour suggests "that modernism in a global frame should be understood not just as an *object* of weak theory but as weak thought *par excellence*—as a set of disparate sites and conversations unified by the aim of weakening the monopolistic hold of transcendental truth claims upon us." This may well be the best description of the global novel that one could ask for. The novel is not only an object that reflects the world, but also a force for building worlds of its own. The novel is, ultimately, perhaps the most narcissistic of all forms, endlessly fascinated by itself and its own powers and potential. And in its self-conscious way of thinking, it produces a form of thought uniquely its own. And paradoxically, it has been at its weakest, relative to literary criticism, precisely when it most forcefully challenges our norms of thinking about what novels can and should do. As the readings contained in the previous chapters have shown, the epistemologies generated by our current paradigms for thinking the novel frequently fail to attend to some of the most interesting things about particular novels, ignoring the conceptual work inherent in the complexities of their form.

In closing, then, this is what I am calling for: instead of a single history, a weak theory of the novel. One that would extend it geographically and chronologically, without claiming any particular mode as definitive. One that would have a suppler and more capacious sense of form. One that would join the novel in the various conversations it has produced in various times and places, without talking over it when it strays from the expected topic. A global formalism that would engage closely and deeply with different kinds of novels and illuminate their offerings to our understanding of the form. A perspective that would make good on the promise for more diverse fiction and offer better ways of valuing it.

NOTES

Introduction · Unreal Histories

1. The canonical example is Watt, *Rise of the Novel*, with Auerbach, *Mimesis*, providing a complementary version. More recent examples include Armstrong, *How Novels Think*; Gallagher, *Nobody's Story*; Brooks, *Realist Vision*; or Slaughter, *Human Rights, Inc.*

2. For a wealth of examples, see Nixon, *Novel Definitions*.

3. A strain of literary scholarship that sees *Don Quixote* as the urtext for the origin of the novel has consistently offered an alternative to the Anglocentric, realism-focused account. See, for instance, Cascardi, "*Don Quixote*"; and Wilson, *Cervantes*.

4. For examples of this Anglocentrism, see, for instance, Schmidt, *The Novel*; or the *Cambridge Companion to the [Eighteenth-Century, Romantic, Victorian,* or *Modernist] Novel*. Similarly, one finds a wealth of texts with titles implying a discussion of the novel at large, and subtitles specifying an English focus, such as Hunter, *Before Novels: The Cultural Contexts of Eighteenth-Century English Fiction*; or Spacks, *Novel Beginnings: Experiments in Eighteenth-Century English Fiction*.

5. See, for example, Mander, *Remapping*; Moore, *The Novel*; Moretti, *The Novel*; and Beecroft, *Ecology of World Literature*.

6. See, for example, Aravamudan, *Enlightenment Orientalism*; Doody, *True Story of the Novel*; Kareem, *Eighteenth-Century Fiction*; Paige, *Before Fiction*; and Spacks, *Novel Beginnings*. On the other hand, Scott Black has recently argued that romance should be seen as distinct, and as central and significant, offering a vision of literary history "without the novel." My critique of rise-of-the-novel paradigms largely overlaps with his. See Black, *Without the Novel*.

7. Although fictionality studies arguably began as an alternative approach to understanding realism (cf. Catherine Gallagher's "Rise of Fictionality"), more recent studies have staked out increasingly assertive claims challenging realism's primacy, or rather, have shown "the so-called realist novel to be *already* rich in estranging marvelous effects." Kareem, *Eighteenth-Century Fiction*, 27. Julie Orlemanski offers a powerful critique of the tendency to equate fictionality with the specific forms it takes in the realist novel. Orlemanski, "Who Has Fiction?"

8. Elaine Freedgood has recently made an argument very similar to my own, using Victorian literature as an entry point. As she writes: "If we displace the nineteenth-century novel from the masterful and still center of a novel history that is as contingent as the genre it tries to track, other novels might have a better chance of getting a reading that is not nineteenth-century-Anglo-Eurocentric" (Freedgood, *Worlds Enough*, xviii).

9. "Minor" is colloquially used to refer to non-major traditions, but it also has a more specific meaning, as described by Deleuze and Guattari, referring to texts written by minorities in a dominant language. Because of the language politics of Ireland, Irish authors are often included in this narrower category. It is rare to see Polish authors, even those such as Joseph Conrad, Jan Potocki, or Jerzy Kosinski, who wrote in English or French rather than Polish, considered in this framework. I discuss this issue further in chapter four.

10. In Pascale Casanova's account, literary capital does not map directly onto political power, though the two are interconnected. But literary capital is intensely bound up with models of development: to possess it is to set the norm of what literature should be, while everyone else struggles to catch up. Casanova uses the metaphor of a Greenwich Mean Time of literature, implying a temporal dimension to the process. Casanova, *The World Republic of Letters*.

11. Moretti, "Conjectures on World Literature," 54–68, 60, 65.

12. See Moretti, *Distant Reading*. For an excellent set of concise responses to this text, see Fitzpatrick, Galloway, and English, "Franco Moretti's *Distant Reading*."

13. This problem is increasingly registered with particular acuteness in discussions of African literature. Taiye Selasi has complained that "to presume that *every* African writer is a closeted sociologist betrays a fundamental disrespect for those writers' artistry. Even where an African novelist has attended to autobiographical material—that is, setting a story in his or her country, observing its social dynamics—we are mistaken in engaging the politics to the exclusion of the poetry" (Selasi, "African Literature Doesn't Exist"). Likewise, Mukoma Wa Ngugi notes that literary criticism has ignored the diverse aesthetics of writing from the African continent, instead reading it as anthropology. Wa Ngugi, *Rise of the African Novel*. Jeanne-Marie Jackson also takes up this problem in a piece on plurality and agonistic form in fiction from Zimbabwe. Jackson, "Plurality in Question."

14. Warwick Research Collective, *Combined and Uneven Development*. Much of the research on magical realism exemplifies this tendency as well.

15. Kandice Chuh makes a similar argument, discussing a sense of fatigue with certain forms of political critique in Asian American studies. Chuh, *The Difference Aesthetics Makes*, 16–17.

16. Françoise Lionnet and Shu-Mei Shih offer a powerful account of the need for, and benefits of, such lateral comparisons among minority groups who are typically discussed in relation to a powerful center. Lionnet and Shih, "Thinking Through the Minor."

17. Tone, *Life of Theobald Wolfe Tone*, 864.

18. Merchant, *Impact of Irish-Ireland*. Brian Earls writes that such comparisons were "a familiar commonplace" in nineteenth-century Irish discourse. Earls, "'By Reason of Past History,'" 9.

19. Wolff, *Inventing Eastern Europe*.

20. Lloyd, *Nationalism and Minor Literature*, ix.

21. See Nycz, *Kultura po przejściach*; or Gosk, *Opowieści „Skolonizowanego/kolonizatora."* It should be noted, however, that the focus of these studies is typically (though not exclusively) on the postsocialist period. In her discussion of the particular position of Poland within these theoretical frameworks, Anita Starosta instead uses the term "postimperial." See Starosta, *Form and Instability*. There is an extensive body of criticism on

the applicability of postcolonial frameworks to a postsocialist context, and on the complexities of thinking about postsocialism, or (post)socialism. See, for instance, Moore, "Is the Post- in Postcolonial?"; Chari and Verdery, "Thinking between the Posts"; Kołodziejczyk and Şandru, "Introduction"; and Jelača and Lugarić, "Introduction."

22. Some scholars would argue that this is not true of Poland during the Cold War, claiming that the Iron Curtain effectively severed Poland's contact with Europe. See, for example, Krasowska, "Po Zaborach i po PRL-u."

23. Foster, "Ascendancy and Union," 134–173, 128, 130.

24. Wandycz, *The Price of Freedom*, 108–109.

25. See, for instance, Jacobson, *Whiteness of a Different Color*; Ignatiev, *How the Irish Became White*.

26. Cleary, *Outrageous Fortune*, 19–22.

27. Andrzej Nowak argues, for instance, that the Polish-Lithuanian Commonwealth should be seen in imperial terms. See Nowak, *History and Geopolitics*. And the history of Polish Jews is extremely complex: for a particularly nuanced and careful account, see Hoffman, *Shtetl*.

28. Adam Zamoyski chronicles a fascinating exception: the Polish soldiers sent by Napoleon to quell the rebellion in Haiti. Upon arrival, the cognitive dissonance of fighting to deprive a people of their nation while they were struggling to regain their own apparently led some soldiers to switch sides. When Jean-Jacques Dessalines became ruler of an independent Haiti, he offered the Poles citizenship, and at least four hundred of them accepted. See Zamoyski, *Holy Madness*, 130–132. This incident is also discussed in Buck-Morss, *Hegel, Haiti, and Universal History*, 75.

29. Poles are quick to note that being written in English gives Irish literature a huge advantage in terms of global readership. Of course, such language issues also shade into the question of the criteria used to consider a given author as "Polish" or "Irish" at all, and the value of such distinctions. These are larger debates, and I do not have the space to pursue them here. Some of the authors discussed in this book have been "claimed" by other national traditions, or as cosmopolitan authors of world literature. This does not, I think, undermine my choice to consider them as Polish or Irish: it should be obvious that there are perfectly legitimate reasons to do so.

30. O'Connor, *Haunted English*. Barry McCrea argues that Irish was especially significant for modernist authors, writing: "As Irish was found less and less 'in the wild' . . . it acquired unusual potential properties for the poetic imagination, as a dream of another, lost, more perfect language hidden beneath the surface of English-speaking Ireland. . . . The underlying meaning the language acquired as it was spoken less as a native language, as a troubling ghost haunting everyday life in English-speaking Ireland, is inseparable from the modernist literary ideas that had such a hold on early twentieth-century Irish writers" (McCrea, *Languages of the Night*, 30).

31. A rare exception is an important recent book by Mary Mullen that argues that not only did Irish literature develop realism, but that it did so in an exemplary way: that a better understanding of the formal features of Irish realism makes central aspects of British writing more visible. But this is an exception that proves the rule; indeed, Mullen presents an image of the landscape of criticism on nineteenth-century Irish fiction that is very similar to the one I offer here. Mullen, *Novel Institutions*.

32. Cleary, "Misplaced Ideas?" 48.

33. Najder, "Development of the Polish Novel," 651–652.
34. Miłosz, *History of Polish Literature*, 255.
35. Eagleton, *Heathcliff and the Great Hunger*, 147.
36. Lloyd, *Anomalous States*, 144.
37. Cited in Lloyd, *Anomalous States*, 134.
38. Wirtemberska, *Malwina, czyli domyślność serca*, 33 (*Malvina, or the Heart's Intuition*, 3).
39. Discussed in Cleary, *Outrageous Fortune*; Lloyd *Anomalous States*; and Murphy, *Irish Novelists*.
40. Hayot, *On Literary Worlds*, 6.
41. Paige, *Before Fiction*, 205.
42. Wai-Chee Dimock similarly offers a model of literary history that would track the "family resemblances" among genres in a more widely dispersed—both geographically and temporally—fashion. Dimock, *Through Other Continents*.
43. Paige, *Before Fiction*, 25.
44. Paige, *Before Fiction*, 25.
45. Lorri Nandrea offers a kind of inverted version of this practice, examining a series of divergent possibilities in the British novel that did not attain dominance, and tracing the resurgence of the formal questions they raise in later works. See Nandrea, *Misfit Forms*.
46. Two recent works, Stephanie Insley Hershinow's *Born Yesterday* and Wendy Anne Lee's *Failures of Feeling*, elegantly exemplify the rising awareness of such structural problems in novel theory, offering corrections to sweeping theoretical narratives of realism, and making more restricted (and extremely compelling) claims about one specific aspect of eighteenth-century fictions. Lee explicitly references Paige's work, saying, "In offering this slanted, skeletal, and multigenre genealogy of fiction, I am persuaded by Nicholas Paige's claim that 'the novel' was never 'born' and so never 'rises.'. . . Insofar as my own study charts a course for what I call a Richardsonian fiction, I do so without making any progressive claims about the nature of that project" (Lee, *Failures of Feeling*, 2).
47. Löwy, "The Current of Critical Irrealism," 195.
48. Anna Kornbluh's recent book offers a different account of realism as engaged in producing an abstract model of reality rather than representation of the real world, a way of describing the work of fiction that is very much in line with the kinds of dynamics that interest me here. Kornbluh, *The Order of Forms*.
49. Nan Z. Da discusses the pressure put on moments of international contact in world literature studies and offers an important corrective. Da, *Intransitive Encounter*.

Chapter 1 · *The Problem with Happily Ever After*

1. Indeed, Jason Pearl has suggested that "*Gulliver's Travels* enjoys a less certain place in the history of the novel, in part because of the centrality of Defoe" (Pearl, *Utopian Geographies*, 152).
2. Along these lines, Mark McGurl notes that "While [*Gulliver's Travels*] restores many of the marvelous improbabilities to the voyage narrative that *Crusoe* had removed, thus provoking its banishment from most discussions of the rise of the novel, it distances itself just as fully as its Whiggish forebear from traditional romance plots and timeless, unspecified identities." He proceeds to offer a more complex explanation of the novel's

relationship to realism, focusing on the notion of scale. McGurl, "Gigantic Realism," 411. Similarly, Clement Hawes writes that "our anachronistic category [of the novel] has lacked the flexibility to deal with a text that simultaneously imitates and violently estranges so-called reality," but he goes on to argue that "eighteenth-century approaches to the real often remained Gulliverian: interwoven with supernatural, surreal, and absurdist tropes" (Hawes, "Gulliver Effects," 187–204, 187, 189).

3. Thus, he writes that Fielding's early works "are really anti-novels in that their almost pervasive sense of parody makes them implicitly critical of the 'naive' realism by which Defoe and Richardson seek to induce a psychological participation which must be identified as the defining quality of the modern novel" (Richetti, *Popular Fiction before Richardson*, 1). In his discussion of Fielding, Ian Watt addresses this divide by counterposing "realism of character" and "realism of assessment," but he acknowledges that Fielding's narratorial intrusions do detract from the overall effect of the text. Watt, *Rise of the Novel*, 286–293.

4. Hunter, "*Gulliver's Travels* and the Novel," 56.

5. Percy Adams suggests that one can place all travel writing on a spectrum. On the far right are wholly invented works that are received as works of imagination, in the center are true stories of travel that are believed and serve as historical documents, and on the far left are false narratives that are believed to be true. Just left of center are accounts that are slightly exaggerated or untrue (such as Chateaubriand), and just right of center are writers such as Defoe, who initially deceived some readers. Adams, *Travelers and Travel Liars*, 2–3.

6. As scholars have noted, in the early eighteenth century, this became a source of genuine confusion. See Adams, *Travelers and Travel Liars*; and Rennie, *Far-Fetched Facts*.

7. As I discuss in the next chapter, similar arguments have been made about the contribution of the Gothic—the emergence of realism arguably depends on works that flirt with the explicitly unreal, in order to test fiction's powers.

8. Said, *Culture and Imperialism*, 9. See also Pratt, *Imperial Eyes*.

9. Wolff, *Inventing Eastern Europe*, 25.

10. See Giraldus Cambrensis (Gerald of Wales), *History and Topography*; Spenser, *Present State of Ireland*; and Harrington, *The English Traveller*.

11. Moryson, *An Itinerary*, Part III, Book 2, Chapter 4, 102. Italics author's.

12. Swift, "On Barbarous Denominations," 281.

13. Swift, *Drapier's Letters*, 103.

14. See McCalman, *The Last Alchemist*; Casanova, *History of My Life*; and Lindemann, *Liaisons Dangereuses*.

15. Louis-Phillippe, comte de Ségur, cited in Wolff, *Inventing Eastern Europe*, 19.

16. Ina Ferris has written specifically about the ways in which early Irish novels were in dialogue with English travel literature, arguing that these works frequently both recycled and parodied the tropes of the travelogue. Ferris, *The Romantic National Tale*.

17. Nemoianu, *The Triumph of Imperfection*, 165.

18. Herbert Marcuse makes a similar claim for the utopian possibilities of art in *The Aesthetic Dimension*. But scholars have also argued for historical examples of such a process. For instance, Joseph Slaughter has suggested that the rise of human rights laws is inextricably bound to the rise of the Bildungsroman, which made "human rights norms both legible and legistable, imaginable and articulable," and Lynn Hunt has claimed that

the epistolary novel paved the way for the Declaration of the Rights of Man by teaching readers new modes of feeling. Slaughter, *Human Rights, Inc.*, 6; Hunt, *Inventing Human Rights*.

19. Jameson, "The Politics of Utopia," 39.

20. See Krasicki, *Historia*. To my knowledge, this book has not been translated into English. Amusingly, this narrator is, we are told, one of the Strudlbrugs described in Gulliver's third voyage, making it clear that Krasicki had read Swift.

21. Swift, *Gulliver's Travels*, 124. Italics author's.

22. Krasicki, *Mikołaja Doświadczyńskiego przypadki*; Krasicki, *Mr. Nicholas Wisdom*. Further quotations and references in the text will be cited with page numbers in parentheses. When both the Polish and the English are quoted, both page numbers will be cited.

23. Fredric Bogel offers a critique of this kind of thinking, arguing that theories of satire have persistently ignored its dual nature, which, he argues, is parallel to the doubleness of irony. Although seemingly invested in distance, satire necessarily registers closeness at the same time; thus, it is never a straightforward attack, but rather, an exploration of the complexity of a given (moral) position. See Bogel, *The Difference Satire Makes*.

24. Watt, "The Ironic Tradition," 314.

25. I describe this as a problem of the reader's attitude toward the text, but Watt frames it differently, as a matter of the character, saying that "insofar as he is an ironic device, his effectiveness is directly proportional to the completeness of his disciplined subordination to his creator's purpose; while, *qua* individual character, the *persona* can become living and effective only by transcending the role he is allotted as the vehicle of the transparently dual or multiple presentations of reality that irony requires. This implicit contradiction becomes manifest if the plot requires that the *persona* not only be lifelike, but actually come to life and be changed by his experiences, just like a real person or a character in a novel" (Watt, "The Ironic Tradition," 314–315).

26. Watt also sees a link between this formal contradiction and the philosophical problem of utopia (what he calls the individual-class dichotomy), but he does not develop the argument in detail.

27. "Gdyby ci, którym złoto zdaje się być najpotrzebniejszym do życia żywiołem; ci, którzy na to wszystkie siły wywnętrzają, żeby jak najwięcej kruszcu tego zgromadzić; gdyby ci, mówię, za każdem na upodobany ten kruszec wejrzeniem, chcieli pomyśleć, jak wielą łzami przy wydobyciu swojem oblany jest; uśmierzyliby chciwość swoję, oszczędziliby miliony nieszczęśliwych ludzi, którzy stają się ofiarą ich łakomstwa" (151). "If he who thinks that gold is life's most indispensable commodity, he who expends all his energy on accumulating as much of it as possible, if only he, I say, were to realize each time he delights in this metal how much its extraction costs in human tears, he would curb his greed and spare millions of unhappy people who become victims of that greed" (110).

28. See Doktór, "Komizm unaiwniony *Mikołaja Doświadczyńskiego przypadków*."

29. Heather Keenleyside offers a fascinating reading of how the novel positions Gulliver in many ways, trying out various literary forms as it posits different relationships between individual and species. Keenleyside, *Animals and Other People*.

30. I have described these critiques in greater detail in an earlier version of this chapter, which also discusses Krasicki's subtle commentary on the colonial project. See Bartoszyńska, "Persuasive Ironies."

31. Nicholas Canny describes the way British landowners expanded tillage farming and introduced technological innovations into eighteenth-century Irish agriculture, noting that native landowners would often follow suit: "While the changing character of the physical environment was closely related to the spread of British landowners and settlers, it was not completely dependent upon this factor. Native proprietors also saw the need to promote innovation, both because they wanted to be considered worthy subjects of the Crown and because innovation could add to their wealth" (Canny, "Early Modern Ireland," 116). For a discussion of Swift's arguments on Irish agriculture, see Landa, "Swift's Economic Views."

32. Ann Laura Stoler has written compellingly on the threat that familial attachments pose to colonial authority, and the struggle of those authorities to police domestic sentiment. Stoler, *Along the Archival Grain*, particularly chapter three, "Habits of a Colonial Heart," 57–104.

33. The mute equines of England seem a humorous presaging of Albert Memmi's argument that it is the "mediocre" colonists who remain. Memmi, *The Colonizer and the Colonized*, especially 48–51.

34. Clifford, "Gulliver's Fourth Voyage."

35. For Ian Watt, it is clear that Swift intended the latter, but the merging of ironic persona and lifelike character destabilizes the tone and detracts from the moral, demonstrating that "the possibilities of combining the effects of character and *persona* are strictly limited; that as readers we cannot, in fact, maintain the separation between the pretended ironic *persona*, and the actual suffering person" (Watt, "The Ironic Tradition," 315). We are meant to view Gulliver ironically, Watt says, but his misery is so compelling that we cannot.

36. Frank Boyle, referring specifically to this episode, offers a defense against this charge. Boyle, *Swift as Nemesis*, 43.

37. Voltaire's *Candide* also takes up this problem. The travelers find themselves in El Dorado, which seems essentially like paradise, and yet, they decide to leave. "A fondness for roving, for making a figure in their own country, and for boasting of what they had seen in their travels, was so powerful in our two wanderers that they resolved to be no longer happy; and demanded permission of the King to quit the country" (47).

38. There is an interesting political undertone to this argument as well: Xaoo argues that travel is the privilege of the wealthy, a luxury unattainable for small—or minor—nations. The costs are too high, not only in terms of expenditure, but also because they deprive society of a useful member: "im kraj uboższy, szkoda większa, a jeżeli nie ma w sobie takich okoliczności, które by do podobnych podróż zwabiały cudzoziemców, nienagrodzona" (125) ("The poorer a nation, the greater the costs. Moreover, if a nation has nothing to attract visitors, the costs are not repaid") (90).

39. Clifford, "Gulliver's Fourth Voyage," 44.

40. The distinction is also physical—the Houyhnhnms seem similar to horses, and the Yahoos seem similar to humans. The physical differences are highlighted in a scene where Gulliver's master comments on his body (219), but they are not as strongly emphasized. For a discussion of the Yahoo-Houyhnhnm distinction in relation to emerging concepts of race, see Malcolmson, *Studies of Skin Color*.

41. Colebrook, *Irony*, 60.

42. Seamus Deane points out that the novel also gives lie to the notion of universal-

ism as such, demonstrating that any theorization of universality is always rooted in a particular time and place, and is thus never genuinely universal. Deane, *Foreign Affections*, 52–53.

43. For example, in paragraph 29 of the *Proposal*: "Therefore, let no man talk to me of other Expedients: Of taxing Absentees at five Shillings a Pound; Of using neither Cloaths, nor Household Furniture except what is of our own Growth and Manufacture: Of utterly rejecting the Materials and Instruments that promote foreign Luxury" (Swift, *A Modest Proposal*).

44. Śniegucka, "Dyptyk z Adamem i Ewą," 183.

45. Clifford summarizes the problem in Swift's novel, saying that it shows that "absolute standards are unattainable by fallen man, and even if they could be achieved would prove unattractive and unsatisfactory. Moreover, all attempts at middle-ground solutions involve a certain amount of self-rationalization and hypocrisy" (Clifford, "Gulliver's Fourth Voyage," 47).

46. It is a curious aspect of the term *utopian* that its literal meaning refers to a given (fictional) place, but its more popular metaphoric usage implies the awareness of the impossibility of such a place.

47. Eagleton, "Nationalism, Irony and Commitment," 30. Italics author's.

48. Eagleton, "Nationalism, Irony and Commitment," 38.

49. Graciotti, "Utopia w Dziełach Ignacego Krasickiego," 1–16. Jason Pearl makes a similar argument about *Gulliver's Travels*: that Gulliver makes utopia a state of mind. See Pearl, *Utopian Geographies*.

50. Śniegucka, "Kilka uwag," 373–380.

51. Attar, *Vital Roots*; Aravamudan, *Enlightenment Orientalism*, 15–17.

52. There is also an interesting piece by Matthew Reilly that instead traces its influence on Pope and Byron. Reilly, "Byron's Babel," 224–245.

53. Hassan, *Hayy bin Yaqzan and Robinson Crusoe*. His argument is based partly on the popularity of Ibn Tufayl's novel during the eighteenth century, and on a survey of Defoe's library, but is predominantly anchored in a comparison of the two texts. Hassan also suggests that the novel may have influenced *Gulliver's Travels*, but his argument is largely based on one sentence (Hassan, 140).

54. Malti-Douglas, *Woman's Body, Woman's Word*, 69.

55. Either because he spontaneously generated there, or because he was placed in a box by his mother and washed up on the shore; the narrator suggests both as plausible explanations.

56. Ibn Tufayl, *Ibn Tufayl's Hayy ibn Yaqzan*, 163.

57. I have since discovered one other truly utopian text, the story of a planned society that offers an ideal existence: Sarah Scott's *Millenium Hall*, written in 1762. The community described, however, is not intended to be universal, but rather, is a kind of shelter for unmarried women or people who are excluded from society because of bodily differences. Thus, it serves as a supplement to "normal" society, akin to the everyday utopias described by Davina Cooper that function as temporary sites of repair, without necessarily leading to social transformation (though they have the potential to do so). See Cooper, *Everyday Utopias*.

58. Khalil Habib offers a similar argument to my own, but with some differences, in Habib, "Ibn Tufayl's Critique."

59. Consider, for example, the paradigmatic case of *Robinson Crusoe*, seemingly the figurehead of such efforts. Crusoe spends most of the novel desperately wanting to leave his island—and ultimately succeeding. Whether his island should be considered a properly utopian space (postcolonial critiques of the novel have, of course, offered extremely persuasive evidence to the contrary), surely it must matter that he chooses to leave it. As the sequel to the book makes clear, moreover, the island descends into turmoil upon his departure, as power struggles ensue among the remaining inhabitants—a strike against the system of government Crusoe establishes.

Chapter 2 · *The Terror of Worlds Unfolding*

1. The primary exception to this is Robert Irwin, who notes that there "are a number of curious resemblances" between them, but he does not elaborate. See Irwin, *The Arabian Nights*, 255. Other scholarly works that mention both texts, though without strictly comparing them, are Teverson, "The Number of Magic Alternatives"; Round, "Gothic and the Graphic Novel"; and Punter, *Rapture*.
2. Baldick, "Introduction," x.
3. See, for instance, McCormack, *Dissolute Characters*.
4. See Baldick, "Introduction."
5. For the most complete and up-to-date chronicle of the different versions and translations, see the introduction to the new Polish translation of the 1810 manuscript. Rosset and Triaire, "Wstęp." For an excellent discussion of some of the differences between the texts, and a consideration of which version should be considered most "authentic," see Białas, "*Fabula Interrupta*."
6. For this reason, in what follows I quote from the Chojecki translation and provide the French in the notes. When relevant, discrepancies between the different languages and versions have been mentioned in the notes.
7. For example: "The whole of Maturin's novel issues from those who have witnessed the traumas endemic to coloniality/modernity. As if offering a phenomenology of this history, Maturin embeds story within story within story, linking witnesses across time and continents" (Doyle, "At World's Edge," 542); or "Maturin's novel merely inverts the brooding pressure of cosmic irony. Mangled remains trumpet the prophetic: home, an Irish home, place and space on Irish soil, can never furnish surcease from wandering, exiled and alienated as it is from itself. Ireland *is* a wandering home. The idea of vagrancy is reinforced by its form: the novel traverses place and space in the process of constructing a nested series of interpolated tales" (Wein, "Wandering Home," 171). Richard Haslam offers further examples of such allegorical readings and a critique of them. Haslam, "Gothic."
8. See Citton, "Potocki and the Spectre."
9. See Krzyżanowski, *Historia Literatury Polskiej*; Miłosz, *History of Polish Literature*; and Skoczek, "Jan Potocki."
10. See, for instance, Fraisse, *Potocki et l'imaginaire*; and the works of François Rosset and Dominique Triaire.
11. Although many people assume that Potocki was a Freemason, there is no final proof. Specifically, his name does not appear on the lists of any Freemason Lodges. Dominique Triaire takes as conclusive a single letter written by Potocki in 1802, which bears a seal containing Masonic symbols, and surmises that in coming years further

evidence will be found in Ukrainian archival documents. See "Jan Potocki Wolnomularzem," in Rosset and Triaire, *Z Warszawy do Saragossy*. I have chosen to use the Polish version of this work rather than the original French text, because, as the authors note in the preface, it is more recent, and was updated to include new findings.

12. For more on Maturin's biography, see Lougy, *Charles Robert Maturin*; and Kelly, *Charles Maturin*.

13. For simplicity's sake, I will hereafter refer to him simply as Melmoth, and to John Melmoth as John.

14. See especially Beecroft, *An Ecology of World Literature*; and Ganguly, *This Thing Called the World*.

15. Paige, "Permanent Re-Enchantments," 173.

16. Lynch, "Gothic Fiction," 62.

17. The most famous example here being, of course, Ann Radcliffe.

18. Todorov, *The Fantastic*.

19. Todorov, *The Fantastic*, 25.

20. *Rękopis znaleziony w Saragossie*, 49; *The Manuscript Found in Saragossa*, 49–50. "Au reste, je m'en rapporte sur toutes ces choses à ceux qui en savent plus que moi. Il me suffit de n'avoir peur ni des revenants, ni des vampires" (*Manuscrit Trouvé à Saragosse*, 47). Further quotations from *Rękopis znaleziony w Saragossie* will be cited as *Rękopis*, with the page number(s). Quotations from *The Manuscript Found in Saragossa* will be cited as *Manuscript*, with the page number(s). And quotations from *Manuscrit Trouvé à Saragosse* will be cited as *Manuscrit*, with the page number(s).

21. *Rękopis*, 16; *Manuscript*, 10. "Ce n'était pas que je fusse convaincu qu'il n'y a point de revenants; mais on verra plus loin que toute mon education avait été dirigé du côté de l'honneur, et je le faisais consister à ne donner jamais aucune marque de crainte" (*Manuscrit*, 9).

22. This is why Todorov says that "All of the 'miracles' are explained rationally at the end of the narrative" (Todorov, *The Fantastic*, 44).

23. *Rękopis*, 91; *Manuscript*, 99; *Manuscrit*, 95. Some scholars argue that Potocki was himself a cabbalist. See especially Otorowski, *Jan Potocki*. A more speculative account appears in Lachman, *A Dark Muse*.

24. *Rękopis*, 221, 302, 330; *Manuscript*, 250, 343, 374; *Manuscrit*, 246, 340, 372. It should be noted, however, that the Wandering Jew does not appear in the 1810 edition of the novel.

25. Walpole, *Castle of Otranto*, 3.

26. Clery, *Rise of Supernatural Fiction*, 54.

27. *Rękopis*, 45; *Manuscript*, 45; *Manuscrit*, 43.

28. *Rękopis*, 557; *Manuscript*, 631; "hostile à la mienne" (*Manuscrit*, 637).

29. Christine Mary Dunford's theatrical adaptation of the novel, staged by Chicago's *Looking Glass Theater* in the fall season of 2005, changes the ending to further emphasize a sense of tolerance and multiculturalism.

30. *Rękopis*, 115; *Manuscript*, 127, translation amended; "j'avoue qu'il y a eu d'ailleurs de grands changements dans le monde démonagorique. Et les vampires, entre autres, sont un invention nouvelle, si j'ose m'exprimer ainsi" (*Manuscrit*, 123).

31. Anna Guéri-Castell mentions this moment in her discussion of the ways in which the film adaptation contains veiled references to twentieth-century Poland. Discussing

this reference to Hungarian and Polish vampires, she notes the resonances with Mickiewicz's 1832 play, *Dziady*, and the idea of vampires as seeking revenge, before discussing the twentieth-century context. Guérin-Castell, "A Film Saved," 172.

32. Potocki's political views were complicated. Initially somewhat active in Polish politics, he became increasingly cynical and disenchanted. See Triaire and Rosset, *Z Warszawy do Saragossy*, especially 41–51.

33. Janion, *Niesamowita Słowiańszczyzna*, 264.

34. Surprisingly, Todorov does not discuss this aspect of the text in relation to its fantastic qualities, though elsewhere he examines how it relates to the idea of character and action. See Todorov, "Narrative-Men."

35. *Rękopis*, 308; *Manuscript*, 350; *Manuscrit*, 346.

36. *Rękopis*, 358; *Manuscript*, 406; *Manuscrit*, 405.

37. *Rękopis*, 416; *Manuscript*, 470, translation modified; "il est dans la nature humaine que lorsqu'elle a goûté au merveilleux, elle y ramène même les événements les plus ordinaires de la vie" (*Manuscrit*, 477). I must note, however, that this line was quite possibly penned by Chojecki rather than Potocki, because it comes up in a plot line that does not exist in either the 1804 or the 1810 manuscript. See footnote on page 598 of Anna Wasilewska's new translation (2015) of the 1810 manuscript of *Rękopis*.

38. Kareem, *Eighteenth-Century Fiction*.

39. Kareem, *Eighteenth-Century Fiction*, 22.

40. Landy, *How to Do Things*.

41. Many of the contemporary articles in popular magazines and newspapers lauding this power of literature draw on research by David Kidd and Emanuele Castano. See Kidd and Castano, "Different Stories," and Kidd and Castano, "Reading Literary Fiction."

42. Landy, *How to Do Things*, 10. To be clear, Kareem's account, and my own in what follows, are more narrowly focused on skills of reading, whereas Landy refers more broadly to skills of living.

43. See Kareem, *Eighteenth-Century Fiction*; Clery, *Rise of Supernatural Fiction*; and Gamer, *Romanticism and the Gothic*.

44. Johnson, *Rambler* No. 4.

45. Examples include *The Female Quixote* by Charlotte Lennox (1752), *Rosella, or Modern Occurrences*, by Mary Charlton (1799), *The Heroine*, by Eaton Stannard Barrett (1813), and *Northanger Abbey*, by Jane Austen (1818), to name only a few.

46. *Rękopis*, 12; *Manuscript*, 5; "cette chaîne sourcilleuse qui sépare l'Andalousie d'avec la Manche" (*Manuscrit*, 5).

47. Gamer, *Romanticism and the Gothic*, 53.

48. Kareem notes a similar problem at work in attitudes toward wonder: that it "must remain disinterested, not credulous, riveted, but not excessively engrossed" (*Eighteenth-Century Fiction*, 41).

49. *Rękopis*, 20; *Manuscript*, 16; *Manuscrit*, 14–15.

50. *Rękopis*, 168, 248, 314, 382, 385; *Manuscript*, 190, 280, 358, 432, 436; *Manuscrit*, 186, 278, 354, 434, 437.

51. *Rękopis*, 140; *Manuscript*, 155; "Cela peut être . . . peut-être Romati a-t-il pris son histoire dans ce livre. Peut-être l'a t-i-l inventée. Toujours est-il sûr que son récit contribua beaucoup à me donner le goût des voyages" (*Manuscrit*, 150).

52. *Rękopis*, 491; *Manuscript*, 506; *Manuscrit*, 516.
53. *Rękopis*, 352; *Manuscript*, 399; *Manuscrit*, 396–397.
54. Scott Black has recently offered a powerful account of the romance that boldly argues for its merits in these very terms, suggesting that one of the pleasures of romance is that it produces a space for play, for incomprehension, for absorption—that it can in fact be beneficial precisely by suspending the kind of formation that Landy describes. See Black, *Without the Novel*, 14–18.
55. *Rękopis*, 94–97; *Manuscript*, 87–89; *Manuscrit*, 89–92.
56. "Ze smutkiem postrzegam, że cnoty twoje zasadzają się na zbyt wygórowanym poczuciu honoru, i uprzedzam cię, że dziś nie ma już tylu pojedynków w Madrycie, ile ich bywało za czasów ojca. Oprócz tego cnoty dziś opierają się na innych, daleko trwalszych zasadach" (*Rękopis*, 49) ("I am sorry to see that your virtues are based on an exaggerated sense of honor. I warn you that you will not find as many duels in Madrid as there were in your father's day. Besides, these days virtue is based on other, more lasting principles") (*Manuscript*, 50); "Je vois avec chagrin que vos vertus reposent sur un point d'honneur beaucoup trop exagéré, et je vous avertis que vous ne trouverez plus Madrid aussi ferraillant qu'il était au temps de votre père. De plus, les vertus ont d'autres principes plus sûrs" (*Manuscrit*, 47).
57. *Rękopis*, 62; *Manuscript*, 65. "Il n'avait cessé de vanter l'honneur, la delicatessen, l'exacte probité des gens à qui l'on aurait fait grâce de les pendre. L'abus de ces mots, dont il se servait avec tant de confiance, brouillait tout mes idées" (*Manuscrit*, 62).
58. *Rękopis*, 115; *Manuscript*, 128, translation amended; "j'eus quelque honte de ma bravade" (*Manuscrit*, 125).
59. Inconsistencies that Landy perceives as well: see especially Landy, *How to Do Things*, 29–39.
60. *Rękopis*, 326; *Manuscript*, 370, translation amended; "convaincue qu'il n'y a pas de femme qui ne se rendît à des arguments pareils" (*Manuscrit*, 367).
61. This, he explains, is the true difference between people, the gap between Eskimos and Hottentots—not race or ethnicity, but intellect—the number of ideas and combinations they have. Preferable, perhaps, to arguments of innate difference, but revolting nonetheless.
62. *Rękopis*, 376; *Manuscript*, 425–426; "L'homme qui a vu toute la terre par les yeux des voyageurs, qui a vu tous les événements dans l'histoire, a réellement une infinité d'images dans la tête . . . et s'il combine ses idées, les rapproche, les compare, cet homme a du savoir et de l'espirit" (*Manuscrit*, 426). I have adapted the English translation here, which has "*read* all the events of history" instead of *seen*, though it notes that the French manuscript has *lu* and not *vu*. However, as seen in the quote, the French translation of the novel that I have uses *vu*, so it is unclear which manuscript the translator is referring to—all the more intriguing, because that is one of the few translator's footnotes in the text. The Polish version uses *seen*, widział. While I have adapted the English so as to remain faithful to the Polish text, this substitution in the English translation neatly confirms my claim that Velásquez is obviously referring to texts as a way of acquiring experience.
63. *Rękopis*, 278; *Manuscript*, 316; "que les romans et les œuvres de ce genre devraient être écrits sur plusieurs colonnes comme les tables chronologiques" (*Manuscrit*, 310).
64. Landy, *How to Do Things*, 10.

65. Kareem, *Eighteenth-Century Fiction*, 24.
66. Maturin, *Melmoth the Wanderer*, 61–62. Further quotations and references in the text will be cited with page numbers in parentheses.
67. A scene that may have served as inspiration for Oscar Wilde's *Picture of Dorian Gray*: see Haslam, "'Melmoth' (OW)."
68. This is, however, generally a problem specific to women—it is notable that the gender is switched in this case.
69. Kelly, *Charles Maturin*, 166.
70. Kelly, *Charles Maturin*, 162.
71. Doyle, "At World's Edge," 533.
72. Conger, *Matthew G. Lewis*, 214; Eagleton, *Heathcliff*, 193. Regina Oost draws a link between this ambivalent attitude toward horror fiction and Maturin's own beleaguered financial position. She argues that this dynamic of resistance to storytelling pervades the novel's entire form, and suggests that it may account for its abrupt and rather unsatisfying ending. As Oost and others have suggested however, the ending may be a product of publisher-author negotiations, or it may have been devised to enable the possibility of a sequel.
73. Maturin, *Melmoth*, 91, 207, 271.
74. Maturin, *Melmoth*, 41, 159, 451.
75. Gallagher, "The Rise of Fictionality," 337.
76. Robert, *The Old and the New*, 125.
77. Morin, *Charles Robert Maturin*, 132.
78. Edgeworth, *Castle Rackrent*, 4.
79. Scott, *The Monastery*, xxix.
80. Ann Rigney discusses the monument to Helen Walker that Scott had made, memorializing her as the prototype for the character of Jeanie Deans in *Heart of Midlothian*, and notes that while such practices make clear that fiction and reality are strongly interconnected for Scott, the fact that both names are given shows that he maintains a meaningful distinction between them. Rigney, *Imperfect Histories*, 13–16.
81. Lukács, *The Historical Novel*, 19.
82. See Gibbons, *Gaelic Gothic*; McCormack, *Dissolute Characters*; and more recently, Doyle, "At World's Edge"; and Morin, *Charles Robert Maturin*.
83. Gallagher, "The Rise of Fictionality," 341.
84. Booth, "Metaphor as Rhetoric," 55.
85. Demata, "Discovering Eastern Horrors," 26.
86. Aravamudan, *Enlightenment Orientalism*, 204–205.
87. Although *Lalla Rookh* may have been intended to be an allegorical treatment of Ireland, nothing in its footnotes makes this connection explicit, and, as J. C. M. Nolan points out, few readers interpreted it in this way. Nolan, "In Search of an Ireland."
88. In this way, too, both novels seem to anticipate a more famous work that involves such mystery-solving through story collection, namely, Bram Stoker's *Dracula*.
89. Ganguly, "The Value of World Making," 205.
90. Hayot, *On Literary Worlds*.
91. *Rękopis*, 128; *Manuscript*, 143; "Il est clair que je fais moi-même partie de cette chaîne invisible. Il est clair que l'on veut m'y retenir encore plus étroitement" (*Manuscrit*, 132). I have amended the English, which has "invisible plot" rather than chain. Although

this elegantly preempts my claims about this chain being one of narrative, it is nonetheless a departure from both the Polish and the French. I have also adapted it to make the chain the agent that binds, as in the Polish.

92. In more recent literature, however, we do find a similar example: Mark Danielewski's *House of Leaves*, where, similarly to *Melmoth the Wanderer*, the novel begins with a mystery and gradually reveals its broad dissemination, thereby revealing unexpected connections between several threads of story. David Mitchell's *Cloud Atlas* could also qualify.

93. Beecroft, *An Ecology of World Literature*, 283.

94. Ganguly, "The Value of World Making," 219.

95. Cheah, *What Is a World?* 42.

96. Lynch, "Gothic Fiction," 56–57.

97. *Rękopis*, 508; *Manuscript*, 574; *Manuscrit*, 582.

98. See, for instance, Sedgwick, *The Coherence of Gothic Conventions*. Sedgwick notes that although the Gothic is governed by extreme conventionality, there is a surprising amount of variety possible within it.

99. Kareem, *Eighteenth-Century Fiction*, 119–120.

100. This joy seems significant in the face of critical accounts that read the form of these texts as symptoms of political trauma. Though it is true that Maturin himself asserted that his works "scarce exhibit vicissitudes more extraordinary than what my life has furnished," supporting the idea that his immediate context was one suited to Gothic romance, he also frequently linked himself to a more universal tradition of supernatural and fanciful writing (Maturin and Scott, *The Correspondence*, 8–9). In an oft-cited quote, he complained of revisions made to his play *Bertram*, saying that they have "*un-Maturined* it completely, they have broken my wand and drowned my Magic Book, and Prospero himself, without his storms, his Goblins, & his Grammary, sinks into a very insignificant sort of Personage" (Maturin and Scott, *The Correspondence*, 59–60). Similarly, when Maturin says "I wish they would let me do that I am good for, sit down by my magic Cauldron, mix my dark ingredients, see the bubbles work, and the spirits rise, and by the pale and mystic light, I might show them 'the best of my delights'" (Maturin and Scott, *The Correspondence*, 9), the emphasis is on "delights" and entertainment. Although Maturin was certainly affected by his environment in ways that are undeniably registered in his works, often with a bitter sharpness, to read his novels solely in terms of the anguish they allude to is to miss the simultaneous pleasure he took in creating them.

Chapter 3 • Queer Tales and Seductive Paintings

1. Of *Dorian Gray*, for instance, Anita Levy says that both it and *Dracula* are "understood to deliver narratives of deviance entirely at odds with bourgeois social conventions, and especially in Wilde's case, contemptuous of dominant aesthetic practices" (Levy, *Reproductive Urges*, 129–130); John Paul Riquelme writes that Wilde straddles the Victorian and post-Victorian worlds, and is post-Romantic. Riquelme, "Between Two Worlds," 126. Of Żmichowska, Grażyna Borkowska writes that she is both old-fashioned and modern, that her works are "*strange*. By this I mean that they cannot be explained by referring to the narrative conventions of the period—of her period or any other" (Borkowska, *Alienated Women*, 100).

2. Mann, *Poganka Narcyzy Żmichowskiej*; Walczewska, *Damy, rycerze, i feministki*; Różewicz, "Miłość lesbijska w romantycznym przebraniu," 128–130.

3. Carla Freccero, for instance, admits "considerable uncertainty about the question of whether what I do in reading queer 'back then' has anything to do with 'back then' or not.... While this sort of critical and analytical juxtaposition could be considered historically illegitimate . . . it is a familiar and valid logic in other kinds of analytical practices, especially those, such as psychoanalysis, that attend to the particularity of the articulating subject and the rhetorical effect of language" (Freccero, *Queer/Early/Modern*, 4).

4. Yeazell, *Art of the Everyday*. See also Brooks, *Realist Vision*.

5. As Yeazell explains, in the case of Dutch painting, it can also refer to historical specificity, an attention to the ordinary or everyday domesticity, interest in "common" people, and "low or vulgar" subjects—all features frequently aligned with literary realism as well. Yeazell, *Art of the Everyday*, 8–9.

6. Notably, where political readings of Wilde such as Jed Esty's tend to see him as expressing resistance to nation/colony, readings of Żmichowska would, until more recently, tend in the opposite direction. Agnieszka Skolasińska offers a wonderfully pithy summary of what was long the standard "political" reading of *Poganka*, saying that "as a good Romantic hero, Beniamin experiences a transformation and declares his affection to be only a fanciful illusion that took him away from his mother. The mother is of course a symbol of Poland, as *The Heathen Woman [Poganka]* was written after the failure of the 1830 November Uprising" (Skolasińska, "Deconstructing the Polish Tradition," 136). This "of course" is, on the one hand, merited, for Żmichowska was certainly responding to a tradition of works written in the spirit of Romantic nationalism, and the mother figure undeniably partakes in the kind of imagery that is typical of this tradition. Yet the status of Romantic nationalism in the text is ambiguous: as Ursula Phillips recounts, one strain of critical interpretations places Romantic martyrdom at the forefront, seeing the novel as offering "an apology for a civic morality subject to the demands of heroic self-sacrifice," narrating Beniamin's moral destruction as a Pole as he abandons the national cause out of a selfish love. Discussing this interpretation, Ursula Phillips inclines, rather, to the interpretation of Grażyna Borkowska (as do I), who argues that Żmichowska worked to deconstruct such stereotypes, and saw slogans of emancipation, in a Polish context, as imposing a new slate of burdens and obligations. Phillips, "Femme Fatale and Mother-Martyr"; Borkowska, Alienated Women, 122.

7. Wilde, *The Picture of Dorian Gray*, 74. Further quotations and references in the text will be cited with page numbers in parentheses.

8. Ginsburg, *Portrait Stories*, 98; Ziolkowski, *Disenchanted Images*.

9. Żmichowska, *Poganka*, 90; Żmichowska, *The Heathen*, 109. Further quotations in the text will be cited with page numbers in parentheses. When both the Polish and the English are quoted, both page numbers will be cited.

10. Grażyna Borkowska also points out that the fantastical elements of the novel are only in the parts that are remembered, effectively quarantining them from "reality." Borkowska, *Alienated Women*, 104.

11. Love, *Feeling Backward*, 21–22.

12. Mann, *Poganka Narcyzy Żmichowskiej*, 13. Translation my own.

13. Phillips, "Femme Fatale and Mother-Martyr," 25.

14. Nunokawa, "Homosexual Desire," 311, 313.

15. Rohy, "Strange Influence," 280. Glick, *Materializing Queer Desire*, 20; Cohen, *Sex Scandal*, 192.

16. Sedgwick, *Epistemology of the Closet*, 165.
17. Esty, *Unseasonable Youth*, 113.
18. Nunokawa, *The Tame Passions of Wilde*, 85–89.
19. Cohen, "Writing Gone Wilde."
20. "For modern readers, the cause of Dorian's desire has come not from the text but from its future, reflecting Wilde's 1895 trials and twentieth-century models of gay identity." Rohy, "Strange Influence," 285.
21. The entrants in this debate are too many to list, but some signal contributions or summations include Halperin, *History of Homosexuality*; Freccero, *Queer/Early/Modern*; Traub, "The New Unhistoricism"; and Lanser, *The Sexuality of History*.
22. Most memorably, in Edelman, *No Future*.
23. Referencing Edelman, among others, Anna Kornbluh argues that the ideal of formlessness, which casts all form as "oppressive containment," denies the crucial fact that the human exists both in and because of collective forms, albeit ones that are ever-changing, and thereby also surrenders the opportunity to better read the work that these forms do. Kornbluh, *The Order of Forms*. Caroline Levine makes a similar argument, noting that "if we imagine that our only option is to critique, shatter, or resist [forms], we reinforce the idea that bounded wholes are always and necessarily dangerous and successful, on their own terms, at organizing experience" (Levine, *Forms*, 28–29).
24. Sue Lanser offers a compelling example, describing the "Sapphic" form of narration in eighteenth-century fiction. She persuasively describes the way that the dialogue form is adapted, in pornographic texts, into one that depicts same-sex desire through the narrative presentation of women speaking to women. She then reads this same mode of address in a series of eighteenth-century novels, demonstrating how such narration queers (or rather, outs) the content, illuminating implicit bonds between female characters. The queerness here is not a feature of the authors' biographies (indeed, she says that the narratives were not penned by women, let alone women with same-sex desires, but by men, for other men's pleasure): it stems from representations of sex in libertine novels, which Lanser argues "finds a muted counterpart" in less sexually explicit texts, forming a "line of continuity" between the two. Lanser, "Sapphic Dialogues," 193. She expands on this argument in Lanser, *The Sexuality of History*.
25. Although some critics have remarked upon an oddity in the structure of *Dorian Gray*, they have described it differently. Neil Hultgren, following Wilde's own contention that the novel is "far too crowded with sensational incident," writes that it has a "surfeit of plotting" (Hultgren, "Oscar Wilde's Poetic Injustice," 214, 215). In a similar vein, Valerie Rohy notes that "the last portion of the narrative provides a generous wadding of irrelevant scenes" (Rohy, "Strange Influence," 283).
26. Jed Esty, one of the few critics to notice this aspect of Wilde's novel, writes that the "combination of lyrical description, epigrammatic discourse, and dramatic dialogue that we find in the opening chapter is characteristic of the entire text—one reason it can be understood as a kind of anti-novel," and points out that "the text's Orientalist tropes cluster and thicken just at the points where Wilde needs to break with the realist mode of presentation or the linear demands of traditional plotting" (Esty, *Unseasonable Youth*, 105).
27. It should be noted that the opening conversation is a later addition to the text. The novel was initially published without it, in 1846, in the journal *Przegląd Naukowy*.

Notes to Pages 84–85   151

The conversation was added in 1861, along with other changes, when the work was reissued as a book. There was another text, *Książka pamiątek* (*Book of Memories*) appended as well, as a kind of sequel. As Grażyna Borkowska notes, the link to this third text is "looser": the opening dialogue is more firmly anchored to the rest of the text through interwoven interjections. Elżbieta Zarych sees the opening as "istotna" ("essential") to the text, and notes that critics disagree whether it was written soon after the original, or much later. Zarych, "Posłowie," 131. I treat *Poganka* as a single novel (that includes the opening conversation), separate from the sequel—a choice arguably validated by its publication in English translation in this form.

28. Brooks, *Reading for the Plot*, 37, 13, 24–25.
29. Brooks, *Reading for the Plot*, 37.
30. Bersani, *A Future for Astyanax*, 65.
31. Bersani, *A Future for Astyanax*, 66.
32. The use of the term "embarrassing" here draws from Elizabeth Freeman, who grapples with a similar dilemma in her reflections on queer form, writing: "While queer antiformalism appeals to me on an intellectual level, I find myself emotionally compelled by the not-quite-queer-enough longing for form that turns us backward to prior moments, forward to embarrassing utopias, sideways to forms of being and belonging that seem, on the face of it, completely banal" (Freeman, *Time Binds*, xiii). Though Freeman calls the longing for form "not-quite-queer-enough," her project ultimately reclaims a view of such formal play as queer, which also reminds us that there is no single queer version of creating, or destroying, form.
33. See, for instance, Cohen, "Writing Gone Wilde."
34. John Paul Riquelme points out, writing about *Dorian Gray*, that "the book we read . . . is also a *Picture*." But of course, as I discuss, it also isn't. Riquelme, "Walter Pater, Dark Enlightenment."
35. Although he focused specifically on painting versus poetry. The question of the difference between poetry and prose is itself a rich one, of course, but I would argue that novelistic fiction aspires, at least, to straddle the divide. Lessing makes the distinction thus, for instance: "The prose writer is satisfied with being intelligible, and making his representations plain and clear. But this is not enough for the poet. He desires to present us with images so vivid, that we fancy we have the things themselves before us, and cease for a moment to be conscious of his words, the instruments with which he effects his purpose" (101) ("Der Poet will nicht bloß verständlich werden, seine Vorstellungen sollen nicht bloß klar und deutlich sein; hiermit begnügt sich der Prosaist. Sondern er will die Ideen, die er in uns erwecket, so lebhaft machen, daß wir in der Geschwindigkeit die wahren sinnlichen Eindrücke ihrer Gegenstände zu empfinden glauben, und in diesem Augenblicke der Täuschung uns der Mittel, die er dazu anwendet, seiner Worte, bewußt zu sein aufhören") (101). This account is strongly reminiscent of Barthes's discussion of realism in "The Rustle of Language," or Jose Ortega y Gasset's account, in "The Dehumanization of Art," of art as window, a description that he clearly applied to fiction as well as visual art.
36. Lessing, *Laocoön*, 110. "Doch, so wie zwei billige freundschaftliche Nachbarn zwar nicht verstatten, daß sich einer in des andern innerstem Reiche ungeziemende Freiheiten herausnehme, wohl aber auf den äußersten Grenzen eine wechselseitige Nachsicht herrschen lassen, welche die kleinen Eingriffe, die der eine in des andern

Gerechtsame in der Geschwindigkeit sich durch seine Umstände zu tun genötiget siehet, friedlich von beiden Teilen kompensieret: so auch die Malerei und Poesie" (Lessing, *Laocoön*, 105). Further quotations in the text will be cited with page numbers in parentheses. When both the German and the English are quoted, both page numbers will be cited.

37. *Laocoön*, 102; "zählt er uns merklich langsam nach und nach zu" (99).

38. *Laocoön*, 102–103; "Welche Mühe, welche Anstrengung kostet es, ihre Eindrücke alle in eben der Ordnung so lebhaft zu erneuern, sie nur mit einer mäßigen Geschwindigkeit auf einmal zu überdenken, um zu einem etwanigen Begriffe des Ganzen zu gelangen!" (99). For an interesting text that takes up this question of how we process what is before our eyes as we read, see Mendelsund, *What We See*.

39. *Laocoön*, 102: "Dem Auge bleiben die betrachten Teile beständig gegenwärtig" (99).

40. In an intriguing piece called "Notes on Form in Art," George Eliot suggests that Form is "the relations of multiplex interdependent parts to a whole which is itself in the most varied & therefore the fullest relations to other wholes." This, she says, is the only definition of Form that would be applicable to art overall (she discusses sculpture, painting, and descriptive poetry). See Eliot, "Notes on Form in Art," 433.

41. Though there is, it seems, widespread consensus that queerness is bound up in representations of time, as Paul Saint-Amour and Stephanie Insley Hershinow have both pointed out, the specific claims of what queer time means can be diametrically opposite. Saint-Amour, "The Literary Present," 367; Saint-Amour, *Tense Future*, 30; Hershinow, "The Incest Plot." For further discussion of "queer time," see also Dinshaw, et al., "Theorizing Queer Temporalities."

42. W. J. T. Mitchell notes some objections to this claim, and the rejoinders to it: although there is a temporal interval involved in looking at an object, it is not determined or controlled by the object: the viewer is always aware that she or he is the one moving or scanning, while the object remains static. Mitchell, *Iconology*, 100.

43. Kornbluh, "We Have Never Been Critical," 401.

44. Brooks, *Reading for the Plot*, 20.

45. Ginsburg, *Portrait Stories*, 6.

46. Some would argue that a painting is instead suspended time. So, for instance, Ruth Yeazell notes that George Eliot's shift to the present tense "intensifies the impression that the story is being suspended for a picture." Yeazell, *Art of the Everyday*, 103.

47. It also suggests a narrator who is a part of the same social milieu, a notable difference from the partly omniscient observer who relates the rest of the story.

48. Hershinow, *Born Yesterday*.

49. Levine, *Serious Pleasures*, 197.

50. Levine, *Serious Pleasures*, 197.

51. Levine, *Serious Pleasures*, 195.

52. Jeff Nunokawa also argues that the text is boring, in a wonderful reading of its representation and embodiment of ennui (as the end of desire), but he does not single out this scene as particularly dull, as I do. Nunokawa, *Tame Passions of Wilde*, 71–89.

53. Levine, *Serious Pleasures*, 198.

54. Żmichowska, *Poganka*, 28; Żmichowska, *The Heathen*, 31.

55. Żmichowska, *Poganka*, 62; Żmichowska, *The Heathen*, 75.

56. Descartes, *Meditations on First Philosophy*, 15.

57. Burke, *A Philosophical Enquiry*, 195, 197.

58. Amanda Anderson offers a different view, arguing that the epigram is actually the form that best serves a program of ethical detachment for Wilde. See Anderson, *The Powers of Distance*.

59. We could say that their pursuit of beauty fails because they do not recognize the necessary link between the beautiful and the good, but I would argue that both texts strongly suggest that beauty is not, in fact, inherently moral.

60. Christopher Craft's wonderful reading of *Dorian Gray* arrives at a similar conclusion, albeit by a somewhat different path, arguing that the novel "point-by-point cites and perverts the idealizing eroto-cognitive itinerary established by Plato" (Craft, "Come See About Me," 117).

Chapter 4 · Impossibly Free

1. Jonathan Ullyot offers a fascinating reading of *Molloy* in relation to the Grail quest. See Ullyot, *The Medieval Presence*.

2. He also claims authorship of some of Beckett's other novels.

3. Focusing on Gerhard Mayer as the critic who developed the concept of the anti-Bildungsroman, Todd Kontje describes the problem with this idea: "The concept enables critics to signal that a particular novel participates in a recognized literary tradition and at the same time to disassociate the text from the conservative ideology associated with the genre's history. Mayer's essay also illustrates one of the main shortcomings of this approach: in developing the notion of a socially critical Antibildungsroman he oversimplifies the Bildungsroman" (Kontje, *The German Bildungsroman*, 65).

4. Such an argument can be found in David Lloyd's *Anomalous States*, or in the work of Declan Kiberd or Terry Eagleton, for example. A more recent example can be found in Patrick Bixby's *Samuel Beckett and the Postcolonial Novel*.

5. For more on the issue of translation in these works, and some of the differences between the two version, see Hill, *Beckett's Fiction in Different Words*, especially chapter 3, "The Trilogy Translated," 40–58.

6. Deleuze and Guattari, *Kafka*, 18.

7. Kronfeld, *On the Margins of Modernism*, 8.

8. Deleuze and Guattari, *Kafka*, 16.

9. Bartosz Lutostański, in his own comparative study of the two authors, similarly notes the lack of attention paid to Gombrowicz. Lutostański likewise focuses on Beckett's Trilogy in his comparison, but does not discuss *Ferdydurke*, instead pairing Beckett's early novels with Gombrowicz's *Trans-atlantyk*, *Kosmos*, and *Pornografia*. Lutostański, *Gombrowicz-Beckett Beckett-Gombrowicz*.

10. Kundera, *The Curtain*, 33–35.

11. Although I make reference to interpretations that draw on sociohistorical aspects of the time, as is the case throughout this book, I do not focus on this dimension. Though there are certainly similarities between the contexts in which the two authors were creating their works—most notably, the newly attained nationhood of both Poland and Ireland—there is also a crucial difference: Gombrowicz's text was written right before the Second World War, and Beckett's after. For a reading of Beckett's Trilogy in a post-Holocaust context, see Anderton, *Beckett's Creatures*.

12. Of course, some would disagree: Lutostański notes the many critics who argue that Beckett is an "antinovelist." Lutostański, *Gombrowicz-Beckett Beckett-Gombrowicz*, 16.
13. Moretti, *The Way of the World*, 16.
14. Moretti, *The Way of the World*, 9.
15. Moretti, *The Way of the World*, 16.
16. "It is not enough that the social order is 'legal'; it must also appear symbolically legitimate. . . . Thus, it is not sufficient for modern bourgeois society simply to subdue the drives that oppose the standards of 'normality.' It is also necessary that, as a 'free individual,' not as a fearful subject but as a convinced citizen, one perceives the social norms as one's own. One must internalize them and fuse external compulsion and internal impulses into a new unity until the former is no longer distinguishable from the latter. This fusion is what we usually call 'consent' or 'legitimation'" (Moretti, *The Way of the World*, 16).
17. Moretti, *The Way of the World*, 7. Moretti contrasts, by way of example, the novel of marriage with unfinished works, or texts whose endings are arbitrary or infinitely deferred. He notes that these two principles are present in most literary works, but are weighted differently, and are, in fact, inversely proportional.
18. Castle, *Reading the Modernist Bildungsroman*, 1.
19. Castle, *Reading the Modernist Bildungsroman*, 2.
20. Sheehan, *Modernism, Narrative, and Humanism*, 5–6.
21. Castle would, I think, agree. While he does not discuss Gombrowicz (his focus is on English and Irish authors), he writes that Beckett departs so far from convention as to no longer belong to the category: "Like the sonnet, the Bildungsroman is tremendously elastic, its conventions so few and relatively simple that resistance to them beyond a certain point is tantamount to putting them aside altogether. Where this does in fact happen, as in the novels of Samuel Beckett, one can still discern the rudiments of the form—a biographical narrative, problems of socialization, the influence of mentors and 'instrumental' women, the problem of vocation—even when such rudiments are pared down to their essence, then to their absence" (Castle, *Reading the Modernist Bildungsroman*, 4).
22. Bixby, *Samuel Beckett*; Starosta, *Form and Instability*.
23. "Wäre aber auch eine Sprache denkbar, in der Einer seine inneren Erlebnisse— seine Gefühle, Stimmungen, etc.—für den eigenen Gebrauch aufschreiben, oder aussprechen könnte?—Können wir denn das in unserer gewöhnlichen Sprache nicht tun?—Aber so meine ich's nicht. Die Wörter dieser Sprache sollen sich auf das beziehen, wovon nur der Sprechende wissen kann; auf seine unmittelbaren, privaten, Empfindungen. Ein Anderer kann diese Sprache also nicht verstehen" (Wittgenstein, *Philosophische Untersuchungen*, 289). Wittgenstein, *Philosophical Investigations*, 88e-89e.
24. It is worth noting here that despite the descriptions of these works as postmodern, both authors clearly do believe that such a private experience is possible. Namely, we have not yet reached a realm where the self is entirely constructed by language.
25. As Anita Starosta points out, however, the distinction between the two is not always clear, and Gombrowicz himself was not consistent in capitalizing it, probably intentionally. Starosta, *Form and Instability*, 101, n 2.
26. Gombrowicz, *Ferdydurke* (Kraków), 79; *Ferdydurke* (New Haven), 80. Further

quotations from *Ferdydurke* will be cited in the text with page numbers in parentheses. If both the Polish edition and the English translation are cited, both page numbers will appear.

27. Lyotard, *The Postmodern Condition*, 16.

28. There is, unfortunately, no good translation for this term. In her English translation of the text, Danuta Borchardt chooses (rightly, I think) to leave it in the original, but she clarifies in her introductory note that it "means the buttocks, behind, bum, tush, rump, but not one of these (nor any others that I considered) adequately conveys adequately the sense in which Gombrowicz uses 'pupa' in the text" (xii). Suffice to say that it refers to the posterior, but in a particularly cutesy, infantile way.

29. Jerzy Jarzębski makes a similar argument, cited in Głowiński, *"Ferdydurke" Witolda Gombrowicza*, 52.

30. Markowski, *Czarny Nurt*, 159. Translation my own.

31. Gombrowicz, *Ferdydurke* (Kraków), 44; *Ferdydurke* (New Haven), 42.

32. I use the word "system" intentionally here: as I've mentioned above, Gombrowicz is intentionally linking the problem of Form with the institution of the school. The individual is indoctrinated into Form through educational institutions, but the teachers are themselves personally dependent on the system for their livelihood as well, as can be seen when the professor pleads with Gałkiewicz to desist by pleading for the sake of his family: "Gałkiewicz, ja mam żone i dziecko! Niech Gałkiewicz przynajmniej nad czieckiem się ulituje!" (44) ("Listen, Gałkiewicz, I have a wife and child! Have pity on the child at least!") (43).

33. This moment can also be read in relation to the text's subversive play with sexuality, a protest not only against the institution of marriage, but also heteronormativity. This is reinforced by the way Gombrowicz deconstructs society's fetishization of young women in the Zuta episode, and bolstered by what is arguably an overall negative portrayal of women in the text, as symbols of conventional traditions of home and family, but also as rather terrifying creatures whose ceaseless demands can never be satisfied. There are many scenes in the novel that are laced with homoeroticism, though they are generally accompanied with brutality, complicating any "queer" readings of the text. For a reading of Gombrowicz's work in terms of queer theory that has clear relevance to *Ferdydurke*, see Sołtysik, "Witold Gombrowicz's Struggle."

34. "Despite this deliberate conflagration, it is nearly impossible for readers not to distinguish different levels in the unnamable's discursive self-projections" (Schwab, *Subjects without Selves*, 134).

35. Rubin Rabinovitz tracks the repetition of various words and faces in the Trilogy, which he points out can be organized into antithetical pairs: I/not I, voice/silence, beginning/end, come/go, will be/will never be. Rabinovitz, *Innovation in Samuel Beckett's Fiction*, 23–30.

36. Sheehan, *Modernism, Narrative, and Humanism*, 173.

37. For example, Paul Davies writes that "another sense of value is always reaching into the discourse, from a level one degree higher than the apparent one." David Hesla, writing on the contradiction at the heart of the second half of Molloy, says that "the novel's value (if that is the right word) is to be discerned in some other dimension than that of its capacity for 'expressing' a world or the author's self." Davies, *The Ideal Real*, 80; Hesla, *The Shape of Chaos*, 102.

38. "Eine absolute Synthesis absoluter Antithesen, der stete sich selbst erzeugende Wechsel zwei streitender Gedanken" (Schlegel, *Athenäums-Fragmente*, 39).

39. Ricoeur, "The Metaphorical Process," 141.

40. Wittgenstein seems to anticipate this in some ways when he writes: "Ein Kind hat sich verletzt, es schreit; und nun sprechen ihm die Erwachsenen zu und bringen ihm Ausrufe und später Sätze bei. Sie lehren das Kind ein neues Schmerzbenehmen. 'So sagst du also, daß das Wort "Schmerz" eigentlich das Schreien bedeute?' - Im Gegenteil; der Wortausdruck des Schmerzes ersetzt das Schreien und beschreibt es nicht" (244) ("A child has hurt himself and he cries; and then adults talk to him and teach him exclamations, and, later, sentences. They teach the child new pain behaviour. 'So are you saying that the word "pain" really means "crying?"—On the contrary: the verbal expression of pain replaces crying and does not describe it') (89e). The difference between expression and description is, I suggest, related to the difference between referential and poetic language."

41. Ricoeur, "The Metaphorical Process," 152–153, italics author's.

42. Ricoeur, "The Metaphorical Process," 152.

43. Metaphor, much like irony, is a slippery term, one whose definitions have been contested for centuries. For a succinct account of these debates, see *The Princeton Handbook of Poetic Terms*. In what follows, I strive to be as specific as possible in my explanation of my particular understanding of the term, which falls under the "interaction" (rather than "substitution") view.

44. Corngold, "Kafka's *Die Verwandlung*," 97.

45. Corngold, "Kafka's *Die Verwandlung*," 97–98.

46. "Imagination does not merely schematize the predictive assimilation between terms by its synthetic insight into similarities nor does it merely picture the sense thanks to the display of images aroused and controlled by the cognitive process. Rather, it contributes concretely to the epoché of ordinary reference and to the projection of new possibilities of redescribing the world" (Ricoeur, "The Metaphorical Process," 152).

47. Cited in Ricks, *Beckett's Dying Words*, 189.

48. Beckett, *Molloy*, 116.

49. Cited in Ricks, *Beckett's Dying Words*, 119.

50. Gabriele Schwab describes it similarly: "By constantly contradicting his own utterances and self-projections, he evokes the fleeting notion of a subject at the vanishing point. The medium of fiction grants him a space for probing epistemologies and ontologies that would be unavailable to either an empirical or a philosophical subject" (Schwab, *Subjects without Selves*, 133).

51. Lloyd Bishop lists six sources of romantic irony in *Molloy*: ambivalent deflation of hero, deflation of narrator, authorial self-parody and self-reflexive irony, self-destruction of narrative, recognition of paradoxical co-existence of contraries, and the "ironic non-dit," "an intangible ironic spirit hovering over the entire work." He does not, however, seem to take into account the fact that the novel is ostensibly penned by Unnamable, and the implications thereof. See Bishop, *Romantic Irony*, 185–203.

52. Beckett, *Molloy*, 84. Further quotations will be cited in the text with page numbers in parentheses.

53. Edgeworth, *Irish Bulls*, 89.

54. See Ricks, *Beckett's Dying Words*, chapter 4.

55. Ewa Płonowska Ziarek sees this in terms of Cavell's writing on skepticism, arguing that a view of language as based on intersubjective understanding serves as an alternative to the traditional subject-object form of knowledge. Płonowska, *The Rhetoric of Failure*, 26.

56. Lyotard, in his writing on language games, says that they are the basis of collective living, "the minimum relation required for society to exist" (Lyotard, *The Postmodern Condition*, 15).

57. Brooks, *Reading for the Plot*, 91.

58. Paul Sheehan describes matters similarly, writing that "events are joined in series, by a process of mutual implication: one event implies the next, which is (retrospectively) implied by all that has gone before. So it could be said that events in series owe their existence to each other" (Sheehan, *Modernism, Narrative, and Humanism*, 9).

59. This is what distinguishes this conceptual labor from that of the novels described in the previous chapter, which instead collect very different moments and insist that they *do* belong together.

60. Admittedly, one finds many readers of the book who have completely forgotten them or simply skipped them while reading.

61. Michael Godddard offers a reading similar to my own, but he uses theoretical armature derived from Deleuze and Guattari, particularly the notion of assemblage and the "body without organs." Goddard, *Gombrowicz*.

62. Bakhtin, *The Dialogic Imagination*.

63. Bishop, *Romantic Irony*, 205.

64. Bishop, *Romantic Irony*, 205.

65. Sheehan, *Modernism, Narrative, and Humanism*, 184.

66. Unless one enjoys that sort of thing, of course, and undoubtedly there are some people who do. But it is undeniably alienating to a vast majority of readers.

67. One sees a similar acknowledgment at the conclusion of Dostoevsky's *Notes from the Underground*, where an editorial intrusion summarily ends the text, saying that "the 'notes' of this paradoxicalist do not end here. He could not help himself and went on. But it also seems to us that this may be a good place to stop." Indeed, Dostoevsky's Underground Man seems like an important predecessor to both Józio and Unnamable. Dostoevsky, *Notes from the Underground*, 130.

68. Sheehan, *Modernism, Narrative, and Humanism*, 153–155.

69. Booth, *A Rhetoric of Irony*, 262.

70. Tomasz Bocheński notes that in such cases the laughter inspired is dangerously close to that of the torturer. See Bocheński, *Czarny Humor*, 14.

71. Booth, *A Rhetoric of Irony*, 264.

72. One thinks here of a wry comment made by Pat Sheeran and Nina Witoszek; "Characters . . . although inhabiting an inner circle of darkness and despair, may well be full of 'warm humanity'—that last saving grace of the Irish, Blacks and Eastern Europeans" (Sheeran and Witoszek, *Talking to the Dead*, 87–88).

Conclusion · Toward a "Weak" Theory of the Novel

1. For a discussion of some of the complexities of postcolonial writers on the international market specifically, see Brouillette, *Postcolonial Writers*.

2. Discussed already in the introduction, Nicholas Paige's work is especially salient

here. Franco Moretti also discusses this in *Distant Reading*. Ted Underwood's work examines how the resources offered by digital humanities shape our sense of these issues: see Underwood, *Distant Horizons*.

3. A problem that is invariably exacerbated with time, as more and more works are published each year. Emily Temple offers an interesting window into the relationship between popularity and canonical status, listing the top ten bestselling books for every year from 1918 to 2018, many of which are largely forgotten today. Temple, "Biggest Fiction Bestsellers."

4. Black, "Quixotic Realism." Eric Hayot also discusses some of the problems with such realist-oriented criticism; see Hayot, *On Literary Worlds*, 125–128.

5. A point also made by Scott Black; see Black, *Without the Novel*, 8.

6. Ma, *The Age of Silver*, 15–28.

7. Ma, *The Age of Silver*, 20.

8. Ma, *The Age of Silver*, 28.

9. I base this on Kengi Hamada's English translation. I am not well versed in scholarship on the text or Japanese literature of this period, so I would not insist too strongly on this reading of the novel, but I hope that the example is sufficient to the point nonetheless.

10. Ma, *The Age of Silver*, 172.

11. Ma, *The Age of Silver*, 11–12.

12. A comparative reading of Defoe and Saikaku that focuses more on narrative technique can be found in Sonnenberg, *At the Roots*.

13. Friedman, *Planetary Modernisms*, 33, 52.

14. Bruce Robbins suggests that this framework depoliticizes the past, leaving out historical violence. He also notes that an account of multiple modernities continues to cast other moments as non-modern, which will "transmit exactly the same othering or denigrating message to its 'before' that Friedman finds unacceptable when transmitted by 'western' modernity" (Robbins, Review of *Planetary Modernisms*, 747).

15. For an excellent discussion of periodization and its function in literary studies, see Underwood, *Why Literary Periods Mattered*.

16. Orlemanski, "Who Has Fiction," 151–153. They are thus analogous to the efforts to rehabilitate nineteenth-century Irish fiction by seeing it as a forerunner of modernism that I describe in the introduction—the structure of the theoretical framework remains intact, even as the particulars are adjusted.

17. Orlemanski, "Who Has Fiction?" 158.

18. Hayot, *On Literary Worlds*, 24.

19. Hayot, *On Literary Worlds*, 6.

20. "A task: to come up with a better theory of the world, and of the relationship between the world and literature. Not to produce a mediating relay between world literature and world-systems, but to see if a third analysis, focusing on the ontology of composed works, can bring 'world' differently into the scene. And to see, then, if such a theory makes any difference to our understanding of world literature or the history of worldedness as an aesthetic and cultural phenomenon—as a symptom and as a compass for the history, in other words, of totality as a function of the human imagination" (Hayot, *On Literary Worlds*, 41).

21. Hayot, *On Literary Worlds*, 44–45.

22. As I discuss in the second chapter, Debjani Ganguly and Pheng Cheah also take up this question of how literary worlding can teach us new ways of theorizing worldedness.

23. Hayot, *On Literary Worlds*, 127. Though aware of this risk, he chooses the names intentionally, so as "by *détournement* to both note their proximity to, and dislocation of, existing literary historical narratives" (127).

24. Black, *Without the Novel*, 10.

25. Though it should be noted that elsewhere Bakhtin, too, emphasizes the kind of dialectic relationship with modernity that is so central to novel theory. For a detailed examination of this current in his work, see Tihanov, *The Master and the Slave*.

26. Saint-Amour, "Weak Theory, Weak Modernism."

Adams, Percy. *Travelers and Travel Liars 1660–1800*. Berkeley: University of California Press, 1962.
Allan, Michael. *In the Shadow of World Literature: Sites of Reading in Colonial Egypt*. Princeton, NJ: Princeton University Press, 2016.
Anderson, Amanda. *The Powers of Distance: Cosmopolitanism and the Cultivation of Detachment*. Princeton, NJ: Princeton University Press, 2001.
Anderson, Benedict. *Imagined Communities: Reflections on the Origin and Spread of Nationalism*. New York: Verso, 1983.
Anderton, Joseph. *Beckett's Creatures: Art of Failure after the Holocaust*. London: Bloomsbury, 2016.
Apter, Emily. *The Translation Zone: A New Comparative Literature*. Princeton, NJ: Princeton University Press, 2011.
Aravamudan, Srinivas. *Enlightenment Orientalism: Resisting the Rise of the Novel*. Durham, NC: Duke University Press, 2012.
Armstrong, Nancy. *How Novels Think: The Limits of British Individualism from 1719–1900*. New York: Columbia University Press, 2006.
Attar, Samir. *The Vital Roots of European Enlightenment: Ibn Tufayl's Influence on Modern Western Thought*. Lanham, MD: Lexington Books, 2007.
Attridge, Derek, and Marjorie Howes, eds. *Semicolonial Joyce*. Cambridge: Cambridge University Press, 2002.
Auerbach, Erich. *Mimesis: The Representation of Reality in Western Literature*. Princeton, NJ: Princeton University Press, 1953.
Bakhtin, Mikhail. *The Dialogic Imagination*. Translated by Caryl Emerson and Michael Holquist. Austin: University of Texas Press, 1981.
Baldick, Chris. "Introduction," *Melmoth the Wanderer*. Oxford: Oxford University Press, 1989.
Banfield, Ann. *Unspeakable Sentences*. Abingdon-on-Thames: Routledge, 1982.
Barthes, Roland. *The Rustle of Language*. New York: Hill and Wang, 1986.
Bartoszyńska, Katarzyna. "From Fantastic to Familiar: Jan Potocki's *Manuscript Found in Saragossa*." *Nineteenth-Century Contexts* 37, no. 4 (2015): 283–300.
———. "Persuasive Ironies: Utopian Readings of Swift and Krasicki." *Comparative Literature Studies* 50, no. 4 (2013).
Bataille, Georges. *Visions of Excess: Selected Writings, 1927–1939*. Translated by Allan

Stoekl with Carl Lovitt and Donald Leslie Jr. Edited and with an introduction by Allan Stoekl. Minneapolis: University of Minnesota Press, 1985.

Beckett, Samuel. *Three Novels: Molloy, Malone Dies, The Unnamable*. New York: Grove Press, 1955, 1956, 1958.

Beecroft, Alexander. *An Ecology of World Literature: From Antiquity to the Present Day*. New York: Verso, 2015.

Berns, Ute. "The Romantic Crisis of Expression: Maturin's Melmoth the Wanderer and Beyond." In *A History of English Laughter: Laughter from Beowulf to Beckett and Beyond*, edited by Manfred Pfister, 83–98. Amsterdam: Rodopi, 2002.

Bersani, Leo. *A Future for Astyanax: Character and Desire in Literature*. New York: Columbia University Press, 1976.

Bhabha, Homi K. *The Location of Culture*. Abingdon-on-Thames: Routledge, 1994.

Białas, Zbigniew. "*Fabula Interrupta*: On Taking (Textual) Liberties." *Comparative Criticism* 24 (2002): 111–120.

Bishop, Lloyd. *Romantic Irony in French Literature from Diderot to Beckett*. Nashville, TN: Vanderbilt University Press, 1989.

Bixby, Patrick. *Samuel Beckett and the Postcolonial Novel*. Cambridge: Cambridge University Press, 2009.

Black, Scott. "Quixotic Realism and the Romance of the Novel." *Novel: A Forum on Fiction* 42, no. 2, Theories of the Novel's Rise Now, Part I (Summer 2009): 239–244.

———. *Without the Novel: Romance and the History of Prose Fiction*. Charlottesville: University of Virginia Press: 2019.

Bocheński, Tomasz. *Czarny Humor w Twórczości Witkacego, Gombrowicza, Schulza*. Kraków: Universitas: 2005.

Bogel, Fredric V. *The Difference Satire Makes: Rhetoric and Reading from Jonson to Byron*. Ithaca, NY: Cornell University Press, 2001.

Booth, Wayne. "Metaphor as Rhetoric: The Problem of Evaluation." In *On Metaphor*, edited by Sheldon Sacks, 47–70. Chicago: University of Chicago Press, 1979.

———. *A Rhetoric of Irony*. Chicago: University of Chicago Press, 1974.

Borkowska, Grażyna. *Alienated Women*. Budapest: Central European University Press, 2001.

Borkowska, Grażyna, and Monika Rudaś-Grodzka. *Między wschodem a zachodem: Europa Mickiewicza i innych: o relacjach literatury polskiej z kulturami ościennymi*. Wrocław: Zakład Narodowy im. Ossolińskich: 2007.

Bowen, Elizabeth. *The Last September*. New York: Penguin, 2000.

Boyle, Frank. *Swift as Nemesis: Modernity and its Satirist*. Palo Alto, CA: Stanford University Press, 2000.

Boym, Svetlana. *The Future of Nostalgia*. New York: Basic Books, 2001.

Broich, Ulrich. *The Eighteenth-Century Mock-Heroic Poem*. Translated by David Henry Wilson. Cambridge: Cambridge University Press, 1990.

Brooks, Peter. *Reading for the Plot: Design and Intention in Narrative*. Cambridge, MA: Harvard University Press, 1992.

———. *Realist Vision*. New Haven, CT: Yale University Press, 2005.

Brouillette, Sarah. *Postcolonial Writers in the Global Literary Marketplace*. London: Palgrave Macmillan, 2007.

Buck-Morss, Susan. *Hegel, Haiti, and Universal History*. Pittsburgh, PA: University of Pittsburgh Press, 2009.

Burke, Edmund. *A Philosophical Enquiry into the Origins of Our Ideas of the Sublime and the Beautiful*. New York: Penguin, 1995.

Canny, Nicholas. "Early Modern Ireland c.1500–1700," in *The Oxford History of Ireland*, edited by R. F. Foster, 88–133. Oxford: Oxford University Press, 1989.

Casanova, Giacomo. *History of My Life*. Vols. 1–12. Translated by William R. Trask. Baltimore: Johns Hopkins University Press, 1997.

Casanova, Pascale. *The World Republic of Letters*. Translated by M. B. DeBevoise. Cambridge, MA: Harvard University Press, 2004.

Cascardi, Anthony. "*Don Quixote* and the Invention of the Novel." In *The Cambridge Companion to Cervantes*, edited by Anthony Cascardi, 58–79. Cambridge: Cambridge University Press, 2002.

Castle, Gregory. *Reading the Modernist Bildungsroman*. Gainesville: University Press of Florida, 2006.

Cavanagh, Claire. "Postcolonial Poland." *Common Knowledge* 10, no. 1 (Winter 2004): 82–92.

Chakrabarty, Dipesh. *Provincializing Europe: Postcolonial Thought and Historical Difference*. Princeton, NJ: Princeton University Press, 2000.

Chari, Sharad, and Katherine Verdery. "Thinking between the Posts: Postcolonialism, Postsocialism, and Ethnography after the Cold War." *Comparative Studies in Society and History* 51, no. 1 (2009): 6–34.

Cheah, Pheng. *What Is a World? On Postcolonial Literature as World Literature*. Durham, NC: Duke University Press, 2016.

———. "World against Globe: Toward a Normative Conception of World Literature." *New Literary History* 45, no. 3 (Summer 2014): 303–329.

Chuh, Kandice. *The Difference Aesthetics Makes: On the Humanities "After Man."* Durham, NC: Duke University Press, 2019.

Citton, Yves. "Potocki and the Spectre of the Postmodern." *Comparative Criticism* 24 (2002): 141–165.

Cleary, Joe. "Misplaced Ideas? Locating and Dislocating Ireland in Colonial and Postcolonial Studies." In *Marxism and Modernity and Postcolonial Studies*, edited by Crystal Bartolovich and Neil Lazarus, 101–124. Cambridge: Cambridge University Press, 2002.

———. *Outrageous Fortune: Culture and Capital in Modern Ireland*. Dublin: Field Day, 2007.

Clery, E. J. *The Rise of Supernatural Fiction, 1762–1800*. Cambridge: Cambridge University Press, 1995.

Clifford, James. "Gulliver's Fourth Voyage: 'Hard' and 'Soft' Schools of Interpretation." In *Quick Springs of Sense: Studies in the Eighteenth Century*, edited by Larry S. Champion. Athens: University of Georgia Press, 1974.

Cohen, Ed. "Writing Gone Wilde: Homoerotic Desire in the Closet of Representation." *PMLA* 102, no. 2 (October 1987): 801–813.

Cohen, Margaret. *The Sentimental Education of the Novel*. Princeton, NJ: Princeton University Press, 1999.

Cohen, William. *Sex Scandal: The Private Parts of Victorian Fiction*. Durham, NC: Duke University Press, 1996.
Colebrook, Claire. *Irony*. Abingdon-on-Thames: Routledge, 2004.
Conger, Syndy. *Matthew G. Lewis, Charles Robert Maturin and the Germans: An Interpretative Study of the Influence of German Literature on Two Gothic Novels*. Salzburg: Inst. f. Engl. Sprache u. Literatur, Univ. Salzburg, 1977.
Cooper, Davina. *Everyday Utopias: The Conceptual Life of Promising Spaces*. Durham, NC: Duke University Press, 2014.
Corngold, Stanley. "Kafka's *Die Verwandlung*: Metamorphosis of the Metaphor." *Mosaic* 3, no. 4 (Summer 1970): 91–106.
Cornwell, Neil. "European Gothic and Nineteenth-Century Russian Literature." In *European Gothic: A Spirited Exchange 1760–1960*, edited by Avril Horner, 104–127. Manchester: Manchester University Press, 2002.
———. "The European 'Nights' Tradition: Potocki and Odoevsky's *Russian Nights*." *Comparative Criticism* 24 (2002): 121–139.
Craft, Christopher. "Come See About Me: Enchantment of the Double in *The Picture of Dorian Gray*." *Representations* 91, no. 1 (Summer 2005): 109–136.
Cronin, Mike. *A History of Ireland*. Basingstoke: Palgrave Macmillan, 2001.
Da, Nan Z. *Intransitive Encounter: Sino-U.S. Literatures and the Limits of Exchange*. New York: Columbia University Press, 2018.
Danielewski, Mark. *House of Leaves*. New York: Pantheon, 2000.
David, Deirdre, ed. *Cambridge Companion to the Victorian Novel*. Cambridge: Cambridge University Press, 2006.
Davies, Norman. *Heart of Europe: The Past in Poland's Present*. Oxford: Oxford University Press, 2001.
Davies, Paul. *The Ideal Real: Beckett's Fiction and Imagination*. Teaneck, NJ: Fairleigh Dickinson University Press, 1994.
Deane, Seamus. *Foreign Affections: Essays on Edmund Burke*. Notre Dame, IN: Field Day Press, 2005.
———. *Strange Country: Modernity and Nationhood in Irish Writing since 1790*. Oxford: Clarendon Press, 1997.
Defoe, Daniel. *Robinson Crusoe*. Edited by Thomas Kaymer. Notes by James Kelly. Oxford: Oxford World Classics: 2009.
Deleuze, Gilles, and Félix Guattari. *Kafka: Toward a Minor Literature*. Translated by Dana Polan. Minneapolis: University of Minnesota Press, 1986.
———. *A Thousand Plateaus: Capitalism and Schizophrenia*. Translated by Dana Polan. Minneapolis: University of Minnesota Press, 1986.
Demata, Massimiliano. "Discovering Eastern Horrors: Beckford, Maturin, and the Discourse of Travel Literature." In *Empire and the Gothic: The Politics of Genre*, edited by Andrew Smith and William Hughes, 13–34. Basingstoke: Palgrave Macmillan, 2003.
Descartes, René. *Meditations on First Philosophy*. Translated by Donald A. Cress. Indianapolis, IN: Hackett, 1993.
Dimock, Wai-Chee. *Through Other Continents: American Literature across Deep Time*. Princeton, NJ: Princeton University Press, 2006.
Dinshaw, Carolyn, Lee Edelman, Roderick A. Ferguson, Carla Freccero, Elizabeth Freeman, Judith Halberstam, Annamarie Jagose, Christopher Nealon, and Nguyen Tan

Hoang. "Theorizing Queer Temporalities: A Roundtable Discussion." *GLQ: A Journal of Gay and Lesbian Studies* 13, no. 2 (January 2007): 177–195.
Doktór, Roman. "Komizm unaiwniony *Mikołaja Doświadczyńskiego przypadków*." *Ruch Literacki* 35, nos. 3–4 (1994): 219–232.
Doody, Margaret. *The True Story of the Novel*. New Brunswick, NJ: Rutgers University Press, 1997.
Dostoevsky, Fyodor. *Notes from the Underground*. Translated by Richard Pevear and Larissa Volokhonsky. London: Vintage Classics, 1993.
Douglas, Mary. *Purity and Danger: An Analysis of Concepts of Pollution and Taboo*. Abingdon-on-Thames: Routledge Classics, 2002.
Doyle, Laura. "At World's Edge: Post/Coloniality, Charles Maturin, and the Gothic Wanderer." *Nineteenth-Century Literature* 65, no. 4 (March 2011): 513–547.
Eagleton, Terry. *Crazy John and the Bishop, and Other Essays on Irish Culture*. Notre Dame, IN: University of Notre Dame Press in association with Field Day, 1998.
——. *Heathcliff and the Great Hunger*. New York: Verso, 1995.
——. "Nationalism, Irony and Commitment." In *Nationalism, Colonialism, and Literature*, by Terry Eagleton, Fredric Jameson, and Edward Said, with an Introduction by Seamus Deane, 23–40. Minneapolis: University of Minnesota Press in association with Field Day, 1990.
Eakin, Paul John. *Fictions in Autobiography: Studies in the Art of Self-Invention*. Princeton, NJ: Princeton University Press, 1985.
——. *How Our Lives Become Stories: Making Selves*. Ithaca, NY: Cornell University Press, 1999.
Earls, Brian. "'By Reason of Past History': Poland through Irish Eyes." *Dublin Review of Books* 8 (Winter 2008).
Edelman, Lee. *No Future: Queer Theory and the Death Drive*. Durham, NC: Duke University Press, 2004.
Edgeworth, Maria. *Castle Rackrent*. Oxford: Oxford University Press, 2009.
——. *An Essay on Irish Bulls*. Dublin: University College Dublin Press [1802] 2006.
Eliot, George. "Notes on Form in Art." In *Essays of George Eliot*, edited by Thomas Pinney, 431–436. London: Routledge, 1963.
Emerson, Caryl. "Answering for Central and Eastern Europe." In *Comparative Literature in the Age of Globalization*, edited by Haun Saussy, 203–211. Baltimore: Johns Hopkins University Press, 2004.
Enright, D. J. *The Alluring Problem: An Essay on Irony*. Oxford: Oxford University Press, 1986.
Esty, Jed. *Unseasonable Youth*. Oxford: Oxford University Press, 2012.
Ferris, Ina. *The Romantic National Tale and the Question of Ireland*. Cambridge: Cambridge University Press, 2002.
Fisk, Gloria. *Orhan Pamuk and the Good of World Literature*. New York: Columbia University Press, 2018.
Fitzpatrick, Kathleen, Alexander R. Galloway, and James F. English. "Franco Moretti's *Distant Reading*: A Symposium." *The Los Angeles Review of Books*, June 27, 2013, http://lareviewofbooks.org/essay/franco-morettis-distant-reading-a-symposium.
Foster, R. F. "Ascendancy and Union." In *The Oxford History of Ireland*, edited by R. F. Foster, 134–173. Oxford: Oxford University Press, 1989.

———. *Modern Ireland: 1600–1972*. London: Penguin, 1989.
Fraisse, Luc. *Potocki et l'imaginaire de la creation*. Paris: Presses Paris Sorbonne, 2006.
Freccero, Carla. *Queer/Early/Modern*. Durham, NC: Duke University Press, 2006.
Freedgood, Elaine. *Worlds Enough: The Invention of Realism in the Victorian Novel*. Princeton, NJ: Princeton University Press, 2019.
Freeman, Elizabeth. *Time Binds: Queer Temporalities, Queer Histories*. Durham, NC: Duke University Press, 2010.
Friedman, Susan Stanford. *Planetary Modernisms: Provocations on Modernity across Time*. New York: Columbia University Press, 2015.
Furst, Lilian R. *Fictions of Romantic Irony in European Narrative, 1760–1857*. New York: Macmillan, 1984.
Gallagher, Catherine. "Formalism and Time." In *Reading for Form*, edited by Susan J. Wolfson and Marshall Brown, 305–329. Seattle: University of Washington Press, 2006.
———. *Nobody's Story: The Vanishing Acts of Woman Writers in the Marketplace, 1670–1920*. Berkeley: University of California Press, 1994.
———. "Nobody's Story: The Vanishing Acts of Women Writers in the Marketplace, 1670–1920." *The American Historical Review* 101, no. 2 (1996): 484.
———. "The Rise of Fictionality." In *The Novel*, vol. 1, edited by Franco Moretti, 336–363. Princeton, NJ: Princeton University Press: 2007.
Gamer, Michael. *Romanticism and the Gothic*. Cambridge: Cambridge University Press, 2004.
Ganguly, Debjani. *This Thing Called the World: The Contemporary Novel as Global Form*. Durham, NC: Duke University Press, 2016.
———. "The Value of World Making in Global Literary Studies." In *The Values of Literary Studies: Critical Institutions, Scholarly Agendas*, edited by Rónán McDonald, 204–219. Cambridge: Cambridge University Press, 2015.
Garber, Frederick, ed. *Romantic Irony*. Budapest: Akademiai Kiado, 1988.
Gibbons, Luke. *Edmund Burke and Ireland: Aesthetics, Politics and the Colonial Sublime*. Cambridge: Cambridge University Press, 2003.
———. *Gaelic Gothic: Race, Colonization and Irish Culture*. Galway: Arlen House, 2004.
———. *Transformations in Irish Culture*. Notre Dame, IN: University of Notre Dame Press, 1996.
Ginsburg, Michal Peled. *Portrait Stories*. New York: Fordham University Press, 2015.
Giraldus Cambrensis (Gerald of Wales). *The History and Topography of Ireland*. London: Penguin, 2006.
Glick, Elise. *Materializing Queer Desire*. Albany: State University of New York Press, 2009.
Głowiński, Michał. *"Ferdydurke" Witolda Gombrowicza*. Warsaw: Wydawnictwa Szkolne i Pedagogiczne, 1991.
Goddard, Michael. *Gombrowicz, Polish Modernism, and the Subversion of Form*. West Lafayette, IN: Purdue University Press, 2010.
Gombrowicz, Witold. *Diary*. Translated by Lillian Vallee. Evanston, IL: Northwestern University Press, 1988.
———. *Ferdydurke*. Kraków: Wydawnictwo Literackie, 1997.
———. *Ferdydurke*. Translated by Danuta Borchardt, with a foreword by Susan Sontag. New Haven, CT: Yale Nota Bene, 2000.

———. *A Kind of Testament.* Edited by Dominique Roux. Translated by Alastair Hamilton, with an introduction by Maurice Nadeau. Philadelphia: Temple University Press, 1973.

———. *Trans-Atlantyk.* Kraków: Wydawnictwo Literackie, 2003.

Gosk, Hanna. *Opowieści „Skolonizowanego/kolonizatora": w kręgu studiów postzależnościowych nad literaturą polską XX i XXI wieku.* Kraków: Universitas, 2010.

Graciotti, Sante. "Utopia w Dziełach Ignacego Krasickiego." *Przegląd Humanistyczny* 16, no. 4 (1972): 1–16.

Guérin-Castell, Anna. "A Film Saved from the Scissors of Censorship." *Comparative Criticism* 24 (2002): 167–192.

Gurewitch, Morton. *The Comedy of Romantic Irony.* Lanham, MD: University Press of America, 2002.

Habib, Khalil M. "Ibn Tufayl's Critique of Cosmopolitanism in *Hayy Ibn Yaqzan.*" In *Cosmopolitanism in the Age of Globalization: Citizens without States,* edited by Khalil M. Habib and Lee Trepanier, 97–116. Lexington: University Press of Kentucky, 2011.

Halperin, David. *How to Do the History of Homosexuality.* Chicago: University of Chicago Press, 2002.

Harrington, John P., ed. *The English Traveller in Ireland: Accounts of Ireland and the Irish through Five Centuries.* Dublin: Wolfhound Press, 1991.

Haslam, Richard. "Gothic: A Rhetorical Hermeneutics Approach." *The Irish Journal of Gothic and Horror Studies* 1, no. 2 (2007).

———. "'Melmoth' (OW): Gothic Modes in *The Picture of Dorian Gray.*" *Irish Studies Review* 12, no. 3 (2004): 303–314.

Hassan, Nawal Muhammad. *Havy bin Yaqzan and Robinson Crusoe: A Study of An Early Arabic Impact on English Literature.* Republic of Iraq Ministry of Culture & Information (Studies Series). London: al-Rashid House for Publication, 1980.

Hawes, Clement. "Gulliver Effects." In *The Oxford Handbook of the Eighteenth-Century Novel,* edited by J. A. Downe, 187–204. Oxford: Oxford University Press, 2016.

Hayot, Eric. *On Literary Worlds.* Oxford: Oxford University Press, 2012.

Hershinow, Stephanie Insley. *Born Yesterday: Inexperience and the Early Novel.* Baltimore: Johns Hopkins University Press, 2019.

———. "The Incest Plot: Marriage, Closure, and the Novel's Endogamy." *Eighteenth-Century Theory and Interpretation* 61, no. 2. Forthcoming.

Hesla, David. *The Shape of Chaos: An Interpretation of the Art of Samuel Beckett.* Minneapolis: University of Minnesota Press, 1971.

Hill, Leslie. *Beckett's Fiction in Different Words.* Cambridge: Cambridge University Press, 1990.

Hoesel-Uhlig, Stefan. "Changing Fields: The Direction of Goethe's *Weltliteratur.*" In *Debating World Literature,* edited by Christopher Prendergast, 26–53. New York: Verso, 2004.

Hoffman, E. T. A. *The Life and Opinions of Tomcat Murr.* London: Penguin, 1999.

Hoffman, Eva. *Shtetl: The History of a Small Town and an Extinguished World.* London: Vintage, 1999.

Hultgren, Neil. "Oscar Wilde's Poetic Injustice in *The Picture of Dorian Gray.*" In *Wilde Discoveries: Traditions, Histories, Archives,* edited by Joseph Bristow, 212–230. Toronto: University of Toronto Press, 2013.

Hunt, Lynn. *Inventing Human Rights: A History*. New York: Norton, 2008.
Hunter, J. Paul. *Before Novels: The Cultural Contexts of Eighteenth-Century English Fiction*. New York: Norton, 1990.
———. "*Gulliver's Travels* and the Novel." In *The Genres of Gulliver's Travels*, edited by Frederick N. Smith, 56–74. Newark: University of Delaware Press, 1990.
Ibn Tufayl, Muhammad ibn'Abd al-Malik. *Ibn Tufayl's Hayy ibn Yaqzan: A Philosophical Tale*. Translated, with an introduction and notes, by Lenn Evan Goddman. Chicago: University of Chicago Press, 2009.
Ignatiev, Noel. *How the Irish Became White*. London: Routledge, 1995.
Immerwahr, Raymond. "The Subjectivity or Objectivity of Friedrich Schlegel's Poetic Irony." *Germanic Review* 26, no. 3 (October 1951).
Irwin, Robert. *The Arabian Nights: A Companion*. Westminster: Allen Lane, 1994.
Jackson, Jeanne-Marie. "Plurality in Question: Zimbabwe and the Agonistic African Novel." *Novel: A Forum on Fiction* 51, no. 2 (August 2018): 339–361.
Jacobson, Matthew Frye. *Special Sorrows: The Diasporic Imagination of Irish, Polish, and Jewish Immigrants in the United States*. Berkeley: University of California Press, 2002.
———. *Whiteness of a Different Color: European Immigrants and the Alchemy of Race*. Cambridge, MA: Harvard University Press, 1998.
Jameson, Fredric. "A Businessman in Love." In *The Novel*, vol. 2: *Forms and Themes*, edited by Franco Moretti, 436–446. Princeton, NJ: Princeton University Press, 2006.
———. *The Political Unconscious: Narrative as a Socially Symbolic Act*. Ithaca, NY: Cornell University Press, 1981.
———. "The Politics of Utopia." *New Left Review* 25 (January/February 2004): 35–54.
———. *A Singular Modernity: Essay on the Ontology of the Present*. New York: Verso, 2002.
Janion, Maria. *Niesamowita Słowiańszczyzna: Fantazmaty Literatury*. Kraków: Wydawnictwo Literackie, 2006.
Jelača, Dijana, and Danijela Lugarić. "Introduction: The 'Radiant Future' of Spatial and Temporal Dis/orientations." In *The Future of (Post)Socialism: Eastern European Perspectives*, edited by John Frederick Bailyn, Dijana Jelača, and Danijela Lugarić, 1–16. Albany: State University of New York Press, 2018.
Johnson, Samuel. *The Rambler* No. 4. Saturday, March 31, 1750. London: J. Payne and J. Bouquet. http://name.umdl.umich.edu/004772607.0001.001.
Joyce, James. *Portrait of the Artist as a Young Man*. London: Penguin, 2003.
Kareem, Sarah Tindal. *Eighteenth-Century Fiction and the Reinvention of Wonder*. Oxford: Oxford University Press, 2014.
Katz, Daniel. *Saying I No More: Subjectivity and Consciousness in the Prose of Samuel Beckett*. Evanston, IL: Northwestern University Press, 1999.
Kay, Magdalena. *In Gratitude for All the Gifts: Seamus Heaney and Eastern Europe*. Toronto: University of Toronto Press, 2012.
Keenleyside, Heather. *Animals and Other People: Living Forms and Literary Beings in the Long Eighteenth Century*. Philadelphia: University of Pennsylvania Press, 2016.
Kellman, Steven. *The Translingual Imagination*. Lincoln: University of Nebraska Press, 2000.
Kelly, Jim. *Charles Maturin: Authorship, Authenticity, and the Nation*. Dublin: Four Courts Press, 2011.

Kiberd, Declan. *Inventing Ireland: The Literature of the Modern Nation*. Cambridge, MA: Harvard University Press, 1995.
Kidd, David, and Emanuele Castano. "Different Stories: How Levels of Familiarity with Literary and Genre Fiction Relate to Mentalizing." *Psychology of Aesthetics, Creativity, and the Arts*, August 8, 2016.
———. "Reading Literary Fiction Improves Theory of Mind." *Science*, October 3, 2013.
Knowlson, James. *Damned to Fame: The Life of Samuel Beckett*. London: Bloomsbury, 1996.
Kołodziejczyk, Dorota, and Cristina Şandru. "Introduction: On Colonialism, Communism, and East-Central Europe: Some Reflections." *Journal of Postcolonial Writing* 48, no. 2 (2012): 113–116.
Kontje, Todd. *The German Bildungsroman: History of a National Genre*. Rochester: Camden House, 1993.
Kornbluh, Anna. *The Order of Forms*. Chicago: University of Chicago Press, 2020.
———. "We Have Never Been Critical." *Novel* 50, no. 3 (November 2017): 397–408.
Kostkiewiczowa, Teresa. *Klasycyzm Sentymentalizm Rokoko: szkice o prądach literackich polskiego Oświecenia*. Warszawa: Państwowe Wydawnictwo Naukowe, 1975.
Krasicki, Ignacy. *The Adventures of Mr. Nicholas Wisdom*. Translated by Thomas H. Hoisington. Introduction by Helena Goscilo. Evanston, IL: Northwestern University Press, 1992.
———. *Historia*. In *Pisma Wybrane*, vol. 4. Warszawa: Państwowy Instytut Wydawniczy, 1954.
———. *Mikołaja Doświadczyńskiego przypadki*. Wrocław: Wydawnictwo Siedmioróg, 1998.
Krasowska, Ewa. "Po Zaborach i po PRL-u: post-zależnościowe niewspółmierności." In *Kultura po przejściach, osoby z przeszłością. Polski dyskurs postzależnościowy – konteksty i perspektywy badawcze*, edited by Ryszard Nycz. Kraków: Universitas, 2011.
Kronfeld, Chana. *On the Margins of Modernism: Decentering Literary Dynamics*. Berkeley: University of California Press, 1993.
Krzyżanowski, Julian. *Historia Literatury Polskiej: Alegoryzm-preromantyzm*. Warszawa: Państwowy Instytut Wydawniczy, 1963.
Kundera, Milan. *The Curtain: An Essay in Seven Parts*. Translated by Linda Asher. New York: HarperCollins, 2005.
Lachman, Gary. *A Dark Muse: A History of the Occult*. New York: Basic Books, 2009.
Landa, Louis. "Swift's Economic Views and Mercantilism." In *Essays in Eighteenth-Century English Literature*. Princeton: Princeton University Press, 1980.
Landy, Joshua. *How to Do Things with Fictions*. Oxford: Oxford University Press, 2012.
Lanone, Catherine. "Verging on the Gothic: Melmoth's Journey to France." In *European Gothic: A Spirited Exchange 1760–1960*, edited by Avril Horner, 71–83. Manchester: Manchester University Press, 2002.
Lanser, Sue. "Sapphic Dialogues: Historical Narratology and the Sexuality of Form." In *Post-Classical Narratology: Approaches and Analyses*, edited by Jan Alber and Monica Fludernik, 186–205. Columbus: Ohio State University Press: 2010.
———. *The Sexuality of History: Modernity and the Sapphic, 1565–1830*. Chicago: University of Chicago Press: 2014.
Lee, Wendy Anne. *Failures of Feeling: Insensibility and the Novel*. Redwood City, CA: Stanford University Press, 2019.

Leerssen, Joep. *Remembrance and Imagination: Patterns in the Historical and Literary Representation of Ireland in the Nineteenth Century*. Dublin: Field Day, 1996.

Lessing, Gotthold Ephraim. *Laocoön: An Essay Upon the Limits of Painting and Poetry*. Translated by Ellen Frothingham. Boston: Roberts Brothers, 1887.

———. *Laokoön, oder Über die Grenzen der Malerei und Poesie*. Berlin: Karl-Maria Guth [1766], 2016.

Levine, Caroline. *Forms: Whole, Rhythm, Hierarchy, Network*. Princeton, NJ: Princeton University Press, 2015.

———. *The Serious Pleasures of Suspense: Victorian Realism and Narrative Doubt*. Charlottesville: University of Virginia Press, 2003.

Levy, Anita. *Reproductive Urges: Popular Novel-Reading, Sexuality, and the English Nation*. Philadelphia: University of Pennsylvania Press, 1999.

Lindemann, Mary. *Liaisons Dangereuses: Sex, Law and Diplomacy in the Age of Frederick the Great*. Baltimore: Johns Hopkins University Press, 2006.

Lionnet, Françoise, and Shu-Mei Shih. "Thinking Through the Minor, Transnationally." In *Minor Transnationalisms*, edited by Françoise Lionnet and Shu-Mei Shih, 1–23. Durham, NC: Duke University Press, 2005.

Lloyd, David. *Anomalous States: Irish Writing and the Postcolonial Moment*. Durham, NC: Duke University Press, 1993.

———. *Ireland after History*. Cork: Cork University Press, 1999.

———. *Nationalism and Minor Literature*. Berkeley: University of California Press, 1987.

Lougy, Robert. *Charles Robert Maturin*. Lewisburg, PA: Bucknell University Press, 1975.

Love, Heather. *Feeling Backward: Loss and the Politics of Queer History*. Cambridge, MA: Harvard University Press, 2007.

Löwy, Michael. "The Current of Critical Irrealism: 'A Moonlit Enchanted Night.'" In *Adventures in Realism*, edited by Matthew Beaumont, 193–206. London: Blackwell, 2007.

Lukács, György. *The Historical Novel*. Translated by Hannah and Stanley Mitchell. Omaha: University of Nebraska Press, 1983.

Lutostański, Bartosz. *Gombrowicz-Beckett Beckett-Gombrowicz: A Comparative Intermodal Study*. Gdańsk: Gdańsk University Press, 2015.

Lynch, Deidre. "Gothic Fiction." In *Cambridge Companion to Fiction in the Romantic Period*, edited by Richard Maxwell and Katie Trumpener, 47–64. Cambridge: Cambridge University Press, 2008.

Lyotard, Jean-Francois. *The Postmodern Condition: A Report on Knowledge*. Translated by Geoff Bennington and Brian Massumi, with a foreword by Frederic Jameson. Minneapolis: University of Minnesota Press, 1984.

Ma, Ning. *The Age of Silver: The Rise of the Novel, East and West*. Oxford: Oxford University Press, 2017.

MacAndrew, Elizabeth. *The Gothic Tradition in Fiction*. New York: Columbia University Press, 1979.

Malcolmson, Cristina. *Studies of Skin Color in the Early Royal Society: Boyle, Cavendish, Swift*. Farnham: Ashgate, 2013.

Malouf, Michael. *Transatlantic Solidarities: Irish Nationalism and Caribbean Poetics*. Charlottesville: University of Virginia Press, 2009.

Malti-Douglas, Fedwa. *Woman's Body, Woman's Word: Gender and Discourse in Arabo-Islamic Writing*. Princeton, NJ: Princeton University Press, 1991.
Mander, Jenny, ed. *Remapping the Rise of the European Novel*. SVEC 10. Oxford: Voltaire Foundation, 2007.
Mann, Maurycy, *Poganka Narcyzy Żmichowskiej: geneza, źródła, artyzm i idea utoworu*. Warszawa: E. Wende: 1916.
Marcuse, Herbert. *The Aesthetic Dimension: Toward a Critique of Marxist Aesthetics*. Translated by Erica Sherover. Boston: Beacon Press, 1978.
Markowski, Michał Paweł. *Czarny Nurt: Gombrowicz, świat, literatura*. Kraków: Wydawnictwo Literackie, 2004.
Maturin, Charles. *Melmoth the Wanderer*. Introduction by Chris Baldick. Oxford: Oxford University Press, 1989.
———. *Melmoth the Wanderer*. Oxford: Oxford University Press, 1998.
Maturin, Charles, and Walter Scott. *The Correspondence of Sir Walter Scott and Charles Robert Maturin, with a Few Other Allied Letters*. Austin: University of Texas Press, 1937.
Maxwell, Richard. "Inundations of Time: A Definition of Scott's Originality." *ELH* 68, no. 2 (Summer 2001): 419–468.
Maxwell, Richard, and Trumpener, Katie. *Cambridge Companion to the Romantic Novel*. Cambridge: Cambridge University Press, 2009.
McCalman, Iain. *The Last Alchemist: Count Cagliostro, Master of Magic in the Age of Reason*. New York: Harper Perennial, 2004.
McCormack, W. J. *Dissolute Characters: Irish Literary History through Balzac, Sheridan Le Fanu, Yeats and Bowen*. Manchester: Manchester University Press, 1993.
McCrea, Barry. *Languages of the Night: Minor Languages and the Literary Imagination in Twentieth-Century Ireland and Europe*. New Haven, CT: Yale University Press, 2015.
McGurl, Mark. "Gigantic Realism: The Rise of the Novel and the Comedy of Scale." *Critical Inquiry* 43 (Winter 2017): 403–430.
McHale, Brian. *Postmodernist Fiction*. Abingdon-on-Thames: Routledge, 1996.
Memmi, Albert. *The Colonizer and the Colonized*. Translated by Howard Greenfeld. New York: Orion Press, 1965.
Mendelsund, Peter. *What We See When We Read*. New York: Penguin, 2014.
Merchant, John. *The Impact of Irish-Ireland on Young Poland, 1890–1918*. New York: Columbia University Press, 2008.
Mercier, Vivian. *The Irish Comic Tradition*. Oxford: Clarendon Press, 1962.
Miller, Robin Feuer. *Dostoevsky's Unfinished Journey*. New Haven, CT: Yale University Press, 2007.
Miłosz, Czesław. *The History of Polish Literature*. Berkeley: University of California Press, 1969.
———. *Native Realm: A Search for Self-Definition*. Translated by Catherine S. Leach. Berkeley: University of California Press, 1981.
———. *Zniewolony Umysł*. Warszawa: Krajowa Agencja Wydawnicza, 1989.
Mitchell, W. J. T. *Iconology: Image, Text, Ideology*. Chicago: University of Chicago Press, 1986.
———, ed. *On Narrative*. Chicago: University of Chicago Press, 1981.

Moore, David Chioni. "Is the Post- in Postcolonial the Post- in Post-Soviet? Toward a Global Postcolonial Critique." *PMLA* 116, no. 1 (January 2001): 111–128.
Moore, Steven. *The Novel: An Alternative History*. London: Bloomsbury, 2011.
More, Sir Thomas. *Utopia*. Translated by Robert Adams. New York: Norton, 1995.
Moretti, Franco. "Conjectures on World Literature." *New Left Review* 1 (January-February 2000): 54–68.
———. *Distant Reading*. New York: Verso, 2013.
———, ed. *The Novel*. Princeton, NJ: Princeton University Press, 2007.
———. *Signs Taken for Wonders: On the Sociology of Literary Forms*. New York: Verso, 2005.
———. *The Way of the World: The Bildungsroman in European Culture*. New York: Verso, 1987.
Morin, Christina. *Charles Robert Maturin and the Haunting of Irish Romantic Fiction*. Manchester: Manchester University Press, 2011.
Moryson, Fynes. *An itinerary vvritten by Fynes Moryson Gent. Containing his ten yeeres trauels thorovv twelue dominions*. London: Iohn Beale, 1617. http://name.umdl.umich.edu/A07834.0001.001.
Muecke, Douglas. *Compass of Irony*. London: Methuen, 1969.
Mullen, Mary. *Novel Institutions: Anachronism, Irish Novels, and Nineteenth-Century Realism*. Edinburgh: Edinburgh University Press, 2019.
Murphy, James. *Irish Novelists and the Victorian Age*. Oxford: Oxford University Press, 2011.
Musil, Robert. *Confusions of Young Törless*. Translated by Mike Mitchell. Oxford: Oxford University Press, 2014.
Najder, Zdzisław. "The Development of the Polish Novel: Functions and Structure." *Slavic Review* 29, no. 4 (December 1970): 651–662.
Nandrea, Lori G. *Misfit Forms: Paths Not Taken by the British Novel*. New York: Fordham University Press, 2015.
Nemoianu, Virgil. *The Triumph of Imperfection: The Silver Age of Sociocultural Moderation in Europe, 1815–1848*. Columbia: University of South Carolina Press, 2006.
Nixon, Cheryl, ed. *Novel Definitions: An Anthology of Commentary on the Novel, 1688–1815*. Peterborough, ON: Broadview, 2009.
Nolan, J. C. M. "In Search of an Ireland in the Orient: Tom Moore's *Lalla Rookh*." *New Hibernia Review* 12, no. 3 (Autumn 2008): 80–98.
Novalis. *Heinrich von Ofterdingen*. Stuttgart: Reclam, 2004.
Nowak, Andrzej. *History and Geopolitics: A Contest for Eastern Europe*. Warszawa: Polish Institute of International Affairs, 2008.
Nunokawa, Jeff. "Homosexual Desire and the Effacement of the Self in 'The Picture of Dorian Gray.'" *American Imago* 49, no. 3 (Fall 1992): 311–321.
———. *The Tame Passions of Wilde: The Styles of Manageable Desire*. Princeton, NJ: Princeton University Press, 2003.
Nycz, Ryszard, ed. *Kultura po przejściach, osoby z przeszłością. Polski dyskurs postzależnościowy – konteksty i perspektywy badawcze*. Kraków: Universitas, 2011.
O'Connor, Laura. *Haunted English: The Celtic Fringe, the British Empire, and De-Anglicization*. Baltimore: Johns Hopkins University Press, 2006.
O'Flaherty, Liam. *The Informer*. San Diego: Harcourt Brace, 1925.

Ohi, Kevin. *Innocence and Rapture: The Erotic Child in Pater, Wilde, James, and Nabokov*. Basingstoke: Palgrave Macmillan, 2005.

Olney, James. *Memory & Narrative: The Weave of Life-Writing*. Chicago: University of Chicago Press, 1998.

Olszewska, Kinga. *Wanderers across Language: Exile in Irish and Polish Literature of the Twentieth Century*. Abingdon-on-Thames: Routledge, 2007.

Orlemanski, Julie. "Who Has Fiction? Modernity, Fictionality, and the Middle Ages." *New Literary History* 50 (2019): 145–170.

Orlowski, Hubert. *"Polnische Wirtschaft": Zum deutschen Polendiskurs der Neuzeit*. Wiesbaden: Harrassowitz Verlag, 1996.

Ortega y Gasset, José. *The Dehumanization of Art*. New York: Doubleday, 1956.

Otorowski, Michał. *Jan Potocki – koniec i początek*. Warszawa: Lampa i Iskra Boża, 2008.

Paige, Nicholas. *Before Fiction: The Ancien Regime of the Novel*. Philadelphia: University of Pennsylvania Press, 2011.

———. "Permanent Re-Enchantments: On Some Literary Uses of the Supernatural from Early Empiricism to Modern Aesthetics." In *The Re-Enchantment of the World: Secular Magic in a Rational Age*, edited by Joshua Landy and Michael Saler, 159–180. Palo Alto, CA: Stanford University Press, 2009.

Pearl, Jason. *Utopian Geographies and the Early English Novel*. Charlottesville: University of Virginia Press: 2014.

Petruszewicz, Marta. "The Modernization of the European Periphery: Ireland, Poland, and the Two Sicilies, 1820–1870: Parallel and Connected, Distinct and Comparable." In *Comparison and History: Europe in Cross-National Perspective*, edited by Deborah Cohen and Maura O'Connor, 145–164. Abingdon-on-Thames: Routledge, 2004.

Phillips, Ursula. "Femme Fatale and Mother-Martyr: Femininity and Patriotism in Żmichowska's *The Heathen*." In *Gender and Sexuality in Ethical Context: Ten Essays on Polish Prose*, edited by Knut Andreas Grimstad and Ursula Phillips, 19–51. Bergen: University of Bergen Press, 2005.

———. "Gombrowicz's Polish Complex." In *New Perspectives in Twentieth-Century Polish Literature: Flight from Martyrology*, edited by Stanislaw Eile and Ursula Phillips. London: School of Slavonic and Eastern European Studies, 1992.

Płonowska Ziarek, Ewa. *The Rhetoric of Failure: Deconstruction of Skepticism, Reinvention of Modernism*. Albany: State University of New York Press, 1996.

Potocki, Jan. *The Manuscript Found in Saragossa*. Translated by Ian Maclean, based on the Radrizzani manuscript. London: Penguin, 1995.

———. *Manuscrit Trouvé à Saragosse*. Translated by René Radzrizzani. Paris: José Corti, 1990.

———. *Manuscrit Trouvé à Saragosse* (version de 1804). Édition établie par François Rosset et Dominique Triaire. Paris: GF Flammarion, 2006.

———. *Manuscrit Trouvé à Saragosse* (version de 1810). Édition établie par François Rosset et Dominique Triaire. Paris: GF Flammarion, 2006.

———. *Rękopis znaleziony w Saragossie*. Translated by Edmund Chojecki. Czerwonak: Vesper, 2007.

———. *Rękopis znaleziony w Saragossie*. Translated by Anna Wasilewska. Warszawa: Wydawnictwo Literackie, 2015.

Pratt, Mary Louise. *Imperial Eyes: Travel Writing and Transculturation*. London: Routledge, 1992.
Preminger, Alex, Frank J. Warnke, and O.B. Hardison, Jr., eds. *Princeton Handbook of Poetic Terms*. Princeton, NJ: Princeton University Press, 2016.
Prendergast, Christopher. "The World Republic of Letters." In *Debating World Literature*, edited by Christopher Prendergast, 1–25. New York: Verso, 2004.
Punter, David. *Rapture: Literature, Addiction, Secrecy*. Sussex: Sussex Academic Press, 2009.
Purdy, Jedediah. *For Common Things: Irony, Trust, and Commitment in America Today*. New York: Knopf, 1999.
Rabinovitz, Rubin. *Innovation in Samuel Beckett's Fiction*. Champaign: University of Illinois Press, 1992.
Reilly, Matthew. "Byron's Babel: Scriblerian Orientalism and the Romantic-Era 'Pope Controversy.'" *Modern Philology* 113, no. 2 (November 2015): 224–245.
Rennie, Neil. *Far-Fetched Facts: The Literature of Travel and the Idea of the South Seas*. Oxford: Clarendon Press, 1995.
Richetti, John, ed. *Cambridge Companion to the Eighteenth-Century Novel*. Cambridge: Cambridge University Press, 2006.
———. *Popular Fiction before Richardson: 1700–1739*. Oxford: Oxford University Press, 1992.
Ricks, Christopher. *Beckett's Dying Words*. Oxford: Oxford University Press, 1993.
Ricoeur, Paul. "The Metaphorical Process." In *On Metaphor*, edited by Sheldon Sacks. Chicago: University of Chicago Press, 1979.
Rigney, Ann. *Imperfect Histories: The Elusive Past and the Legacy of Romantic Historicism*. Ithaca, NY: Cornell University Press, 2001.
Riquelme, John Paul. "Between Two Worlds and Beyond Them: John Ruskin and Walter Pater." In *Oscar Wilde in Context*, edited by Kerry Powell and Peter Raby, 125–136. Cambridge: Cambridge University Press, 2013.
———. "Walter Pater, Dark Enlightenment, and *The Picture of Dorian Gray*." In *Gothic and Modernism: Essaying Dark Literary Modernity*, edited by John Paul Riquelme, 25–45. Baltimore: Johns Hopkins University Press: 2008.
Robbins, Bruce. Review of Susan Stanford Friedman's *Planetary Modernisms*. *Interventions* 18, no. 5 (2016): 746–748.
Robert, Marthe. *The Old and the New: From Don Quixote to Kafka*. Translated by Carol Cosman. Berkeley: University of California Press, 1977.
Rohy, Valerie. "Strange Influence: Queer Etiology in *The Picture of Dorian Gray*." In *Narrative Theory Unbound: Queer and Feminist Interventions*, edited by Sue Lanser and Robyn Warhol, 275–292. Columbus: Ohio State University Press, 2015.
Rosset, François, and Dominique Triaire. *De Varsovie à Saragosse. Jean Potocki et son oeuvre*. Leuven: Peeters, 2001.
———. "Wstęp." *Rękopis Znaleziony w Saragossie*. Translated by Anna Wasilewska. Edited by François Rosset and Dominique Triaire. Warszawa: Wydawnictwo Literackie, 2015.
———. *Z Warszawy do Saragossy: Jan Potocki i jego dzieło*. Translated by Anna Wasilewska. Warszawa: Instytut Badań Literackich Polskiej Akademii Nauk, 2005.
Round, Julia. "Gothic and the Graphic Novel." In *A New Companion to the Gothic*, edited by David Punter, 335–349. Hoboken, NJ: Blackwell, 2012.

Różewicz, Tadeusz. "Miłość lesbijska w romantycznym przebraniu." In *Przygotowania do wieczoru autorskiego*, 128–130. Warszawa: Państwowy Instytut Wydawniczy, 1977.
Said, Edward. *Culture and Imperialism*. London: Vintage, 1993.
Saint-Amour, Paul. "The Literary Present." *ELH* 85, no. 2 (Summer 2018): 367–392.
———. *Tense Future: Modernism, Total War, Encyclopedic Form*. Oxford: Oxford University Press, 2015.
———. "Weak Theory, Weak Modernism." *Modernism/Modernity* 25, no. 3 (2018).
Schlegel, Friedrich. *Athenäums-Fragmente*. In *Kritische Schriften*. Munich: Carl Hanser Verlag, 1956.
———. *Philosophical Fragments*. Translated by Peter Firchow. Minneapolis: University of Minnesota Press, 1991.
Schmidt, Michael. *The Novel: A Biography*. Cambridge, MA: Harvard University Press, 2014.
Schwab, Gabriele. *Subjects without Selves: Transitional Texts in Modern Fiction*. Cambridge, MA: Harvard University Press, 1994.
Scott, Sarah. *Millenium Hall*. Edited by Gary Kelly. Peterborough, ON: Broadview, 1995.
Scott, Walter. *The Monastery*. Edinburgh: Edinburgh University Press, 2000.
Sedgwick, Eve Kosofsky. *The Coherence of Gothic Conventions*. New York: Arno Press, 1980.
———. *Epistemology of the Closet*. Berkeley: University of California Press, 1990.
Selasi, Taiye. "African Literature Doesn't Exist." Opening Address, 13th International Literature Festival, Berlin, 2013.
Sheehan, Paul. *Modernism, Narrative, and Humanism*. Cambridge: Cambridge University Press, 2002.
Sheeran, Pat, and Nina Witoszek. *Talking to the Dead: A Study of Irish Funerary Traditions*. Amsterdam: Rodopi, 1998.
Shiach, Morag. *The Cambridge Companion to the Modernist Novel*. Cambridge: Cambridge University Press, 2007.
Skoczek, Anna. "Jan Potocki." *Historia Literatury Polskiej. Oświecenie* 4, no. 2. Gdów: Wydawnictwo SMS: 2005.
Skolasińska, Agnieszka. "Deconstructing the Polish Tradition in Tadeusz Różewicz's *Marriage Blanc*." In *Studies in Language, Literature, and Cultural Mythology in Poland: Investigating 'The Other,'* edited by Elwira M Grossman, 131–149. Lewiston, NY: Edwin Mellen Press, 2002.
Slaughter, Joseph. *Human Rights, Inc.: The World Novel, Narrative Form, and International Law*. New York: Fordham University Press, 2007.
Śniegucka, Agnieszka. "Dyptyk z Adamem i Ewą, czyli o *Alegorii* i *Mikołaja Doświadczyńskiego przypadkach* Ignacego Krasickiego." *Prace Polonistyczne* 60 (2005): 177–185.
———. "Kilka uwag o wątku romansowym w *Mikołaja Doświadczyńskiego przypadki* Ignacego Krasickiego." *Ruch Literacki* 4–5 (2010): 373–380.
Sołtysik, Agnieszka. "Witold Gombrowicz's Struggle with Heterosexual Form: From a National to a Performative Self." In *Gombrowicz's Grimaces: Modernism, Gender, Nationality*, edited by Ewa Płonowska Ziarek, 245–265. Albany: State University of New York Press, 1998.
Sonnenberg, Katarzyna. *At the Roots of the Modern Novel: A Comparative Reading of Ihara Saikaku's* The Life of an Amorous Woman *and Daniel Defoe's* Moll Flanders. Kraków: Jagiellonian University Press, 2015.

Spacks, Patricia Meyer. *Novel Beginnings: Experiments in Eighteenth-Century English Fiction*. New Haven, CT: Yale University Press, 2006.

Spenser, Edmund. *A View of the Present State of Ireland*. Oxford: Clarendon Press, 1970.

Spivak, Gayatri Chakravorty. *Death of a Discipline*. New York: Columbia University Press, 2003.

Starosta, Anita. *Form and Instability: Eastern Europe, Literature, Postimperial Difference*. Evanston, IL: Northwestern University Press, 2015.

Stoler, Ann Laura. *Along the Archival Grain: Epistemic Anxieties and Colonial Common Sense*. Princeton, NJ: Princeton University Press, 2009.

Swift, Jonathan. *Drapier's Letters and Other Works, 1724–1725*. Edited by Herbert Davis. Oxford: Shakespeare Head Press, 1941.

———. *Gulliver's Travels*. London: Penguin 2001.

———. *A Modest Proposal and Other Writings*. London: Penguin, 2009.

———. "On Barbarous Denominations." In *Prose Works of Jonathan Swift*, vol. 4. Edited by Herbert J. Davis. Oxford: Blackwell, 1957.

Szczeszak-Brewer, Agata. *Empire and Pilgrimage in Conrad and Joyce*. Gainesville: University Press of Florida, 2011.

Taylor, Lawrence. "Irony and Self-Irony in Irish Culture." In *Irony in Action: Anthropology, Practice, and the Moral Imagination*, edited by James Fernandez and Mary Taylor Huber, 172–187. Chicago: University of Chicago Press, 2001.

Temple, Emily. "Here Are the Biggest Fiction Bestsellers of the Last 100 Years (And What Everyone Read Instead)." *LitHub*, November 27, 2018. https://lithub.com/here-are-the-biggest-fiction-bestsellers-of-the-last-100-years/.

Teverson, Andrew. "The Number of Magic Alternatives: Salman Rushdie's 1001 Gothic Nights." In *Empire and the Gothic: The Politics of Genre*, edited by Andrew Smith and William Hughes, 208–228. Basingstoke: Palgrave Macmillan, 2003.

Tihanov, Galin. *The Master and the Slave: Lukács, Bakhtin, and the Ideas of Their Time*. Oxford: Oxford University Press, 2000.

Todorov, Tzvetan. *The Fantastic: A Structural Approach to a Literary Genre*. Translated by Richard Howard. Ithaca, NY: Cornell University Press, 1975.

———. "Narrative-Men." In *The Poetics of Prose*. Translated by Richard Howard. Ithaca, NY: Cornell University Press, 1977.

Tone, Theobald Wolfe. *Life of Theobald Wolfe Tone, Compiled and Arranged by Himself*. Edited by Thomas Bartlett. Stoneybatter: Lilliput Press, 1998.

Traub, Valerie. "The New Unhistoricism in Queer Studies." *PMLA* 128, no. 1 (2013): 21–39.

Trumpener, Katie. *Bardic Nationalism: The Romantic Novel and the British Empire*. Princeton, NJ: Princeton University Press, 1997.

Ullyot, Jonathan. *The Medieval Presence in Modernist Literature: The Quest to Fail*. Cambridge: Cambridge University Press, 2016.

Underwood, Ted. *Distant Horizons: Digital Evidence and Literary Change*. Chicago: University of Chicago Press, 2019.

———. *Why Literary Periods Mattered: Historical Contrast and the Prestige of English Studies*. Redwood City, CA: Stanford University Press, 2013.

Voltaire, Francoise. *Candide, or Optimism*. Translated by Theo Cuffe. London: Penguin, 2005.

Walczewska, Sławomira. *Damy, rycerze, i feministki: Kobiecy dyskurs emancypacyjny w Polsce*. Kraków: eFKa, 1999.
Walpole, Horace. *The Castle of Otranto*. New York: Penguin, 2002.
Wandycz, Piotr. *The Price of Freedom: A History of Central Europe from the Middle Ages to the Present*. Abingdon-on-Thames: Routledge, 1992.
Wa Ngugi, Mukoma. *The Rise of the African Novel: Politics of Language, Identity, and Ownership*. Ann Arbor: University of Michigan Press, 2018.
Warwick Research Collective. *Combined and Uneven Development: Towards a New Theory of World-Literature*. Liverpool: Liverpool University Press, 2015.
Watt, Ian. "The Ironic Tradition in Augustan Prose from Swift to Johnson." In *The Character of Swift's Satire: A Revised Focus*, edited by Claude Rawson, 305–326. Newark: University of Delaware Press, 1983.
———. *The Rise of the Novel*. Berkeley: University of California Press, 1957.
Wein, Toni. "Wandering Home: Charles Robert Maturin and the Subliming of Ireland." In *Land and Landscape in Nineteenth-Century Ireland*, edited by Úna Ní Bhroméil and Glenn Hooper, 171–186. Dublin: Four Courts Press, 2008.
Weisberg, David. *Chronicles of Disorder: Samuel Beckett and the Cultural Politics of the Modern Novel*. Albany: State University of New York Press, 2000.
Whelan, Kevin. *The Tree of Liberty: Radicalism, Catholicism and the Construction of Irish Identity 1760–1830*. Notre Dame, IN: University of Notre Dame Press, 1996.
Wilde, Oscar. *The Picture of Dorian Gray*. Oxford: Oxford University Press, 1998.
Wilson, Diana de Armas. *Cervantes, the Novel, and the New World*. Oxford: Oxford University Press, 2002.
Wirtemberska, Maria. *Malwina, czyli domyślność serca*. Kraków: Universitas, 2002.
———. *Malvina, or the Heart's Intuition*. Translated and with an introduction by Ursula Phillips. DeKalb: Northern Illinois University Press, 2012.
Witoszek, Nina. *The Theatre of Recollection: A Cultural Study of the Modern Dramatic Tradition in Ireland and Poland*. Stockholm: Almqvist and Wiksell, 1988.
Wittgenstein, Ludwig. *Philosophical Investigations*. Translated by G. E. M. Anscombe. New York: Macmillan, 1953.
———. *Philosophische Untersuchungen*. Frankfurt am Main: Suhrkamp, 2003.
Wolff, Larry. *Inventing Eastern Europe: The Map of Civilization on the Mind of the Enlightenment*. Palo Alto, CA: Stanford University Press, 1994.
Woolf, Virginia. *The Voyage Out*. New York: Mariner, 2003.
Yeazell, Ruth Bernard. *Art of the Everyday: Dutch Painting and the Realist Novel*. Princeton, NJ: Princeton University Press, 2008.
Zamoyski, Adam. *Holy Madness: Romantics, Patriots, and Revolutionaries: 1776–1871*. London: Penguin, 1999.
Ziolkowski, Theodore. *Disenchanted Images: A Literary Iconology*. Princeton, NJ: Princeton University Press, 1977.
Żmichowska, Narcyza. *The Heathen*. Translated by Ursula Phillips. DeKalb: Northern Illinois University Press, 2012.
———. *Poganka*. Kraków: Wydawnictwo Zielona Sowa, 2003.

INDEX

abstraction, 13, 113, 127; and fictionality, 97, 124; and persuasion, 24–26; and political theory, 17, 34–35, 38; and queer theory, 76, 84; and travel writing, 20–22; and worlding, 132

Adventures of Mr. Nicholas Wisdom (Krasicki). See *Mikołaja Doświadczyńskiego przypadki*

African literature, 5, 136n13

anomaly, Polish and Irish literature as, 2, 6, 8, 10, 101, 102–3; and novel theory, 4, 12, 13, 101, 126–27

anthropological approach to fiction, 5, 125–6

anti-novels, 75, 127; anti-Bildungsroman, 104

Aravamudan, Srinivas, 67

Bakhtin, Mikhail, 122, 133

beauty, 75; and morality, 97–100

Beckett, Samuel, 104–5; *Malone Dies*, 103, 114; *Molloy*, 13, 102–4, 114, 117–18, 123–24, 127; Trilogy, 13, 102–4, 114; *The Unnamable*, 13, 102–4, 108, 113–18, 122–24, 127

Beecroft, Alexander, 72

Bersani, Leo, 84

Bildung, 14, 23, 110–11, 119; and time, 90

Bildungsroman, 86, 127, 139n18; history of, 103–4; and modernism, 103–4; problem of, 106–8; standard features of, 113, 115, 119

Black, Scott, 126, 128, 133, 135n6, 146n54

Bogel, Fredric, 140n23

Bonaparte, Napoleon, 6, 137n28

Booth, Wayne, 67, 123–24

Borkowska, Grażyna, 148n1, 149n6, 150–51n27

Brooks, Peter, 77, 86, 106, 121

Burke, Edmund, 98–99

Burns, Robert, 59

Cabbalism, 40, 71; cabbalist in *Rękopis*, 41, 45, 46, 47, 54; Potocki and, 144n23

Cagliostro, Alessandro di, 19

Canterbury Tales, The (Chaucer), 71

Casanova, Giacomo, 19

Casanova, Pascale, 136n10

Castle, Gregory, 107

Catholicism, 1, 58, 67

Cervantes, Miguel, *Don Quixote*, 51, 129

Chuh, Kandice, 136n15

Cleary, Joe, 7, 8

Clery, E. J., 46

clues, 58

colonialism, 6–7, 26–28, 40, 67, 149n6

compromise: in Bildungsroman, 106–7; of history and form, 4; in *Mikołaja Doświadczyńskiego przypadki*, 35

Conger, Syndy, 59

Conrad, Joseph, 136n9

contradiction, 38, 114–15; and impossibility, 14, 117–18, 102; and tension between irony and identification, 17, 26, 28; and totality, 120–23

Decameron, The (Boccacio), 71

Defoe, Daniel, 3, 129; *Robinson Crusoe*, 16, 17, 36–37, 139n5, 143n59

Deleuze, Gilles, and Felix Guattari, 7, 136n9, 157n61; and modernism, 105–6

delusion, 99; and romance, 51–52; and the supernatural, 48–49
Descartes, René, 98
Diderot, Denis, *Supplement to the Voyage of Bougainville*, 19
Doyle, Laura, 59, 143n7
Dracula (Stoker), 147n88, 148n1

Eagleton, Terry, 8, 34–35, 59
Earls, Brian, 136n18
Edgeworth, Maria 8–9, 63–64
Eliot, George, 152n40; *Middlemarch*, 8
empathy, 53
Enlightenment, the, 6, 7, 40, 47; and universalism, 34–35; and utopian fiction, 13, 16, 36–37
Esty, Jed, 82, 149n6, 150n26

fantastic, 40, 43, 44–45, 113; differences from, 78–79, 111, 117
Ferdydurke (Gombrowicz), 13, 102–4, 108–13, 118–24, 127
Ferris, Ina, 19n16
fictionality: as capability, 18, 102–3, 122, 124; and difference from realism, 39, 60–69, 73; and history, 64–66; and idealism, 97–100; and impossibility, 117–18; and pedagogy, 50–56; and rise of the novel, 3, 12, 42–43, 127, 131; as travel, 60, 67–69
Form (in Gombrowicz), 109–13, 118–21
formalism, 76; need for, 5, 126, 134; queer, 13, 77, 81, 83, 85, 97
formative fictions, 50, 55
Freedgood, Elaine, 135n8
freedom, 14, 18, 29, 38; in Bildungsromans, 106–8; and creativity, 123, 127; as irrationality, 34–36, 127
Freeman, Elizabeth, 151n32
Freemasonry, 40
Foster, R. F., 7
Friedman, Susan Stanford, 14, 128, 130–31, 132

Gallagher, Catherine, 61, 66, 135n1, 135n7
Gamer, Michael, 51
Ganguly, Debjani, 69, 72, 159n22
genocide, 33

Ginzburg, Michal Peled, 79, 87
Gombrowicz, Witold, 104–6; *Ferdydurke*, 13, 102–4, 108–13, 118–24, 127
Gothic, the, 39, 50, 57, 79; and epistemology, 60–61; and history, 65; and rise of the novel, 2, 3, 13, 42–43, 46–47, 61, 73, 139n7, and sociohistorical development, 43–47
Gulliver's Travels (Swift), 13, 16–18, 20, 21–23, 26–35, 37–38, 124, 127

Haiti, 137n28
Hayot, Eric, 10–11, 14, 69–70, 132–33
Heathen, The (Żmichowska). See *Poganka*
Hershinow, Stephanie Insley, 90, 138n46, 152n41
historical trauma, 2, 40, 66, 100, 148n100; and Gothic, 65; and irrealism, 5, 143n7, 148n100
historicism, 40; challenges to, 11, 78, 82, 100; and queer theory, 76, 78, 82–83; and rise of the novel, 4–5, 14, 105, 125–28, 125–28, 130–31, 133
Holocaust, 153n11
Houyhnhnms, 17, 27–28, 30–33, 98
humor, 1, 28, 123–24
Hunter, J. Paul, 17–18

idealism, 76, 97, 101, 127
identification with fictional characters, 18, 22–28, 38
influence, 14, 140n20
Irish Bulls, 116–18
irony, 2, 13, 19, 38, 57, 59, 127; and argument, 33–35; and identification with characters, 21–28; and Irish Bulls, 116–18; and metaphor; 103, 106, 115–18, 120–22, 124; and realism, 17–18; and travel writing, 20–21
irrealism, 5, 12

Jameson, Fredric, 20
Janion, Maria, 47
Johnson, Samuel, 50

Kareem, Sarah Tindal, 42, 49–50, 53, 73, 135n7
Kelly, Jim, 59

Kornbluh, Anna, 86, 138n48, 150n23
Kosinski, Jerzy, 136n9
Krasicki, Ignacy: *Historia*, 21; *Mikołaja Doświadczyńskiego przypadki*, 13, 16–18, 20, 21–27, 29–38, 124, 127
Kundera, Milan, 106

Landy, Joshua, 50, 53–55, 146n54
language games, 109–13
language politics, 7–9; different versions of texts, 40, 104–5; and modernism, 105–6
Lanser, Susan, 150n24
Lessing, Gotthold Ephraim, *Laocoön*, 76, 85–87, 90
Levine, Caroline, 90–92, 94, 150n23
Lloyd, David, 6, 8
Love, Heather, 81
Lukács, György, 65, 107, 128
Lynch, Deirdre, 42–43, 73
Lyotard, Jean-Francois, 109, 157n56

Ma, Ning, 14, 128–30
magic, 13, 75, 78–80, 84, 98, 148n100
magical realism, 136n14
Manuscript Found in Saragossa (Potocki). See *Rękopis znaleziony w Saragossie*
Markowski, Michał Paweł, 111
Maturin, Charles, 39; *Melmoth the Wanderer*, 13, 39–44, 56–74, 127
McCrea, Barry, 137n30
Melmoth the Wanderer (Maturin), 13, 39–44, 56–74, 127
Merchant, John, 6
metaphor: and irony, 106, 115–17, 121–22; as virtual travel, 60, 67–68
Mikołaja Doświadczyńskiego przypadki (Krasicki), 13, 16–18, 20, 21–27, 29–38, 124, 127
Miłosz, Czesław, 8, 106
"minor" literature, 4, 7, 12; and modernism, 105–6
misogyny, 29
Mitchell, W. J. T., 152n42
modernism: and Ireland and Poland, 9, 102–7; and "minor" literature, 105–6; theories of, 126, 130, 132, 133–34
modernity, 3; alternative theorizations of, 14, 126–33

modernization, 9, 72; and supernatural, 47
Molloy (Beckett), 13, 102–4, 114, 117–18, 123–24, 127
money, 23–24
Montesquieu, *Persian Letters*, 19
morality, 50, 97–101
Moretti, Franco, 3n1, 3n5, 4, 106–7, 158n2
Morgan, Lady (Sydney Owenson), 64
Moryson, Fynes, 19

Najder, Zdzisław, 8
Nemoianu, Virgil, 20
novelistic pedagogy, 16–17, 50–55; and assertion, 86; and empathy, 53; and history, 65–69; and irony, 23–28; and morality, 50–51, 99; and utopianism, 20
Nunokawa, Jeff, 82, 152n52

1,001 Nights, 71, 143n1
Oost, Regina, 59, 147n72
Orientalism, 40, 46–47, 56, 67–68, 71–72
Oriental tale, 3, 67
Orlemanski, Julie, 10–11, 14, 128, 131–32, 135n7
Otto, Peter, 42

Paige, Nicholas, 10–12, 42, 157n2
painting: difference from prose, 85–101; and realism, 76–80
paratext, 60–68, 71; as authentication, 60–63; as transportation, 65–68
Partitions of Poland, 6–7, 40, 47
periphery, 72; and colonialism, 28, 108; and modernism, 104–6; and travel, 20; in world literature, 1–2, 4–6, 10, 12
Phillips, Ursula, 81, 149n6
Picture of Dorian Gray, The (Wilde), 13, 75–101, 127, 147n67
Plato, 75, 100
Poganka (Żmichowska), 13, 75–101, 127
postcolonial theory, 108; and Ireland and Poland, 6–8; and travel writing, 19
postsocialism, 136n21
post-zależność, 6
Potocki, Jan, 40, 136n9; *Rękopis znaleziony w Saragossie*, 13, 39–56, 68–74, 127
private language, 108; and contradiction, 114–15, 117–18; and erasure of self,

private language (*continued*)
113–14; and Form, 109–13, 118–22; metaphor as, 115–16

queerness, 75–77, 80–85, 101

Rabinovitz, Rubin, 155n35
race, 7, 141n40, 146n61
realism, 56, 61, 70, 100, 102, 107; alternatives to, 38, 42, 116; claims of, 63; and historical trauma, 5; and irony, 17–18; and painting, 76; and rise of the novel, 2–3, 8, 9, 12, 16, 73–74, 125–32, 134, 139n5
reason, critique of, 33–35
Rękopis znaleziony w Saragossie (Potocki), 13, 39–56, 68–74, 127
Richetti, John, 17
Ricoeur, Paul, 115–116
rise of the novel, 3, 8, 125–28, 131; and Gothic, 42–43, 61; non-developmental accounts of, 10–13, 133–34
romance, 36, 42, 50–51, 69, 133, 146n54

Saint-Amour, Paul, 14, 128, 133–34, 152n41
satire, as argument, 26–28, 33; and realism, 17
Schlegel, Friedrich, 115, 122
Schwab, Gabriele, 114
Scott, Walter, 64, 65
1798 Rebellion, 40, 66
Sheehan, Paul, 107, 114, 122, 123, 157n58
Sheeran, Pat, and Nina Witoszek, 125, 157n72
Starosta, Anita, 108, 136n21, 154n25
stereotypes, 1, 19, 25, 58–59
supernatural, 70, 73, 99, 111; how to represent, 41–49, 56–60; representations of, 78–80; and truth, 64
Swift, Jonathan, 19; *Gulliver's Travels*, 13, 16–18, 20, 21–23, 26–35, 37–38, 124, 127; *A Modest Proposal*, 33

teleology, in novel theory, 9–10, 126
time, 85–96, 133; and detective fiction, 93; and development, 91–96; and painting, 85–87; and portraits, 87
Todorov, Tzvetan, 44–45, 121, 145n34
Tone, Theobald Wolf, 6

totality: in painting, 85–96, 101; world-building and, 70–72, 120–23
translation, 9; and authoritative version, 40, 105; and private language, 108, 115; transcultural, 67, 105
travel, 31–32, 35, 54; metaphor as, 60, 66–68
travel writing, 13, 16, 18–22, 38; and irony, 21–22; and postcolonial theory, 19–20; and utopianism, 31–32; and verisimilitude, 18
Tufayl, Ibn, *Hayy ibn Yaqzan*, 36–37

Underwood, Ted, 158n2, 158n15
uneven development, 2, 5, 9–10, 14
universalism, 20, 131; and particular, 22; problem of, 18, 34–35, 36, 37
Unnamable, The (Beckett), 13, 102–4, 108, 113–18, 122–24, 127
utopia, 13, 16, 21, 28–38
utopian fiction, 16, 20, 37

vampires, 44, 47
violence, 100; in history, 2, 8, 9, 27, 67, 131; and humor, 123; and utopianism, 31–33, 38

Walpole, Horace, 60; *Castle of Otranto*, 42, 46
Wandycz, Piotr, 7
Warwick Research Collective, 5
Watt, Ian, 23, 135n1, 139n3, 141n35
weak theory, 126, 128, 133–34
Wilde, Oscar, 75; *The Picture of Dorian Gray*, 13, 75–101, 127, 147n67
Williams, Tennessee, 1
Wirtemberska, Maria, 9
Wittgenstein, Ludwig, 108–9, 115
Wolff, Larry, 6, 19
worlding, 77; and idealism, 97–101; and impossibility, 117–18, 124; and interlaced tales, 39, 41–42, 44, 69–74; and rise of the novel, 3, 127, 132, 134; and totality, 70–71
world literature, 2, 3, 10, 40, 69, 125–26

Zbyszewska, Paulina, 81
Ziołkowski, Theodore, 79
Żmichowska, Narcyza, 76; *Poganka*, 13, 75–101, 127

www.ingramcontent.com/pod-product-compliance
Lightning Source LLC
Chambersburg PA
CBHW030121240426
43673CB00041B/1357